MICROINTERVENTION STRATEGIES

MICROINTERVENTION STRATEGIES

WHAT YOU CAN DO TO DISARM AND DISMANTLE INDIVIDUAL AND SYSTEMIC RACISM AND BIAS

DERALD WING SUE

CASSANDRA Z. CALLE

NAROLYN MENDEZ

SARAH ALSAIDI

ELIZABETH GLAESER

Teachers College, Columbia University

WILEY

The right of Derald Wing Sue, Cassandra Z. Calle, Narolyn Mendez, Sarah Alsaidi and Elizabeth Glaeser to be identified as the authors of this work has been asserted in accordance with law.

Registered Office(s)
John Wiley & Sons, Inc., 111 River Street, Hoboken, NJ 07030, USA

Editorial Office
111 River Street, Hoboken, NJ 07030, USA

For details of our global editorial offices, customer services, and more information about Wiley products visit us at www.wiley.com.

Wiley also publishes its books in a variety of electronic formats and by print-on-demand. Some content that appears in standard print versions of this book may not be available in other formats.

Library of Congress Cataloging-in-Publication Data

Names: Sue, Derald Wing, author.
Title: Microintervention strategies : what you can do to disarm and dismantle individual and systemic racism and bias / Derald Wing Sue [and four others].
Description: Hoboken, NJ : John Wiley & Sons, Inc., 2021. | Includes bibliographical references and index. | Description based on print version record and CIP data provided by publisher; resource not viewed.
Identifiers: LCCN 2020037753 (print) | LCCN 2020037754 (ebook) | ISBN 9781119769989 (epub) | ISBN 9781119769972 (pdf) | ISBN 9781119769965 (paperback) | ISBN 9781119769965q(paperback) | ISBN 9781119769972q(pdf) | ISBN 9781119769989q(epub)
Subjects: LCSH: Microaggressions. | Discrimination. | Racism.
Classification: LCC BF575.P9 (ebook) | LCC BF575.P9 S84 2021 (print) | DDC 305.8--dc23
LC record available at https://lccn.loc.gov/2020037753 LC record available at https://lccn.loc.gov/2020037754

Cover image: The Light of the Gospel Rekindled by the Reformers, Courtesy of Kunstsammlungen der Veste Coburg
Cover design by Wiley

Set in 10/14.5pt Palatino by Integra Software Services Pvt. Ltd, Pondicherry, India

SKY10024120_011821

Dedication

George W. Ashburn 1868
Emmett Till 1955
Rev. George Lee 1955
Lamar Smith 1955
Willie Edwards Jr. 1957
Mack Charles Parker 1959
Herbert Lee 1961
Cpl. Roman Ducksworth Jr. 1962
Medgar Evers 1963
Virgil Lamar Ware 1963
Louis Allen 1964
Henry Hezekiah Dee 1964
Charlies Eddie Moore 1964
James Chaney, Andrew Goodman,
Michael Schwerner 1964
Lt. Col. Lemuel Penn 1964
Jimmie Lee Jackson 1965
Oneal Moore 1965
Willie Brewster 1965
Malcolm X 1965
Johnathan Myrick Daniels 1965
Samuel Leamon Younge Jr. 1966
Vernon Ferdinand Dahmer 1966
Ben Chester White 1966
Wharlest Jackson 1967
Benjamin Brown 1967
Samuel Hammond Jr. 1968
Delano Middleton 1968
Henry Smith 1968
Martin Luther King Jr. 1968
Fred Hampton 1969
Ahmadou Diallo 1999
Kendra James 2003
Oscar Grant 2009
Aiyanna Stanly Jones 2010
Trayvon Martin 2012
Mohamed Bah 2012
Alesia Thomas
Shantel Davis 2012
Shelly Frey 2012
Rekia Boyd
Kyam Livingston 2013
Miriam Carey 2013
Kayla Moore 2013
Michelle Cusseaux 2014
Pearlie Golden 2014

Yvette Smith 2014
Eric Garner 2014
John Crawford 2014
Michael Brown 2014
Ezell Ford 2014
Dante Parker 2014
Laquan McDonald 2014
Tamir Rice 2014
Ruman Brisbon 2014
Jerame Reid 2014
Phillip White 2014
Aura Rosser 2014
Akai Gurley 2014
Gabriella Nevarez 2014
Meagon Hockaday
Natasha Mckenna 2015
Alexa Christian 2015
Samuel DuBose 2015
Jeremy McDole 2015
Tanisha Anderson 2014
Tony Terrell Robinson Jr. 2015
Anthony Hill 2015
Mya Hall 2015
Eric Harris 2015
Walter Scott 2015
William Chapman II 2015
Alexia Christian 2015
Victor Manuel Larosa 2015
India Kager 2015
Jonathan Sanders 2015
Freddie Carlos Gray Jr. 2015
Salvado Ellswood 2015
Sandra Bland 2015
Albert Joseph Davis 2015
Darrius Stewart 2015
Billy Ray Davis 2015
Samuel Duaose 2015
Michael Sabbie 2015
Christian Taylor 2015
Felix Kumi 2015
Keith Harrison McLeod 2015
Dominic Hutchinson 2015
Anthony Ashford 2015
Lavante Biggs 2015
Michael Lee Marshall 2015
Jamar Clark 2015

Nathaniel Harris Pickett 2015
Benni Lee Tignor 2015
Miguel Espinal 2015
Michael Noel 2015
Kevin Matthews 2015
Bettie Jones 2015
Quintonio Legrier 2015
Keith Childress Jr. 2015
George Mann 2015
Frank Swart 2015
Kisha Michael 2016
Janet Wilson 2016
Richard Perkins 2016
Joseph Mann 2016
Asshams Pharoah Manley 2016
Lamontez Jones 2016
Paterson Brown 2016
Richard Perkins 2016
Janet Wilson 2016
Randy Nelson 2016
Antronie Scott 2016
Wendell Celestine 2016
David Joseph 2016
Calin Roquemore 2016
Dyzhawn Perkins 2016
Marco Loud 2016
Peter Gaines 2016
Torrey Robinson 2016
Darius Robinson 2016
Kevin Hicks 2016
Demarcus Semer 2016
Willie Tillman 2016
Terrill Thomas 2016
Sylville Swth 2016
Alton Sterling 2016
India Beaty 2016
Symone Marshall 2016
Jessica Williams 2016
Korryn Gaines 2016
Deborah Danner 2016
Philando Castile 2016
Terence Crutcher 2016
Kionte Spencer 2016
Mary Truxillo 2016
Christopher Davis 2016

Junior Prosper 2017
Alonzo Smith-Tyree Crawford 2017
Alteria Woods 2017
Jordan Edwards 2017
Aaron Bailey 2017
Ronell Foster 2018
Stephon Clark 2018
Botham Jean 2018
Brendon Glenn 2018
Ronell Foster 2018
Stephon Clark 2018
Antwon Rose II 2018
Pamela Turner 2019
Dominique Clayton 2019
Atatiana Jefferson 2019
Christopher Whitfield 2019
Christopher McCorvey 2019
Eric Reason 2019
Michael Lorenzo Dean 2019
Brian Keith Day 2019
Shukri Abdi 2019
Matthew Ajibade 2019
Breonna Taylor 2020
Ahmaud Arbery 2020
Tony Mcdade 2020
George Floyd 2020
Layleen Polanco 2020
Nina Pop 2020
Monika Diamond 2020
Dominique "Rem'mie" Fells 2020
Riah Milton (2020)
Robert Fuller (2020)
Rayshard Brooks (2020)

*... and many more who are unnamed and
have been brutalized and murdered at the
hands of police, White supremacists, hate
mongers, anti-Blackness and systemic
oppression.*

*... and to any and all other victims who are
subject to discriminatory based violence due
to their minoritized, oppressed identities
or allyship.*

... #SayTheirNames

Contents

CHAPTER EIGHT
Microintervention Strategy and Tactics to Disarm
Microaggressions and Macroaggressions

CHAPTER NINE
Microintervention Strategy and Tactics for Using
External Support and Alliances

CHAPTER TEN

Preface

Microintervention Strategies: What You Can Do to Disarm and Dismantle Individual and Systemic Racism and Bias is a book aimed at organizing and providing a conceptual framework of antibias strategies and tactics that can be used by targets, parents/significant others, allies, and well-intentioned bystanders to counteract, challenge, diminish, or neutralize the individual (microaggressions) and institutional/societal (macroaggressions) expressions of prejudice, bigotry, and discrimination.

Since the murder of George Floyd on May 25, 2020, and the historical and continuing killing of many unarmed Black Americans, our nation has seemingly experienced a racial awakening of its racist historical past, and its continuing oppression, denigration, and silencing of Black, Indigenous, and People of Color. The COVID-19 pandemic has laid bare the existence of systemic racism that threatens the well-being of humankind as a whole, but differentially impacts communities of color. While experts and the general public initially believed that COVID-19 affected all individuals – regardless of race and SES, we have come to recognize how communities of color, especially African Americans, Latinx Americans, and Indigenous people, suffer from the virus at disproportionate high rates when compared to their White counterparts. Macroaggressions that exist in structural inequities, programs, policies, and practices become visible due to the discriminating impact of COVID-19.

The admonition "Do Something!" echoes the sentiment of many social justice advocates regarding the appalling worldwide silence and inaction of people in the face of injustice, hatred, and oppression directed toward socially marginalized group members. In the United States, the omnipresence of racial bias and bigotry has led many to question the reasons for their persistence in light of widespread public condemnation. In many cases, bias and discrimination go unchallenged because the behaviors and words are disguised in ways that provide cover for their expression and/or the belief that they are harmless and insignificant. Even when the biased intent and detrimental impact are unmasked, the possible actions to be taken are unclear and filled with potential pitfalls. The reasons for inaction appear particularly pronounced and applicable in the expression of racial microaggressions and racial macroaggressions.

In this book, we introduce a new concept, *microinterventions*, the everyday antibias actions taken by targets, parents, significant others, allies, and well-intentioned bystanders to counteract, challenge, diminish, or neutralize individual and systemic racism. Although we discuss and offer solutions to the many barriers to antibias actions, we focus upon a central feature of microinterventions: Arming social justice advocates with specific and concrete strategies and tactics to challenge racism, bias, and bigotry. There is strong consensus that in the face of interpersonal and systemic racism, microinterventions not only disarm and dismantle racism but also ward off the negative consequences of silence and inaction as well as promote positive outcomes associated with self-respect, self-efficacy, and self-worth. For targets, they defend one's integrity, self-esteem, and self-worth; increase the repertoire of effective tools to take action; and contribute to a sense of control and empowerment. For significant others (parents, relatives, teachers, and neighbors), microinterventions offer opportunities to immunize targeted loved ones against the forces of racism, to communicate empathy and support, and to teach them functional survival skills. For allies, taking action transmits to targets and onlookers support and validation, but – more importantly – aligns with and reinforces their own values of social justice and equity. For bystanders, studies suggest that antiracism action is associated with personal satisfaction, self-pride rather than guilt, and the knowledge of behaving in harmony with equalitarian values.

This book is about developing a repertoire of microintervention strategies to combat bias and discrimination. Being motivated to help is simply not enough when well-intentioned individuals lack the necessary strategies and tools required for effective antibias actions. As a result, we hope to provide the knowledge, skills, and tactics that well-intentioned social justice advocates can use in their continuing efforts to disarm and dismantle racism and bias.

As our dedication page indicates, this book is dedicated to the memory of the many named and unnamed individuals who have been killed and brutalized by racism, bias, and bigotry. We cherish their memories in the hope that others will have the courage to step forward and become allies in the struggle for equal rights.

Derald Wing Sue (on behalf of all coauthors)

A Note to Those Who Inspire Us

This book would not have been possible without the work of frontline community activists and grassroots' organizations. To our thought leaders, community organizers, and local community members – we see you, we hear you, we are inspired by you, and we appreciate you. Your inspirational work has protected marginalized communities, demanded systemic change, and inspired others to engage in activism work at various levels.

We understand the way that knowledge is constructed in our society is based on larger systemic inequities. It was our goal to recognize the power dynamics that keep community-based activists from having a larger platform by highlighting the wisdom that has inspired us to do this work. Activists have modeled support in their own communities by sharing coping tools and response strategies that individuals can use when faced with systemic oppression and individual-level microaggressive experiences. As students in academia, we saw this wisdom and wanted to uplift these voices by compiling these resources and creating a framework for responding that can reach more people and larger institutions. We recognize that we have a platform because of our access to the "Ivory Tower" (academia) and professors and mentors such as Derald Wing Sue, and with this, we wanted to navigate these privileges to benefit marginalized communities and individuals. In order to ensure that we amplify activist voices and continue to support them: (1) we have cited all our sources in this book (from journal articles, books, and to forums and social media accounts) and (2) we will be donating our portion of the proceeds from this book to various activist organizations that continue to do this groundwork.

Activists, we thank you. Thank you for protecting, supporting, teaching, and inspiring us. No words can truly capture our gratitude. The work is never done, *siempre adelante.*

With gratitude,
Sarah Alsaidi, Cassandra Calle,
Lizzie Glaeser, and Narolyn Mendez

CHAPTER ONE

Taking Responsibility to Address Bias and Discrimination

We will have to repent in this generation not merely for the hateful words and actions of the bad people but for the appalling silence of the good people.

– Dr. Martin Luther King Jr.

I am only one, but still I am one. I cannot do everything, but still I can do something; and because I cannot do everything I will not refuse to do the something that I can do.

– Helen Keller

These two quotes are reflective of attempts to answer several questions echoed in this chapter and throughout the rest of the book: (a) what makes it so difficult for people, whether targets of discrimination or those in the majority group to engage in antibias actions when prejudice, racism or xenophobia rear their ugly heads; (b) can the actions of a single person actually do any good in overcoming the immensity of racism; (c) what changes must occur in

Microintervention Strategies, First Edition. Derald Wing Sue, Cassandra Z. Calle, Narolyn Mendez, Sarah Alsaidi, and Elizabeth Glaeser.
© 2021 John Wiley & Sons, Inc. Published 2021 by John Wiley & Sons, Inc.

well-intentioned individuals to make them valuable social advocate allies; and (d) what are the tools and strategies that have proven effective in combatting racist expressions on individual and institutional levels? To answer these key questions, we must first understand the internal struggle and complex array of embedded or nested emotions that keep each of us from confronting the meaning of racism.

For White Americans, this confrontation and the fears it generates are elo-quently expressed by Tatum (2002):

> Fear is a powerful emotion, one that immobilizes, traps words in our throats, and stills our tongues. Like a deer on the highway, frozen in the panic induced by the lights of an oncoming car, when we are afraid it seems that we cannot think, we cannot speak, we cannot move…What do we fear? Isolation from friends and family, ostracism for speaking of things that generate discomfort, rejection by those who may be offended by what we have to say, the loss of privilege or status for speaking in support of those who have been marginalized by society, physical harm caused by the irrational wrath of those who disagree with your stance?
>
> (pp. 115–116)

For people of color, the barriers to confronting biases are summed up in these narratives by a Latina and African American about the racism they experience.

> "It seems to never end. 'You're different, you're stupid. You don't belong!' You get angry but have to hold it in. How does it make me feel? It hurts a lot, especially if it comes from your friends and even your teachers. Explaining, doesn't help. They will just say, 'It wasn't my intention.' 'Why are you always so sensitive?' 'Can't you take a joke?' And, I can't say anything because I am so emotional. I don't want them to see me cry or they'll think I'm weak." (Latina participant)

> "I have to stop and think sometimes. 'Are they being racist? Or, is that just how they act? Or, are they just not being friendly because they had a bad day?' I feel like there's nothing I can do. Show my anger or say something, I'll get in trouble. I try to walk away sometimes, but it just eats away at you. Then you take it out on yourself, 'Why didn't you stand up for your rights?' You begin to feel like a weak coward." (African American participant)

Increasingly, scholars and practitioners in the fields of psychology and education have stressed the responsibility of all concerned citizens to address issues of interpersonal bias/discrimination and systemic oppression (APA, 2019c; Brown & Ostrove, 2013; Obear, 2017; Olle, 2018; Ratts, Singh, Nassar-McMillan, Butler, & McCullough, 2016; Sue, 2017b). The call to action was especially urgent when on May 25, 2020, a video of a Minneapolis police officer kneeling on the neck of George Floyd for nearly nine minutes surfaced. Floyd died from asphyxiation and four officers were arrested for participating in his murder. The event sent shock waves throughout the nation, sparked weeks of widespread protests, resulted in calls for police reform, energized the Black Lives Matter (BLM) movement, and ignited public debate about individual and systemic racism. Unlike other unarmed killings of Black men, the George Floyd murder seemed different as it somehow pricked the conscience of the nation and the rest of the world. Ironically, despite the protests and renewed concern with police brutality, Jacob Blake, a Black man was shot seven times in the back that left him paralyzed by a White police officer on August 23, 2020.

For years, social justice advocates have underscored the social responsibility of everyone to (a) take action against prejudice and discrimination (Tatum, 1997); (b) develop the awareness, knowledge and skills necessary to confront individual and institutional manifestations of oppression (Spanierman & Smith, 2017a); and (c) actively promote conditions that allow for equal access and opportunities for marginalized groups in our society (Goodman, Wilson, Helms, Greenstein, & Medzhitova, 2018). Despite these pressing calls to combat bias and bigotry, many have noted the appalling silence and inaction that often accompanies an incident or expression of prejudice and discrimination in our everyday lives (Byrd, 2018; Potok, 2017; Sue & Spanierman, 2020). Because of their often-unintentional nature and invisibility, this seems particularly true for expressions that take the form of micro and macroaggressions (Nadal, Griffin, Wong, Hamit, & Rasmus, 2014; Torino, Rivera, Capodilupo, Nadal, & Sue, 2018).

Sue, Alsaidi, Awad, Glaeser, Calle, and Mendez (2019) have introduced the concept of "microinterventions" or interpersonal antibias strategies used by targets, allies and bystanders to disrupt, diminish, and terminate prejudice and discrimination arising from the actions of individual perpetrators. In their original formulation, they focused on interpersonal microinterventions directed toward offenders who deliver everyday affronts that communicate race-based "put-downs," insults, and invalidations. These antiracism strategies were organized under four conceptual categories: (1) making the "invisible" visible, (2) disarming the microaggression, (3) educating the offender, and (4) seeking external support and intervention. The authors also called for the development of individual actions and tactics that would change, nullify or minimize the expression of macroaggressions (biased institutional policies, practices, structures, and social norms) as distinct from microaggressions (interpersonal slights).

In this book, we extend and expand the concept of microinterventions to include their role in nullifying the harmful impact of not only microaggressions but also macroaggressions directed toward marginalized groups in our society. Although we primarily use racial bias as an example, it is important to note that women, LGBTQ individuals, people with disabilities, and other socially devalued groups in our society can also experience micro- and macroaggressions in the form of unfair and biased institutional policies and practices. Many of these antibias strategies seem equally applicable to combat sexism, heterosexism, ableism, and classism as well.

In this chapter, we make a major conceptual distinction between micro- and macroaggressions, and explicate the manifestation, dynamics and impact of both forms on the lived experience of marginalized groups in our society. We reveal how microaggressions are often hidden in the implicit biases of individuals and describe how macroaggressions can be disguised in the customs and practices of institutions, the public policies of our society, and the racialized ideological beliefs of the general public.

In Chapter 2, we provide a new conceptual framework and working definition of microinterventions and organize them into three types: microaffirmations, microprotections and microchallenges. We explore how each uniquely immunizes targets against and/or nullifies and minimizes the negative impact of micro- and macroaggressions.

In Chapter 3, we review literature that discuss the positive benefits that often accrue to targets, significant others, allies, well-intentioned bystanders, and interestingly to our broader social norms when concerned individuals engage in microinterventions. In addition, we cite scholarly work that explicates the personal costs of inaction (to the target or onlooker) in the face of racially biased and unfair actions.

In Chapter 4, we identify major barriers to acting against prejudice and discrimination, and how they often force silence and complicity on targets, White allies, and bystanders into accepting the manifestation of bias. Among one of the major forces to overcome is the fear of personal and professional retribution.

In Chapter 5, we spend considerable time suggesting solutions for overcoming these challenges. Receiving and providing social support from like-minded individuals or groups may represent a major strategy in combatting racism. The old adage that there is strength and safety in numbers not only applies to individual, but to group action as well.

In Chapters 6–9, we add to the original conceptual framework of microinterventions, formulate new strategies associated with social advocacy principles, and provide examples of effective and functional antibias actions and tactics that can potentially be used by targets, parents, teachers, significant others, allies and bystanders. These chapters are organized around four strategic goals:

- Chapter 6 – Make the "invisible" visible.
- Chapter 7 – Educate perpetrators and stakeholders.
- Chapter 8 – Disarm and neutralize micro- and macroaggressions.
- Chapter 9 – Seek external help from authoritative individuals, groups and organizations.

Finally, in Chapter 10, we discuss the implications of microintervention work, summarize our findings, and provide suggestions and actions for caretakers, educators, and other concerned citizens and professionals.

THE FAILURE TO ACT

The notable quotes at the start of this chapter echo the sentiment of many social justice advocates regarding the appalling worldwide silence and inaction of people in the face of injustice, hatred and oppression directed toward socially marginalized group members (Freire, 1970; Potok, 2017; Tatum, 1997). In the United States, the omnipresence of racial bias and bigotry has led many to question the reasons for their persistence in light of widespread public condemnation. Social scientists have proposed a number of reasons for people's failure to act: (a) the invisibility of modern forms of bias; (b) trivializing an incident as innocuous; (c) diffusion of responsibility; (d) fear of repercussions or retaliation; and (e) the paralysis of not knowing what to do (Goodman, 2011; Kawakami, Dunn, Karmali, & Dovidio, 2009; Latane & Darley, 1968; Scully & Rowe, 2009; Shelton, Richeson, Salvatore, & Hill, 2006; Sue, 2003).

These reasons apply equally to targets of discrimination, White allies, and "innocent" bystanders (Scully & Rowe, 2009; Sue, 2015a). In many cases, bias and discrimination go unchallenged because the behaviors and words are disguised in ways that provide cover for their expression and/or the belief that they are harmless and insignificant. Even when the biased intent and detrimental impact are unmasked, the possible actions to be taken are unclear and filled with potential pitfalls. The reasons for inaction appear particularly pronounced and applicable to the expression of racial microaggressions (Sue et al., 2007) and racial *macro*aggressions, a concept to be introduced shortly (Huber & Solorzano, 2014).

The bombardment of racial micro-/macroaggressions in the life experience of persons of color has been described as a chronic state of "racial battle fatigue" that taxes the resources of target groups (Smith, Hung, & Franklin, 2011). In the stress-coping literature, two forms of managing stress have been identified: emotion-focused coping and problem-focused coping (Lazarus & Folkman, 1984). The former is a strategy utilized by individuals to reduce or manage the intensity of the emotive distress (internal self-care) and tends to be more passive, while the latter is used to target the cause of the distress (external). Problem-focused strategies are more long-term solutions that are proactive and directed to altering, or challenging the source of the stressor. Although there is considerable scholarly work on general models of stress coping (Lazarus, 2000; Lazarus & Folkman, 1984), there is less research that take into consideration how people of color cope with prejudice and discrimination (Brondolo, Brady Ver Halen, Pencille, Beatty, & Contrada, 2009). Even when race-related stress and coping are discussed, it seldom explores questions about what people of color can do to disarm, challenge and change perpetrators or institutional systems that oppress target populations (Mellor, 2004). Throughout this book, we anchor our proposed race-related coping strategies to the more active problem-focused strategies in navigating prejudice and discrimination, preserving well-being, and promoting institutional and societal equity.

Additionally, scholars have largely ignored the role that White allies and well-intentioned bystanders play in the struggle for equal rights (Scully & Rowe, 2009; Spanierman & Smith, 2017). Most research and training have attempted to identify how White Americans become allies, but there is an absence of work on the types of actions or strategies that can be used to directly combat racism (Sue, 2017b). In this chapter, we (a) distinguish between individual microaggressions that arise interpersonally and *macroaggressions* that arise on a systemic level, (b) highlight the importance of disarming and neutralizing harmful micro- and macroaggressions, and (c) discuss the unique challenges of targets, allies and bystanders to engage in microinterventions.

THE RELATIONSHIP BETWEEN MACROAGGRESSIONS AND MICROAGGRESSIONS

The use of the term *macroaggression* is a relatively new one that is often confused, confounded or mistakenly differentiated from microaggressions (Pérez Huber & Solorzano, 2015; Sue et al., 2019). Although both are entirely different concepts, the confusion surrounds the misperception that microaggressions (a) refer to relatively small slights and possess minimal harmful impact, (b) are always unintentional acts outside the level of conscious awareness, and (c) do not include overt displays of bigotry such as voicing demeaning group-based epithets. White parents who forbid their sons or daughters from dating or marrying a Latinx, police who profile and shoot an unarmed African American suspect, or calling an Asian American a "Chink" or "Jap" hardly seem like *micro* acts but rather *macro* ones. For these behaviors, some have mistakenly referred to them as macroaggressions (Torino et al., 2018). Yet, it is important to note that intentionality, harmful impact, and overtness are criteria that do not necessarily distinguish one from the other.

Sue and colleagues (Sue et al., 2007) originally defined microaggressions as brief and commonplace daily verbal and behavioral interpersonal indignities, whether intentional or unintentional, which communicate hostile, derogatory, or negative slights, invalidations, and insults to an individual because of their marginalized status in society. Racial microaggressions are the everyday slights, insults, put-downs, invalidations, and offensive behaviors that people of color experience in daily interactions with generally well-intentioned White Americans who may be unaware that they have engaged in racially demeaning ways toward target groups. The taxonomy of microaggressions includes microassaults, microinsults and microinvalidations.

A microassault is an explicit racial derogation characterized primarily by a verbal or nonverbal attack meant to hurt the intended victim through name-calling, avoidant behavior, or purposeful discriminatory actions. Referring to someone as "Colored" or "Oriental," using racial epithets, discouraging interracial interactions, deliberately serving a White patron before someone of color, and displaying a swastika are examples. Microassaults are most similar to what has been called "old-fashioned" racism conducted on an individual level. They are most likely to be conscious and deliberate, although it is generally expressed in limited "private" situations (micro) that allow the perpetrator some degree of anonymity. In other words, people are likely to hold notions of minority inferiority privately and will only display it publicly when they (a) lose control or (b) feel relatively safe to engage in a microassault. With the election of President Trump and the rise of right-wing groups, however, overt expressions of racism, sexism, and heterosexism have increased. For many, the public statements from the president and the Twitter expressions of racial bias have seemingly given permission for others to do likewise.

A microinsult is characterized by communications that convey rudeness and insensitivity and demean a person's racial heritage or identity. Microinsults represent subtle snubs, frequently unknown to the perpetrator, but clearly convey a hidden insulting message to the recipient of color. When a White employer tells a prospective candidate of color that "I believe the most qualified person should get the job, regardless of race" or when an employee of color is asked "How did you get your job?," the underlying message from the perspective of the recipient may be twofold: (a) people of color are not qualified and (b) as a minority group member, you must have obtained the position through some affirmative action or quota program and not because of ability. Such statements are not necessarily microaggressions, but context is important. Hearing these statements frequently when used against affirmative action makes the recipient likely to experience it as such. Microinsults can also occur nonverbally, as when a White teacher fails to acknowledge students of color in the classroom or when a White supervisor seems distracted during a conversation with a Black employee by avoiding eye contact or turning away (Hinton, 2004). In this case, the message conveyed to persons of color is their contributions are unimportant.

Microinvalidations are characterized by communications that exclude, negate, or nullify the psychological thoughts, feelings, or experiential reality of a person of color. When Asian Americans (born and raised in the United States) are complimented for speaking good English or repeatedly asked where they were born, the impact is to negate their American heritage and conveys that they are perpetual foreigners. When Blacks are told that "I don't see color" or "We are all human beings," the effect is to negate their experiences as racial/cultural beings (Helms, 1995). When a Latinx couple is given poor service at a restaurant and shares their experience with White friends, only to be told "Don't be so oversensitive" or "Don't be so petty," the racial experience of the couple is being nullified and its importance is being diminished.

The two latter forms of microaggressions are generally outside the level of conscious awareness of the perpetrator but may vary in their degrees of consciousness. Microassaults, however, are frequently confused as macro-aggressions because they are overt, intentional and have an obvious distressing impact. As stressed earlier, microassaults are most similar to blatant overt racism where no guesswork is involved in determining the conscious intent of the perpetrator. The overtness (name-calling) of micro-assaults, conscious intentionality (expressing racial inferiority), and harmful consequences (shooting an unarmed African American suspect) are forms of microaggressions, and calling them macroaggressions is a misnomer. Pierce (1974) first coined the term (*micro*) aggressions to mean *everyday* racism that are *commonplace* and delivered *interpersonally* by offenders. Microaggressions can and do result in macro harm to targets, but they are not macroaggressions.

How Macroaggressions Differ from Microaggressions

Macroaggressions are the active manifestation of systemic or institutional biases that reside in the philosophy, policies, programs, practices and structures of institutions and communities (Pérez Huber & Solorzano, 2015; Sue et al., 2019). Oftentimes, they may be codified into laws, such as gerrymandering, where voting districts are drawn up to favor a particular party or constituency. They are the primary culprits for creating disparities in education, employment, and health care, and result in harmful detrimental consequences to a socially devalued group's standard of living and quality of life (Jones, 1997). There are three major differences between macroaggressions and microaggressions summarized in Table 1.1. First, while the manifestation of microaggressions resides in the biased attitudes and behaviors of an individual (the perpetrator), macroaggressions reside in the biased programs, policies, and practices of institutions, communities, and society (Sue et al., 2019). Second, microaggressions are generally directed toward a specific individual target, while macroaggressions are group-focused and

Table 1.1 Differences between microaggressions and macroaggressions

	SOURCE	TARGET	INTERVENTION
Microaggression	Reside in biased attitudes and behaviors of individuals	Directed toward an individual	Changing or neutralizing the bigotry of an individual
Macroaggression	Reside in biased programs, policies, practices and customs of institutions, communities, and society	Directed toward large classes of socially marginalized groups of people	Altering institutional policies and practices that oppress and deny equal access and opportunity to marginalized groups

affect an entire socially marginalized class of people. Third, although remedying microaggressions involves changing or neutralizing the bigotry of the person, combatting macroaggressions means altering institutional policies and practices that oppress and deny equal access and opportunity to marginalized groups.

Central to understanding the dynamism and distinction between racial macroaggressions and microaggressions is the multidimensional model of racism (MMR) proposed by Jones (Jones, 1972; Jones & Rolon-Dow, 2018b). The MMR describes three levels of racism analysis: individual racism, institutional racism, and cultural racism.

Cultural racism comprises the cumulative effects of a racialized worldview, based on belief in essential racial differences that favor the dominant racial group over others. These effects are suffused throughout the culture via institutional structures, ideological beliefs, and personal everyday actions of people in the culture, and these effects are passed on from generation to generations.

(Jones, 1997, p. 472)

From this definition, it is our contention that individual racism is the source of microaggressions; institutional/societal racism is the source of macroaggressions; and cultural racism is the overarching umbrella that gives rise to both through the expression and enforcement of a White supremacy doctrine. In other words, cultural racism is the individual and institutional expression of the superiority of one group's cultural heritage over another (arts, crafts, language, traditions, beliefs, and values) with the power to impose and enforce these beliefs upon people of color and their communities (Sue, 2006). It is the glue that holds together an interlocking set of ideological beliefs and principles (White superiority and non-White inferiority) that justifies discrimination, segregation, and domination of people of color through individual actions of perpetrators (microaggressions) and through the practice of institutional/societal racism (macroaggressions). Micro- and macroaggressions are active manifestations of bias that detrimentally affect individual targets or whole classes of people. For microaggressions, the bias resides in the prejudicial beliefs, attitudes and behaviors of an individual, while macroaggression bias resides in societal social policies and standards of practice (SOP) in institutions.

It is important to note, however, that most active manifestations of macroaggressions are still individually mediated: people act as agents of institutions by practicing and applying their biased rules and regulations. Macroaggressions are most likely enforced by people in positions of power, authority or leadership: employers who decide who to hire, fire, retain and promote; judges who make judicial rulings about the fate of defendants; educators who administer school policies that affect curriculum and acquisition of knowledge; politicians who pass laws and social policies; and health-care providers who determine the quality and quantity of care for patients or clients (Sue, 2006). What makes biased decisions and actions especially deleterious is that they are backed by the full force and power of an institution or community. Like microaggressions, macroaggressions vary in terms of their visibility and conscious intentionality. Institutional and societal macroaggressions can be quite blatant or they can be hidden, considered fair, reasonable, and race-neutral in impact (Jones, 1997; Jones & Dovidio, 2018).

Macroassaults in Institutional Policies and Practices

Macroassaults are social or institutional policies and practices (laws, rules and regulations) that are *highly visible, purposeful* and *relatively undisguised* in their intended racial impact upon people of color. In our society, there is a long history of the deliberate use of societal philosophy, laws, and policies to oppress and to force compliance (assimilation), to treat people of color as lesser human beings (second-class citizens), to restrict or reduce their number in the United States (immigration policies), and to disempower them (restricting voting rights) (Cortes, 2013; Huber & Solorzano, 2014; Jones, 1997). There are numerous historical examples of macroaggressions that evolved from racist institutional and societal practices, often with devastating results: (a) the nineteenth-century philosophy of "manifest destiny" justified the forced removal of Native Americans from their lands; (b) the passage of state and local Jim Crow laws enforced racial segregation in the South; (c) the laws and practice of slavery based on Black individuals being less than human and/or property; (d) the Chinese Exclusion Act of 1882 that forbid the immigration of Chinese to the United States because their presence led to "a race problem"; and (e) the internment of 110,000 Japanese Americans, two-thirds were citizens by virtue of birth in the United States during World War II because they "posed a threat to national security."

Ironically, history seems to be repeating itself in the present day. The proposed building of the southern border wall and the passage of a travel ban on individuals from Muslim majority countries are prime examples of macroaggressions (Potok, 2017). Passing strict voter ID laws that inconvenience and discourage voters of color, attempting to end the Deferred Action for Childhood Arrivals (DACA) puts at risk some 700,000 immigrant children for deportation, creating policies to erode transgender rights (i.e. inability to serve in the military), and diverting educational funds from public to private schools all have catastrophic harmful impact upon those groups targeted (SPLC, 2018). Fortunately, with respect to DACA, the US Supreme Court ruled on June 18, 2020, that the President could not immediately end the program with the justification they provided. Especially harmful has been President Trump's May 2018 "Family Separation Policy" for migrants attempting to escape persecution and violence in their own countries by entering the United States. It has resulted in the separation of thousands of children (including infants) from their parents and families under the guise of national security and disavowing the real reasons of bias and discrimination (Rhodan, 2018).

Macroaggressions as Systemic Racism

The COVID-19 crisis has created a threat to the physical well-being of humankind as a whole. The novel virus has spread throughout the globe and has created widespread panic and anxiety, killing hundreds of thousands and leaving uncertainty and fear. The level of panic and threat has unfortunately bred negative sentiments, more specifically anti-Asian sentiment and xenophobia toward this group (CDC, 2020). This response to pandemics and foreign agents is not a new sentiment or reaction; it mirrors the reaction to the AIDS epidemic when an early "diagnosis" named the disease as "gay-related-immune deficiency" (Hussain, 2020). Unfortunately, the effects have also laid bare the continuing existence of systemic racism in our society.

While experts and the general public initially believed that COVID-19 impacted all individuals – regardless of race and socioeconomic status equally, all have come to see how communities of color, especially African Americans, Latinx Americans, and Indigenous peoples, suffer from the virus at a disproportionate high rate when compared to their White counterparts (CDC, 2020; Dorn, Cooney, & Sabin, 2020; Jean-Baptiste & Green, 2020; Kaur, 2020). Macroaggressions that exist in structural inequities, programs, policies and practices become visible due to the discriminating impact of COVID-19. Systemic racism and the dangers associated with this societal virus span across various institutions (i.e. health care, education, justice system, employment, law enforcement, and housing). As stated by Laurencin and McClinton (2020), while COVID-19 itself does not discriminate, years of racial and economic disparities defined how the virus disproportionately impacted Black and Brown communities.

An important aspect of understanding how macroaggressions operate via systemic racism is to acknowledge how structural factors (inadequate health care, poverty, housing inequalities, etc.) prevented communities of color from practicing social distancing, obtaining access to personal protective equipment, avoiding use of public transportation, and so forth in the same manner as more privileged individuals (Dorn et al., 2020). When thinking specifically about the impact of COVID-19 in Black and Brown communities, there are three major systems/institutions to focus on: (a) healthcare, (b) housing, and (c) employment. According to the CDC (2020), Latinx individuals are three times as likely to be uninsured and Black individuals are almost two times as likely to be uninsured. In addition to this statistic, African Americans and Latinx Americans suffer from higher rates of preexisting conditions when compared to their White counterparts (Dorn et al., 2020). This medical fact makes them more vulnerable to infections and deaths. The disparities within the healthcare system in the United States have impacted Black and Brown communities for many years and the outcomes of COVID-19 have only highlighted this long-lasting disparity. Native American (and

Indigenous) individuals also suffer from much higher levels of underlying conditions including diabetes and heart disease, which make individuals more susceptible to more dire symptoms of COVID-19 (Dorn et al., 2020).

Another major factor that has contributed to the differential impact of COVID-19 is housing inadequacies and discrimination experienced by communities of color, especially Black and Latinx Americans. According to the CDC (2020), housing plays a large role in outcomes of COVID-19 in communities of color due to the following reasons: (a) Marginalized individuals often live in densely populated areas due to housing segregation and discrimination against communities of color. This reality makes it more difficult for individuals to follow preventative care and social distancing. (b) African Americans and Latinx Americans often live in areas that are further away from grocery stores and medical facilities, which in turn make it increasingly difficult to seek care, and stock up on supplies that would allow them to isolate at home. (c) People of color more often live in multigenerational households, which therefore make it more difficult to socially distance and protect more vulnerable family members.

Finally, employment within Black and Brown communities is a major and important factor that has impacted how COVID-19 discriminates between groups. During the COVID-19 pandemic, essential workers have been on the frontlines, and therefore at the highest risk to virus exposure. While nurses and doctors have worked directly with COVID-19-positive patients, they have also received (for the most part) protective gear to lessen the possibility of becoming ill. On the other hand, other essential workers such as retail, grocery, food, agriculture, delivery, and cleaning workers typically do not have the same, if any, protective gear. Of course, this puts all essential workers at a higher risk than the average population, but there are important trends to highlight within the aforementioned essential workers. About 25% of employed Latinx and Black people work in service industry jobs as compared to 16% of their White counterparts (CDC, 2020). Additionally, Latinx workers make up about 17% of total employment in the United States but account for approximately 53% of agricultural workers. African Americans make up 12% of total employment in the United States but approximately 30% of licensed practical and vocational nurses (CDC, 2020). Other discriminating factors that unfairly impact people of color include lack of financial stability and economic resources, inability to work from home, and lack of paid sick leave within essential jobs (not including high-paying medical fields). With these employment trends, it becomes evident how Black and Latinx communities were at a higher risk of contracting COVID-19 in the first place. As concluded by Jean-Baptiste and Green (2020), *"COVID-19 is illuminating disparities that have been long been denied, ignored, and continue exasperating a significant majority of the Black population,"* as well as other communities of color.

Macroaggressions in Standard Operating Procedures

Another form of macroaggressions that may be equally insidious are those hidden in the standards of practice of institutions or society and appear unbiased, fair, and necessary for smooth operation and efficiency. They are often referred to as standard operating procedures (SOPs) that are applied equally to everyone, across all domains and situations (Jones, 1997). The potential inherent biases in policies and practices, for example, are especially difficult to unmask because there is a confounding belief that equal treatment is fair treatment and cannot be discriminatory. Biased SOPs, for example, inundate nearly all aspects of institutional and societal life: (a) criterion for admissions into college (test scores); (b) performance appraisal systems that use a common standard to hire, retain, promote or fire employees; (c) bank lending practices for home mortgages that consider creditworthiness on the basis of location; (d) law enforcement "stop and frisk" policies; (e) biased curricula, books and reading materials that affirm the identity of one group, but ignore or denigrate the contributions of people of color; and (f) media portrayals that foster stereotypes rather than realistic images of people of color.

Sue (2008) provides a real-life example of how SOPs embedded in performance appraisal systems of organizations may appear gender and race neutral, but in fact produce biased outcomes that disadvantage certain groups, but advantage others. A Fortune 500 company hired Sue to provide assertiveness training for an Asian American technical workforce and to help them develop leadership skills. The company made the request because a survey of employees revealed many Asian and Asian American workers planned to seek employment elsewhere. They complained of bias from management who failed to recommend them for promotion when otherwise qualified. The company, however, explained the underrepresentation of Asian Americans in management, as due to "lack of leadership and social skills," and their need to be "more assertive, commanding, and competitive." They disavowed any bias in their promotion of employees to management-level positions, and pointed to company-defined leadership criteria used for all workers regardless of race and gender.

Interestingly, the problem definition paralleled societal stereotypes of the group: Asian Americans are passive, inhibited, and unassertive, make poor leaders and managers, are poor in people relationships, but make good scientists and technical workers (Sue, Sue, Zane, & Wong, 1985). Furthermore, the hiring and promotion criteria outlined in the job description for managers valued "assertiveness and aggressiveness," "taking charge," "being competitive," and "being highly visible." To make a long story short, Sue was able to show the management team that Asian communication styles were often culturally determined (subtlety and indirectness), and that Western definitions of leadership were strongly influenced by culture. Asians, for example, consider leadership competence to be a person who is able to work behind the scenes, building group consensus, and motivating the team to increase productivity. When work units at the company were asked to identify members who were most instrumental in the success of their teams, Asian American employee names would consistently be mentioned. Thus, while not outwardly visible as leaders, they were nevertheless central in getting fellow workers to increase both efficiency and productivity (important qualities of a leader). Interestingly, the company never considered these individuals as candidates for promotion to the managerial ranks.

Sue notes that he was able to help the company examine closely their performance appraisal system (job description criteria) used for hiring and promotion of employees. In essence, their performance appraisal system was culture-bound, and potentially biased toward Asian Americans and women who operate from a much more collaborative and cooperative group approach (Lee, Soto, Swim, & Bernstein, 2012). Biased performance appraisal systems serve powerful gate-keeping functions that allow certain groups to benefit, while holding others back. Applying biased standards may not be an intentional or deliberate act, but the issue is still one of control, power and privilege. Just as promotion and tenure systems in higher education serve gate-keeping functions that determine rank and security, the criteria used for promotion in businesses may be fraught with bias and account for many of the inequities in senior leadership positions, and the standard of living for marginalized groups in our society (Holder, 2019b; Kim, Nguyen, & Block, 2019).

In conclusion, macroaggressions are many times more harmful to marginalized group members because they affect large classes of people and create disparities in education, employment, health care, and the standard of living for people of color (Jones, 1997; Mazzula & Campon, 2018). Systemic change, however, is quite different from dealing with relational microaggressions that focus on the interpersonal actions of individuals. In the case of macroaggressions, biased policies and organizational structures that inherently discriminate are often not directly amenable to change. Change comes from presenting convincing evidence to those in leadership positions, and/or increasing public pressure on them to (a) end discriminatory policies and (b) create new programs and practices that allow for equal access and opportunity (Goodman et al., 2018; Kozan & Blustein, 2018).

THE NEED TO TAKE ACTION: PEOPLE OF COLOR, WHITE ALLIES, AND BYSTANDERS

Given the immense harm inflicted on individuals and groups of color via prejudice and discrimination, it becomes imperative for our nation to begin the process of disarming, disrupting, and dismantling the constant onslaught of micro- and macroaggressions. In this section, we describe the potential antiracist actions of three major groups – *targets, allies* and *bystanders* – in their struggle against racism; we advocate the need for these constituents to take a proactive stance against the discriminatory actions of perpetrators.

Targets

Targets are people of color who are objects of racial prejudice and discrimination expressed through microaggressions or macroaggressions. The experience of a microaggression can often feel isolating, painful and filled with threat (Sue, 2010b). In the race-related stress-coping literature, the first rule of thumb for targets is to *take care of oneself* (Holder, Jackson, & Ponterotto, 2015; Mellor, 2004). In this respect, it is important to distinguish between the internal (survival and self-care goals of the target) and the external (confronting the source) objectives in dealing with bias and discrimination. It is often problematic to ask people of color to educate or confront perpetrators when the sting of prejudice and discrimination pains them. A number of coping or self-care strategies in the face of racism have been identified: social support (Shorter-Gooden, 2004), spirituality and religion (Holder et al., 2015), humor (Houshmand, Spanierman, & De Stephano, 2017), role shifting (Jones & Shorter-Gooden, 2003), armoring

(Mellor, 2004), cognitive reinterpretation (Brondolo et al., 2009), withdrawing for self-protection (Mellor, 2004), self-affirmations (Jones & Rolon-Dow, 2018), and directly or indirectly confronting the racism (Obear, 2017). It is this last proactive response that we believe merits much more attention as it is one of the main explanations for inaction in the face of microaggressions.

Little has been done to offer people of color the tools and strategies needed to disarm, diminish, deflect, and challenge experiences of bias, prejudice, or aggression (Mellor, 2004). Although it is important not to negate the functional survival value of self-care for people of color, it represents a defensive or reactive strategy that does not eliminate the source of future acts of bias. The experiences of discrimination can be jarring and can cause a "freeze effect" (Goodman, 2011). Without knowing what to do or how to respond, targets often experience great anxiety, guilt, and self-disappointment. People of color often wish to confront the aggressor, but their lack of action or paralysis leads to later rumination about the situation and to negative self-evaluations (Shelton et al., 2006; Sue et al., 2007). Additionally, individuals who do not stand up for themselves often experience feelings of helplessness and hopelessness. The result may be a fatalistic attitude and belief that racism is normative and must be accepted (Williams & Williams-Morris, 2000).

Rather than perpetuate a sense of resignation, it would be beneficial to (a) provide targets with a repertoire of interpersonal responses to racism, (b) arm them with the ability to defend themselves, (c) offer guiding principles and a rationale behind using external intervention strategies, and (d) decrease the negative impact on their mental health and well-being. Response strategies provide targets with the tools to be brave in the face of adversity and to feel dignified, leading to an increased sense of self-worth. They also provide targets with the ability to dispel racist attitudes of perpetrators through educational and action-oriented approaches, leading to a greater sense of self-efficacy. Unfortunately, not responding often leads to internalizing prevalent racist attitudes and negative beliefs about oneself (Speight, 2007).

White Allies

Allies are individuals who belong to dominant social groups (e.g. Whites, males, heterosexuals) and, through their support of nondominant groups (e.g. people of color, women, LGBTQ individuals), actively work toward the eradication of prejudicial practices they witness in both their personal and professional lives (Broido, 2000; Brown & Ostrove, 2013). Allies surpass individuals who simply refrain from engaging in overt sexist, racist, ethnocentrist, or heterosexist behaviors. But rather, because of their desire to bolster social justice and equity, to end the social disparities from which they reap unearned benefits, and to maintain accountability of their actions to marginalized group members, they are motivated to take action at the interpersonal and institutional levels by actively promoting the rights of the oppressed (Brown & Ostrove, 2013). Like targets, allyship development involves internal and painful self-reckoning and a commitment to external action.

The internal component for potential White allies involves soul searching as to who they are as racial/cultural beings, acknowledging and overcoming their biases, confronting their motivations for engaging in antiracism work, and recognizing how their lives would be changed for the better in the absence of oppression (Edwards, 2006; Helms, 1995). As indicated by Helms (1996), developing a nonracist White identity is a major step toward social justice work; allies are motivated by an intrinsic desire to advocate for equity rather than by White guilt or to seek glorification as a "White savior." Her theory of White racial identity development addresses this issue profoundly and is central to our understanding of the difference between the development of a nonracist identity (interpersonal reconciliation with whiteness) and an antiracist identity (taking external actions against racism). When individuals expect credit for being an ally, broadcast their self-righteousness to others, or do not accept criticism (especially from persons of color) thoughtfully, their work as an ally becomes questionable (Spanierman & Smith, 2017).

Scholars in the field of racism have been advocating for dialogue, openness, and social action for many years (Helms, 1996; Sue, 2015a; Tatum, 1997). These works have often been the basis of colloquial strategies for breaking down racism and developing an "allied" identity for White people. It is a concerted movement from words toward action, from privilege toward understanding one's positionality in oppression, and from identifying oppression to making a daily effort to resist that make allies distinct from bystanders, families, friends (Brown, 2015; Reason & Broido, 2005b). Allies possess affirmative attitudes on issues of diversity (Broido, 2000), consciously commit to disrupting cycles of injustice (Waters, 2010), and do not view their work as a means to a measurable end but a constant dismantlement of the individual, and institutional beliefs, practices, and policies that have impeded the social growth and well-being of persons of color.

The shift from a nonracist identity to an action-oriented approach, however, assumes that activists have in their response repertoire the knowledge and skills to combat racism effectively. This may be a fallacious assumption as most educational and training programs often fall far short of teaching White allies the concrete and direct action strategies needed to influence perpetrators and social systems (Scully & Rowe, 2009; Sue, 2017b).

Bystanders

Bystanders can be anyone who become aware of and/or witness unjust behavior or practices that are worthy of comment or action (Scully & Rowe, 2009). In many respects, the definitions of targets, allies, and bystanders may overlap, but research on White allyship suggests that allies are more likely to have an evolved awareness of themselves as racial/cultural beings and to be more attuned to sociopolitical dynamics of race and racism (Broido, 2000; Helms, 1996). Although anyone can be a bystander, including targets (witnessing discrimination against a member of their group), we reserve this term for individuals who may possess only a superficially developed or a nebulous awareness of racially biased behaviors and of institutional policies and practices that are not fair to a person of color or racial group. These individuals do not fall into the classes of targets or White allies but represent the largest plurality of people in society.

Most bystanders experience themselves as good, moral, and decent human beings who move about in an invisible veil of whiteness (Sue & Sue, 2015), have minimal awareness of themselves as a racial/cultural being (Helms, 1996), and possess limited experiences with people of color (Jones, 1997). Their naiveté about race and racism makes it very difficult for them to recognize bias or discrimination in others, and/or how institutional policies and practices advantage select groups and disadvantage groups of color. When they witness a discriminatory incident, for example, they may have difficulty labeling it as a racist act or they may excuse or rationalize away the behavior as due to reasons other than racism (Dovidio, Gaertner, Kawakami, & Hodson, 2002; Obear, 2017). Even when right or wrong behavior is recognized, inaction seems to be the norm rather than the exception.

Considerable scholarly work has attempted to explain the passivity of bystanders, even in the face of clear normative violations (Latané & Darley, 1968, 1970; Scully, 2005). Diffusion of responsibility, fear of retaliation, fear of losing friends, not wanting to get involved, and other anticipated negative consequences have all been proposed as inhibiting active bystander interventions. A number of social scientists, however, have begun to turn their attention to exploring conditions that would enhance or enable bystanders to intervene (Ashburn-Nardo, Morris, & Goodwin, 2008; Rowe, 2008; Scully, 2005). Four requirements for bystander action seem important: (a) the ability to recognize acceptable and unacceptable behaviors; (b) the positive benefits that accrue to the target, perpetrator, bystander, and organization through taking action; (c) providing a toolkit for active bystander interventions; and (d) the use of bystander training and rehearsal (Scully & Rowe, 2009).

CHAPTER TWO

What Are Microinterventions?

Your silence will not protect you.

– Audre Lorde

The time is always right to do what is right.

– Dr. Martin Luther King Jr.

Microinterventions are antibias actions used by targets, parents/significant others, allies and well-intentioned bystanders to counteract, challenge, diminish, or neutralize the individual (microaggressions) and institutional/societal (macroaggressions) expressions of prejudice, bigotry and discrimination. In their original formulation of microinterventions, Sue, Alsaidi, Awad, Glaeser, Calle, and Mendez (2019) defined them as everyday words or deeds whose primary purpose is to validate the worth of the target, to minimize the sense of helplessness, and to challenge or terminate biased behaviors or situations. They focused on two aspects of microinterventions. First, they indicated that microinterventions helped overcome one of the primary reasons for inaction: the sense of powerlessness and futility often experienced by both targets and onlookers who

Microintervention Strategies, First Edition. Derald Wing Sue, Cassandra Z. Calle, Narolyn Mendez, Sarah Alsaidi, and Elizabeth Glaeser.
© 2021 John Wiley & Sons, Inc. Published 2021 by John Wiley & Sons, Inc.

experience or witness a racially biased transgression but find themselves "paralyzed" and at a loss of "how to respond" (Byrd, 2018; Jones & Rolon-Dow, 2018b; Scully & Rowe, 2009). Second, although they acknowledged the harmful impact of macroaggressions and the need to address systemic bias, they concentrated their work primarily on interpersonal antibias strategies directed toward microaggressions. In this book, we include the use of microinterventions for macroaggressions as well.

DISTINGUISHING MICROINTERVENTIONS FROM MACROINTERVENTIONS

Our primary focus in this book is on the *everyday actions* (microinterventions) that responsible individuals can take in their *everyday lives* to combat bias and bigotry expressed through micro- and macroaggressions. Just as there may be confusion surrounding the use of the terms microaggressions and macroaggressions, so too readers may mistakenly misunderstand the distinction between *microinterventions* and *macrointerventions*. The individual and group actions taken by social justice advocate to address systemic bias as opposed to individual acts of bigotry, for example, do not make them macrointerventions. Voicing disapproval of biased policies and practices, signing petitions, engaging in letter writing campaigns, boycotting, or appealing to those in authority are individual or collaborative forms of microinterventions aimed at (a) eliminating a biased policy, program or practice and/or (b) creating a policy that mitigates harm and allows for fairness. These are *individual* actions that ordinary citizen can take to voice disapproval, educate others, and pressure those in authority to make changes. In almost all cases, however, institutional and societal changes require the efforts of many individuals using numerous strategies and tactics (microinterventions) to eliminate a biased policy and/or implement a new and fair one.

Macrointerventions, on the other hand, are the *actual implementation of large-scale changes in tradition, policy, custom or law.* Perhaps the most recent and significant macrointervention example is the June 15, 2020, ruling by the US Supreme Court that LGBTQ individuals cannot be fired from jobs because they are gay or transgender. They are protected under Title VII of the Civil Rights Act of 1964. The ruling sent shock waves through the conservative community and promises to have "seismic" implications for protection of

LGBTQ rights in all facets of life. Macrointerventions are attempts to formulate an overarching guiding policy to neutralize and change biased or unfair practices of an organization or community. A macrointervention is often the result of public pressure in which the voices of many compel decision makers and those in authority to implement institutional change. For example, the relationship of social justice activism and institutional change is seen in the impact of microaggression research on college campuses. The language of microaggressions validated and made real the racialized experiences of many marginalized group members, but it also had a profound impact on institutions of higher education by raising awareness of the harm inflicted on students of color (Young & Anderson, 2019). During the early and middle 2000s, for example, discrimination protests erupted across college campuses throughout the country (Hartocollis & Bidgood, 2015: Sue, 2019).

Two particularly noteworthy movements placed high pressure on colleges and universities to respond with institutional changes (macrointerventions). First, the "I Too, Am Harvard" (2014) photo campaign in which Black students at Harvard described their experiences with microaggressions spread rapidly like a prairie fire on social media. It resonated with the experiential reality of many students of color and soon found its expression on numerous college campuses throughout the United States, and even internationally (Sue, 2019). Second, the "Black Lives Matter" movement, a national protest against the killing of unarmed Black men by law enforcement officers added pressure on colleges and universities to recognize the embeddedness of racism in their institutions. This brought about a chain reaction among many students of color who called on administrators to take act against microaggressions (Anderson & Svrluga, 2015; Neville, Gallardo, & Sue, 2016). In most cases, students engaged in microintervention strategies (demonstrations, protests, sit-ins, social media, etc.) to educate the public and to make visible the rationale for their complaints.

The outcry against racism on college campuses resulted in a number of macrointerventions in higher education. For example, Janet Napolitano, former Homeland Security Chief and former President of the University of California system, implemented a policy (macrointervention) of sensitivity training (although voluntary) on microaggressions for employees on all 10 California campuses. Some institutions, like Teachers College, Columbia University, however, require all new employees to undergo microaggression training. Other forms of macrointerventions in higher education include implementing policies that require the hiring of chief diversity officers, creating safe spaces for students of color to discuss their concerns, forming affirmative action committees to insure that candidates of color are recruited, developing guidelines on when racial trigger warnings should be included on course syllabi, insuring the presence of multicultural content in coursework, and renaming or removing offensive monuments on campuses (Eligon, 2016; Young & Anderson, 2019).

Likewise, an example of a societal macrointervention occurred when Nikki Haley, former Governor of South Carolina, decided no longer to fly the Confederate flag at the State Capitol. Her actions did not come about easily but from years of protests by African Americans and social justice advocates who viewed the flag as a symbol of White supremacy, racism and hatred. Symbols of White supremacy such as the Klan hood, a burning cross, statues and monuments, and those that derogate or demean other groups like Native Americans have been found to not only be offensive to targeted groups but also be psychologically harmful (Steinfeldt, Hyman, & Steinfeldt, 2019). The movement to remove dehumanizing symbols was further fueled in the aftermath of the George Floyd murder, which led to calls for the removal of statues honoring confederate soldiers, and the removal of names of military bases named after confederate generals. Shortly after, NASCAR banned the flying of the confederate flag at its races, and many states have moved to take down statues of soldiers from the historical Southern confederacy. Weeks later, Uncle Ben, Mrs. Butterworth, and Cream of Wheat removed or plan "to evolve" their stereotypical depiction of African American in advertising and promotion; Aunt Jemima has been retired. In essence, these symbols are examples of *environmental macroaggressions* because they are offensive, dehumanizing, and harmful to a large class of people.

At this point, it is important to distinguish between environmental micro- and macroaggressions. In their original article, Sue et al. (2007) indicated that microaggressions are not limited to simply human encounters, and that they could be manifested verbally, nonverbally and environmentally. They did not distinguish, however, the differences between environmental micro- and macroaggressions. *Environmental microaggressions are generally confined to individual actions* such as a White person appearing at a fraternity social function in blackface, male employees displaying nude playmate photos in their offices, a person wearing a Klan hood as a Halloween costume, or an individual displaying a confederate flag. *They become macroaggressions when such displays no longer are individual actions, but become a sanctioned societal or organizational policy, practice or custom.* For example, one's racial identity can be minimized or made insignificant through the intentional or unintentional exclusion of decorations or literature that does not represent various racial groups, through use of Native American mascots by sports teams, racial caricatures to promote products, or monuments that glorify the confederacy.

Former Governor Haley's decision to remove the flag (change community custom) was also prompted by the despicable actions of 21-year-old Dylann Roof, an avowed White supremacist, who murdered nine Black parishioners in the basement Church of Mother Emanuel. The horrific incident occurred in Charleston, South Carolina, in 2015. In internet postings, Roof was often seen proudly waving the confederate flag and embraced its symbolism of hatred toward African Americans.

Table 2.1 provides a conceptual framework that identifies the individual and systemic forms of microinterventions used to address micro- and macroaggressions. In Quadrants I (microaggressions) and II (macroaggressions) are listed sample individual actions that citizens can take to challenge the manifestation of both forms. Note, however, that microinterventions for microaggressions in most cases involve directly addressing an individual perpetrator, while microinterventions for macroaggressions may include an individual perpetrator (decision-maker), but is often more indirect because the bias is systemic. Microinterventions in Quadrant II involve garnering the support of constituencies, engaging in social advocacy, and challenging the legitimacy of institutional rules and regulations. The ultimate purpose of microinterventions in this domain is to implement macrointerventions. As Quadrants III and IV illustrate, macrointerventions are aimed at creating new policies, practices or customs that end or undermine micro- and macroaggressions, and/or creating new ones that rectify a systemic injustice (i.e. affirmative action). Macrointerventions usually are the result of sustained public pressure using all the social advocacy tools available to force institutions to effect systemic change. Thus, the ultimate goal of microinterventions is not only to end individual biases but also to create a society with equal access and opportunity.

Table 2.1   Micro and Macro Distinctions in Expressions of Bias and Antibias Interventions

───▶ EXPRESSION OF BIAS	MICROAGGRESSIONS: INDIVIDUAL	MACROAGGRESSIONS: SYSTEMIC
Antibias Interventions	Interpersonal manifestations of individual biases that reside in the attitudes, beliefs and behaviors of an individual.	Systemic institutional biases that reside in the customs, policies, programs, practices, and structures of institutions and society.
Microinterventions: Individual Individual antibias actions used to counteract, challenge, diminish, or neutralize the individual and institutional/societal expressions of prejudice, bigotry and discrimination.	**I** • Interrupt the telling of a racist joke • Disagree with the expression of a stereotype • Point out discriminatory behaviors • Ask for clarification of a biased statement • Support the perspective of a person of color	**II** • Educate decision-makers or those in authority • Join and build coalitions for change • Sign petitions for change • Take part in rallies and demonstrations • Engage in civil disobedience
Macrointerventions: Systemic Systemic implementation of large-scale changes in tradition, policy, custom, practice or law that neutralize and change biased practices of individuals, organizations or society.	**III** • Implement microaggression training • Create safe places for students of color • Require trigger warnings in course content • Make educational curricula multicultural • Incorporate antibias training in schools	**IV** • End the Family Separation Policy • Remove demeaning mascots and racist monuments • Change culture-bound performance appraisal systems • End gerrymandering • Reinforce the Voting Rights Act • US Supreme Court Ruling that forbid job discrimination against LGBTQ individuals

Systemic change, however, often disrupts standard operating procedures, customs, and firmly entrenched practices that frequently attain "Godfather" like status in organizations or society. Former Governor Haley's actions directly opposed a 54-year cherished tradition among many Southerners who responded with outrage and has resulted in a strong backlash (Lerner, 2016).

Likewise, macrointervention initiatives on college campuses have been ridiculed (Schacht, 2008; Thomas, 2008), and universities have been accused of cowering to the unwarranted demands of protestors, perpetuating an infantilized culture, and "coddling minority" students (Lukianoff & Haidt, 2015). Some have even concluded that these policy initiatives foster a dangerous culture of dependency and victimhood (Campbell & Manning, 2014) and have warned of dangers it posed to First Amendment Rights (Lukianoff & Haidt, 2015). It is clear that macrointervention initiatives do not mean that the battle has been won, but rather a realization that the journey to social justice has just begun, and that even hard-fought gains must be sustained and defended.

THREE FORMS OF MICROINTERVENTIONS: STRATEGIES AND TACTICS

A number of scholars have stressed the importance of developing anti-racism strategies (everyday actions or best practices) that can be used to defend against or challenge not only microaggressions but macroaggressions as well (Anderson & Stevenson, 2019; Byrd, 2018; Dotterer & James, 2018; Pérez Huber & Solorzano, 2015). In a content analysis of the counseling psychology literature related to anti-racism practice recommendations, investigators found three universal endorsements for addressing racism: validation, psychoeducation, and critical consciousness (Miller et al., 2018). Validation includes actions that affirm the target's experiential reality; psychoeducation involves teaching culturally responsive coping; and critical consciousness is an analytical understanding of racism. They noted, however, that of 51 scholarly publications, 96% provided practice recommendations primarily targeting the individual level (microaggressions), while only 12% offered suggestions for addressing structural or institutional biases (macroaggressions). They speculated that the finding was not surprising in light of psychology's focus on individualism. They also observed that advocacy efforts aimed at addressing systemic racism require a different set of knowledge and skills infrequently integrated into psychology training programs.

Given this last observation, it is highly probable that microintervention strategies aimed at macroaggressions involve another class of antibias actions that complement those originally identified by Sue et al. (2019). Although they focused primarily on describing the strategic goals of individual antibias actions, they did not explore their complex categorical differences that

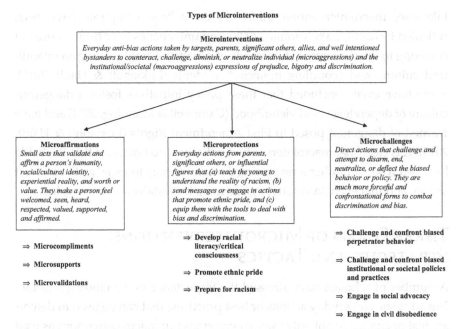

Figure 2.1 Types of Microinterventions.

would make microinterventions applicable to addressing both micro- and macroaggressions. From a review of the literature, we create and provide a conceptual framework that organizes microinterventions into three types: (1) microaffirmations, (2) microprotections, and (3) microchallenges. Figure 2.1 illustrates and defines three forms of microinterventions and their categorical goals and actions. It is important to note, however, that while all three types of microinterventions are characterized by their own emphases, they often overlap with one another in terms of their goals and impact.

Microaffirmations

An African American student had just finished answering a challenging question posed by the White male professor. Surprised but impressed by the student's analysis, the professor loudly exclaimed, "Jamal that was a most artic- ulate and surprisingly insightful explanation!" Although seemingly a compli- ment, Jamal felt uncomfortable as the professor continued his lecture. While the professor and many White students seemed oblivious to the possible offensive statement (microaggression), **nearly all the students of color made immediate eye contact with Jamal** (microaffirmation).

During a meeting conducted by the CEO, Patricia, a Latina manager, made several suggestions about dealing with a company crisis. The White male managers on the team seemed to ignore her comments, cut her off in midsentence, and consistently talked over her (microaggressions). One of her male colleagues, however, noticed the ready dismissal of Patricia's ideas and made the following observation, **"There are many good options here, but I'm interested in what Patricia is suggesting." Could you expand upon your solution** (microaffirmation)?" At that point, everyone turned to Patricia and listened to her ideas.

These examples illustrate two common forms of microaggressions identified by people of color (Sue, 2010b). In the former, the professor is expressing surprise that a "Black" student could possibly be so bright and articulate, and in the latter, the Latina manager seems invisible to the other White males on the team. The microaggressive message sent to the Black student is "Blacks are usually inarticulate and less intelligent. Jamal must be an exception, and not like other Blacks." Likewise, the message sent to the Latina manager is that her contributions (as a Latinx and a woman) are less worthy than that of White men, and that she is "invisible." Both microaggressions are not consciously intended and if the issue is brought to the attention of perpetrators, the tendency is to deny the accuracy of the interpretation. The Black student would be told that the professor's comment was a compliment, and that Jamal is simply too overly sensitive or paranoid. The Latina manager who complains that she feels unseen/unheard by others, that no one takes her comments seriously, and that others speak over her is often told that she should "speak up more" and "be more forceful." In both situations, the Black student and Latina manager will have their experiential realities questioned; they are misreading the situation, externalizing blame, or even accused of playing "the race or gender card" (Sue, 2015a).

Although these two situations are excellent examples of microaggressions, so too are they prime examples of microaffirmations. Mary Rowe (2008) coined the term "microaffirmation" as a counterforce to micro-inequities (microaggressions). She believed that the everyday indignities, put-downs, insults and invalidations that women and employees of color suffered in the workplace could be minimized and even overcome through the use of microaffirmations. Rowe defined microaffirmations as "small acts" in the workplace that make a person feel welcomed, seen, heard, respected, valued, supported, and affirmed. They are words or deeds that reside on the opposite end of the continuum from micro- and macroaggressions that denigrate, invalidate, exclude, and render marginalized group members invisible (Franklin, 2004; Powell, Demetriou, & Fisher, 2013). Microaffirmations have positive impact for socially devalued groups because they affirm, recognize, and convey a counter message to discriminatory racial encounters or situations (Perez Huber & Solorzano, 2015). A review of studies in counseling psychology has identified four validation themes that benefit targets: (1) validating racism encounters and race-related stress, (2) acknowledging and accepting the reality of racism experiences, (3) empowering and supporting strengths of targets, and (4) affirming existing resilience and coping strategies (Miller et al., 2018).

In the aforementioned example of Jamal, note that other students of color engaged in a nonverbal microaffirmation. When they all turned and made eye contact with Jamal, they were in essence telling him "That was a microaggression. Do not doubt yourself. You are not crazy. It did happen." They were not only validating his experiential reality but also providing him support. "You aren't alone. We are all in the same boat." When Patricia's suggestions were ignored and her attempts to make contributions were cut off in mid-sentence by male colleagues, the manager who interrupted the dialogue by expressing interest in her ideas was communicating: "You have good ideas that are worthy of consideration. I value you as a colleague. I view you as a competent member of this team, so do not give up. I support you. I see and hear you."

These two "small acts," whether verbal or nonverbal, intentional or unintentional, are microaffirmations that validate the target's experiential race/ gender reality, affirm their worth as racial/cultural beings, communicate support and encouragement, and make them feel visible, capable and included (Koch, Knutson, Loche, Loche, Lee, & Federici, manuscript under review). In a study of 524 first-generation college students' lived experiences in a predominantly White public research university, researchers identified three forms of microaffirmation: (1) microcompliments, (2) microsupports, and (3) microvalidations (Ellis, Powell, Demetriou, Heurta-Bapat, & Panter, 2019). They define microcompliments as statements or actions that imply praise, admiration and respect for the person's identity, heritage, or for taking courageous actions in the face of trying and difficult times. Microsupports are communications that are provided in situations where the person feels unwelcome or, as in the case of Patricia, "invisible." It may also communicate to targets or socially devalued groups that they are valued, understood, and not alone (Laughter, 2014). Microvalidations are communications that express appreciation for the lived realities of people of color, their thoughts, abilities and feelings. In the face of constant racial invalidations, these forms of communication counteract the negating message by actively validating the racial realities of people of color.

Microaffirmations may appear to be small acts, but they have macro or big impact on targets and onlookers as well. Witnessing a microaffirmation makes the "invisible" visible, models positive behaviors, and creates an inclusive environment for marginalized group members in our society (Jones & Rolon-Dow, 2018; Rowe, 2008). It is important to note, however, that microaffirmations are more than small gestures of kindness and empathy that can be delivered to or by anyone regardless of race, gender or sexual orientation or identity. Microaffirmations explicitly recognize and operate within the social and institutional context of group marginality, exclusion, and disempowerment. When delivered within such a framework, they directly and indirectly counter prejudice, bias and discrimination, and their negative consequences on both the individual and institutional levels (Jones & Rolon-Dow, 2018; Powell, Demetriou, et al., 2013).

Microprotections

I (Chinese American) was eight years old when my family moved to an all-white neighborhood from Chinatown. My first week of school was filled with taunting and teasing by classmates who called me a "Chink," and would push their eyelids up to be slanted like mine. The older kids in the neighborhood called my family the "yellow peril" and would laugh hysterically when they echoed nonsensical sounds, "eeeaah, ooowee, ching chong chinaman" that they thought was our language. I would fight back tears and secretly wished I could be white. One day, my mother sensing something was wrong sat me down and asked what was going on. When I shared with her my experiences, she asked a series of questions: "What do you think is happening?" How did it make you feel? What can we do to feel better? In her warm, caring and supportive way, she acknowledged my pain, talked about prejudice, how there was nothing wrong with being different, that she was proud to be Chinese, and that we would always encounter ignorant people who would dislike us because we were different. It was the beginning of many racial conversations that prepared me to deal with racism.

In the example here, the mother was intuitively engaging in *microprotections* by countering the racist scripts delivered by White classmates: "Differences are deviant. There is something wrong with being Chinese. You are a lesser human being. You don't belong here." She was (a) teaching her son to deconstruct and understand racism through a series of analytic questions (developing racial literacy), (b) expressing her own ethnic self-esteem and dignity in being Chinese American (promoting racial pride), and (c) preparing her son for the bias and bigotry he is likely to experience in life (preparation to encounter racism).

The concept of *microprotections* originates from work on racial socialization, particularly among African American youths whose parents prepare them to function in a racialized world that denigrates their humanity (Anderson & Stevenson, 2019), diminishes their racialized experiences (Jones & Rolon-Dow, 2018), and threatens their physical and psychological well-being (Dotterer & James, 2018). James (2016) defines microprotections as "small daily caring, supportive, and loving behaviors... enacted by parents of Black children to counteract the debilitating microaggressions Black children are sure to face, through the life course... whether unknowingly or knowingly" (p. 2). There are three major goals of microprotections that are part of the behaviors and strategies used by parents of color and significant others: (1) teach the young to develop racial literacy (Anderson & Stevenson, 2019), (2) send messages or engage in actions that promote ethnic pride (Jones & Rolon-Dow, 2018a), and (3) prepare children of color to deal with bias and discrimination (Byrd, 2018; Dotterer & James, 2018).

Racial Literacy and Critical Consciousness
The development of racial literacy or critical consciousness is an important function of microprotections that buffer against the persistent and deleterious consequences of racial discrimination. One of the primary characteristic of micro- and macroaggressions is their often invisible nature, but each contain hidden scripts that communicate denigrating messages to marginalized group members about their worth as human beings and positionality in society (Dotterer & James, 2018; Sue, 2015a). Macroaggression and microaggression themes are likened to a master narrative, in script form, that reinforce and legitimize the position of the dominant group, suggest it is the natural order of things, and imply these arrangements were achieved through fairness (Warren, 2000). These denigrating communications and subsequent actions are painful, strike at the core of racial/ethnic identity (racial pride), and are meant to marginalize and keep people of color in their places (Anderson & Stevenson, 2019). Macroaggressions through the mass media, schools, and neighborhoods reinforce the microaggression scripts delivered by classmates and teachers.

Microprotections through racial literacy and critical consciousness are attempts to accurately decode, decipher, interpret, appraise and reappraise the true meaning of the scripts and messages being communicated (Anderson & Stevenson, 2019). It supplants the master narrative with a counter narrative (White Talk vs. Black Talk) that reveals the true meaning of the hidden communication (Sue, 2015b). In addressing the issue of immunizing and preparing children of color to confront discriminatory racial encounters, Anderson and Stevenson (2019) write, "To successfully navigate these encounters, families must translate these scripts, investigate how congruent they are with their own narratives of humanity, and jettison dehumanizing meanings" (p. 66).

Developing racial literacy is not only important for targets but also for allies and bystanders who can only address racism when they are able to decipher the hidden messages and codes of racism. Sternberg (2003) coined the term *perspicacity* as the wisdom to see beyond the obvious, penetrating discernment, and clarity of vision in recognizing the hidden manifestation and meaning of racism. Paulo Freire (1970) in *Pedagogy of the Oppressed* indicates that the first step to liberation and empowerment is the ability to discern the true message of the oppressor because it demystifies, deconstructs and makes the "invisible" visible. Racial literacy is liberating and empowering to targets because it provides a language to describe their experiences, validates their racial realities, and reassures them that they are "not crazy." For White allies and bystanders, racial literacy is the precondition to their ability to take action against racism.

Promote Ethnic Pride
Racial identity theorists have long emphasized the importance of sociopolitical influences in the development of racial/cultural identities among people of color (Cross, 1991; Helms, 1995). Unfortunately, in a racialized society, the predominant messages sent to youth of color are: (a) White lifestyles, value systems, cultural/physical characteristics, arts, crafts, language and traditions are the most desired and superior, and (b) all other lifestyles, ways of being and knowing, and cultural/physical differences are undesirable and inferior (Jones, 1997). Assimilation and acculturation in the form of forced compliance have detrimental consequences for youths of color in which they begin to feel negatively about themselves, their own race, ethnicity and culture. Constantly bombarded on all fronts with messages (from peers, neighbors, media, institutional customs, policies, and practices, and social

beliefs) that uphold White Western standards, they may begin to view themselves as inadequate, wonder whether their own group is to blame for their current situation, and ponder whether subordination and subjugation are not justified. The term *internalized racism* refers to the process by which youth of color absorb racist messages omnipresent in our society and internalize or come to believe them (Liu et al., 2019).

Research indicates that positive racial identities act as buffers to the impact of discriminatory racial encounters by immunizing youngsters of color to the impact of race-related trauma, building resilience and hardiness, and developing better coping skills (Dotterer & James, 2018; Jones & Rolon-Dow, 2018). In one study of 7-year olds, for example, researchers found that children's ethnic-racial identity moderated the impact of early discriminatory experiences on child behavior problems (Marcelo & Yates, 2018). Strong ethnic racial identities seemed to protect children from discriminatory experiences that lead to behavior problems. The importance of parents and significant others in using microprotections to promote racial/ethnic pride, and to provide an accurate, realistic, cultural history and heritage of their group is a major goal of racial socialization. For parents of color, conveying positive and accurate messages that dispute racist messages and providing affirmative but truthful ones are a monumental task. Liu et al. (2019) have stressed the importance and urgency of developing forms of microprotections to help buffer children of color from microaggressions and their many daily negative racial encounters. They note that the study of microprotections is a pressing and valuable matter for parents of color who would benefit from knowing how to talk to their children about race. The American Psychological Association has provided a "tip tool" of racial ethnic socialization suggestions for parents in a list of microprotective actions that enhance positive self and group identities (APA, 2019c).

Preparation for Racism

Racism is deeply embedded in individual, institutional and societal levels and places the lives of people of color in constant danger. Three recent incidents attest to the danger of being Black in America. On February 23, 2020, Ahmaud Arbery (Black man) was chased down in Georgia and murdered by White men while jogging. The men argued that he appeared to look like an individual who had committed multiple burglaries in the neighborhood. On March 13, 2020, Breonna Taylor (Black woman) was shot eight times in her apartment and killed by Louisville, Kentucky police attempting to serve an erroneous no-knock search warrant. On May 25, 2020, in a video-recorded act that bore a chilling resemblance to the 2014 police killing of Eric Garner, George Floyd, while handcuffed and face down on the ground, was killed by police officers in Minneapolis as he pleaded repeatedly, "I can't breathe." One of the four officers was later arrested for murder, after a huge public outcry in Minneapolis. The arrested officer had put his knee on the back of Floyd's neck for nearly nine minutes, even when he became nonresponsive through suffocation. The incident resulted in days or demonstrations and protests, some violent, in many cities and across the world in sympathy.

It is important to note that microprotections are not meant to protect youngsters of color from the *experience of racism*, but rather to prepare for, buffer against, build resilience to, and cope effectively with the *harmful impact of racism*. This statement, of course, recognizes that forms of racism, which overwhelms the resources of the person, are dangerous and should be curtailed as much as possible. Ironically, parents of color who attempt to prevent or minimize all racism exposure may be undermining their children's ability to build effective cognitive, emotive and behavioral coping skills when dealing with prejudice and discrimination (Sue & Sue, 2015). Developing racial literacy and promoting ethnic pride are part of the preparation for bias because they serve as protective factors against the detrimental effects of micro- and macroaggressions. Preparation for racism, however, usually involves broader discussions of bias and discrimination that people of color are likely to experience, or they may involve situation-specific incidents that include teaching strategies of how to navigate challenging racial terrain (Harris-Britt, Valrie, Kurtz-Costes, & Rowley, 2007).

Racial socialization is best used and most effective prior to encountering discriminatory racial situations (Anderson & Stevenson, 2019). In many cases, however, this form of microprotection is utilized after a critical incident has occurred that proves painful, hurtful and confusing, such as our earlier example of the Chinese American student who was negatively impacted by the racial taunts of fellow classmates. The mother helped the child deconstruct the meaning of classmate behaviors (racial literacy), used herself as a proud Chinese role model (promote ethnic pride), explored his son's feelings to the incident, indicated that he would always encounter people with biases, and explored possible coping solutions to future discriminatory racial encounters (preparation for future similar biases) (APA, 2019; Anderson & Stevenson, 2019; Dunbar, 2017). Microprotections are powerful because they help people of color anticipate and prepare for encountering micro- and macroaggressions that threaten harm at both the psychological and physical levels. Sue and Sue (2015) provide an example of how micro-protections learned from the past prepare a person of color to deal with racialized environments:

> One of our male African American colleagues gives the example of how he must constantly be vigilant when traveling in an unknown part of the country. Just to stop at a roadside restaurant may be dangerous to his physical well-being. As a result, when entering a diner, he is quick to observe not only the reactions of the staff (waiter/waitress, cashier, cook, etc.) to his entrance but the reactions of the patrons as well. Do they stare at him? What type of facial expressions do they have? Do they fall silent? Does he get served immediately, or is there an inordinate delay? These non-verbal cues reveal much about the environment around him. He may choose to be himself or to play the role of a "humble" Black person who leaves quickly if the situation poses dangers.
>
> (p. 269)

This example exemplifies another major realistic concern and fear of people of color – living in highly racialized and racially charged situations that threaten their physical well-being and survival. Referred to as, *The Talk*, African American parents communicate to their children, especially Black males, how to respond to the police during a conflictual encounter (Anderson & Stevenson, 2019). In light of the frequent killing of unarmed Black men by the police, many parents of color know this to be a reality and teach their children how to exercise self-control and manage their anger and hostility (Jones, 1997). For example, in the face of threatening racial encounters, Black mothers teach their children (a) to express aggression indirectly, (b) to read the thoughts of others while concealing their own, and (c) to engage in ritualized accommodating and subordinating behaviors designed to create as few waves as possible (Boyd-Franklin, 2010; Jones, 1997). Something more difficult for parents of color to teach, however, is separating out behaviors of forced compliance from the overwhelming sense of betraying one's own integrity.

Microchallenges

Microchallenges are direct action strategies and tactics that challenge and attempt to disarm, neutralize, deflect or end the biased behavior of a perpetrator and/or to challenge and change a biased institutional policy, practice or societal custom. They are usually more forceful, confrontive, and undisguised than other forms of microinterventions, but may also be subtle and indirect (Sue et al., 2019). While microaffirmations and microprotections primarily focus on fortifying individual targets and/or their communities, the focus of microchallenges is directly aimed at the perpetrator's behavior (microaggressions) and/or biased institutional policies and practices (macroaggressions) (Byrd, 2018; O'Bear, 2017).

Challenge and Confront Biased Perpetrator Behaviors

In the face of personal racial affronts, three options seem available to targets. First, they may engage in a passive strategy, ignore the behavior, and withdraw from the unpleasant situation. Second, targets may vent their anger by striking back at perpetrators with the intent to hurt and harm. Third, the person may engage in an active microchallenge that is strategic and functional in nature. Sue et al. (2019) outlined a number of microchallenges directed at microaggressions that they classify under the strategic goal of *disarm the microaggression*. The goal of this strategy is to immediately disarm, stop or challenge the biased behavior or statement of the individual because of its injurious nature. Microchallenges attempt to (1) stop or deflect the microaggression, (2) force the perpetrator to consider what they have said or done, and (3) communicate disagreement or disapproval toward the behavior of the perpetrator.

Studies suggest that active forms of coping with discrimination have better mental health outcomes for socially devalued group members than taking a passive stance (Dickter, 2012; Miller & Major, 2000). A failure to confront or challenge the aggressor is frequently associated with questioning of one's competency, feelings of guilt and/or powerlessness, and negative rumination (Czopp & Ashburn-Nardo, 2012; Shelton, Richeson, Salvatore, & Hill, 2006; Sue et al., 2007). Likewise, bystanders who intervene on behalf of targets also experience a greater sense of self-efficacy and self-esteem (Dickter & Newton, 2013). It is important to note that becoming angry, irritated, and frustrated in the face of discrimination is a normal response, and being able to express such feelings contributes to an overall sense of emotional well-being. It may prove dysfunctional, however, if it represents an out-of-control response meant solely to hurt the aggressor. Although it may provide satisfaction in the moment, it often evokes a defensive counter reaction from offenders that may prove detrimental to targets. Some have indicated that effective interventions balance a message of disapproval or discomfort without irreversible damage to the interpersonal relationship (Hyers, 2010; Plous, 2000). Hostile confrontations, for example, generated defensiveness, backlash, and threatened the interpersonal relationship. More importantly, hostile confrontations did not seem to increase its effectiveness over measured and calm appeals.

Although individual and interpersonal microchallenges can be used to contest and neutralize the biased behaviors of individuals, when applied to macroaggressions, a different class of strategies aimed at systemic change is needed. Microchallenges intended to combat biased institutional policies and practices, for example, often require advocacy strategies that mobilize a larger constituency to bring pressure to bear upon the individual in a position of authority or to convince, persuade, compel, or even force a change in the detrimental and biased institutional practice. Microchallenges to macroaggressions are manifested in three different ways.

Challenge and Confront Biased Institutional or Societal Policies and Practices

It is important to note that despite the presence of institutional racism in organizations or in the public sphere, the application of regulations still resides in people who occupy positions of authority; the rules and procedures are still individually mediated. Thus, challenging, confronting, and changing macroaggressions mean convincing those in authority about their inherent biases. Many of the strategies outlined for dealing with microaggressions are similar to that aimed at decision-makers and those responsible for creating policies and practices (Sue et al., 2019). For example, an African American mother may be able to educate and convince the Superintendent and teachers at her child's school district to change curriculum policy by including culturally sensitive texts for students that accurately portray the life experiences of people of color.

Engage in Social Advocacy

Many systemic changes, however, are not amenable to the actions of a single individual because they remain embedded in an interlocking network of policies that can only be changed by those in even higher authority far removed from those who are asked to carry out policy (Olle, 2018). Furthermore, many policies may be supported by legal precedence and can only be changed through court decisions and/or legislative action. In this case, mobilizing large groups of concerned citizens who desire modifications represents a powerful advocacy tool in which many voices are brought to bear on the issue at hand. Thus, educating the public, forming advocacy groups, and using legal and political means constitute a class of microintervention strategies that focus on group empowerment and pressure. It must be noted, however, that most microintervention strategies directed at social change fall within legal boundaries that are considered acceptable and peaceful channels of protest. They are means of working within the accepted confines of organizations or within the established social system (Kozan & Blustein, 2018).

Engage in Civil Disobedience

Related to this last class of microinterventions, however, are direct-action methods that confront, provoke, defy, and even sabotage unjust rules and regulations by (a) refusing to carry them out, (b) flagrantly disobeying them, or (c) purposefully breaking the law to call attention to the unfairness of policies (DeLeon, 2010). These actions are not necessarily aimed at appealing directly to people with the power to make change, but rather acting directly, as an individual or a group, to challenge the legitimacy of the authority (Fox, 2011). When Rosa Parks refused to give up her seat to a White passenger, when Black patrons challenged segregation by purposely sitting at all-White lunch counters, and when demonstrators refused to disband when ordered by law enforcement, they were in essence "breaking conventional laws" to achieve a higher purpose (Jones, 1997). We are well aware that these microinterventions may mean taking "unlawful" actions, and that serious personal consequences can result. Advocating illegal actions or civil disobedience to achieve social justice are strategies that must be carried out with cautious deliberation. We note that, historically, they have played an important role in changing unjust customs, laws and regulations, and we will devote considerable discussion to this topic shortly.

CHAPTER THREE

Psychological Benefits of Microinterventions vs. the Psychological Costs of Inaction

There may be times when we are powerless to prevent injustice, but there must never be a time when we fail to protest it.

– Elie Wiesel

On April 12, 2018, two young Black men walked into a Philadelphia Starbucks and asked if they could use the restroom. The barista in a curt manner stated "it's for paying customers only," and walked away mumbling under her breath. In less than 10 minutes, two police officers entered the premises, approached the barista, and she was overheard saying "those two gentlemen in the corner are refusing to leave." It was obvious that she had called the police about the unwanted customers. The officers walked over to the Black men and told them to leave, but both demanded to know "why?" Within minutes, two other cops

Microintervention Strategies, First Edition. Derald Wing Sue, Cassandra Z. Calle, Narolyn Mendez, Sarah Alsaidi, and Elizabeth Glaeser.
© 2021 John Wiley & Sons, Inc. Published 2021 by John Wiley & Sons, Inc.

arrived, followed by two others, and then another two that totaled eight officers! Soon, the two Black patrons found themselves in handcuffs.

This ugly racial encounter, and many similar ones, would ordinarily remain invisible to the public were it not for the intervention of two brave customers who witnessed the incident and recorded it on a cell phone. One was a Black female bystander, Michelle Saahene, who saw a different series of events unfold. The two black men had done nothing wrong, she said, and were waiting for another friend who showed up later during the police confrontation. The barista was less than truthful about her interactions with the two Black customers, and accused them of trespassing. When Saahene tried to explain to the officers that she had witnessed the entire episode, the policemen chose to believe the barista instead. At about the same time, the friend of the two African American men, who was White, arrived and implied that racial profiling was occurring and exclaimed, "This is racist."

As the encounter escalated, Melisssa DePino, a middle-aged white woman, also watched the entire incident unfold, and later tweeted the video which went viral with 13 million views. She came to the support of Saahene and corroborated her story. DePino recounts that she did not know what compelled her to intervene, but states she felt angry for the Black customers, ashamed that this was happening in her primarily White neighborhood, and knew it was important to speak out. The Starbuck interaction went viral on the internet causing Starbucks' CEO to issue a public apology, and subsequently shutting down all 8000 Starbucks for mandatory employee unconscious bias training.

(Gassam, 2019)

This racial encounter represents only one of countless stories told by people of color about racially biased incidents they experience in their everyday lives. Most of the time, these discriminatory behaviors occur in the presence of onlookers who seldom act to intervene. The presence of these two Black customers in a primarily all-White neighborhood automatically drew suspicion, and the word of the barista (White) was taken over that of the men, and Saahene without question. It was only after another White woman (DePino) and the White friend of the two Black men spoke in defense that a different description challenged the story of the barista. The fact that in most cases the word of White people is taken over that of Black people attests to a prevalent "master narrative" in our society; the image of the fearsome character of Black people and the belief that African Americans are potential criminals, "up to no good," dangerous, and not to be trusted. But that alone would probably not have been enough to accept the alternative explanation, but for the existence of a video watched by many.

Unlike Saahene and DePino, most witnesses to a racist incident will remain silent for fear of bringing attention to themselves and the possible negative consequences. We will shortly explore the personal and societal barriers to taking antibias actions, but in this chapter we focus on the personal benefits of engaging in microinterventions and the costs of inaction. Some of these are illustrated in the lessons learned from the Starbucks' incident.

1. First, and foremost, none of us are completely powerless or helpless, and taking individual action to confront racism and injustice can have a potent impact on altering the course and eventual outcome of a situation. Not only did the actions of the two women call public attention to the prevalence of racism in our society, but it had a large-scale impact on a major employer in our nation resulting in instituting a macrointervention at their worksites (mandatory implicit bias training for all employees of Starbucks).

2. The actions of Saahene and DePino modeled for onlookers (targets, White allies, and bystanders) the importance of taking antibias actions, rather than remaining silent and allowing racism to continue unabated. When more than one person speaks out against racism, it is more likely to be heard.

3. It is rare that a racially immoral transgression occurs outside the view of other bystanders, so when others act to challenge racism, it creates an environment that reinforces positive behaviors and discourages negative ones.

4. Both Saahene and DePino experienced personal benefits from their anti-racist actions that motivated them to form a movement "From Privilege to Progress," a national anti-racist organization. Apart from the environmental impact they had in stopping and disarming the biased incident, both felt a sense of satisfaction about acting in accordance with their values of equity, the realization they had done the right thing, and the accompanying feeling of empowerment, efficacy, and increased self-esteem.

5. Last, the costs of inaction are incalculable for both society and on a personal level. A failure to confront bias and discrimination leads to the perpetuation of racism and enhances its continued expression in our

society. Furthermore, from a personal perspective, remaining silent has personal costs to onlookers whose failure to act is often accompanied by a sense of guilt, shame, helplessness, and lowered self-esteem.

We opened this chapter with a quote from Elie Wiesel that indicates protesting injustice is important (do the right thing) despite our inability to change it directly. We would add, however, that the *benefits of microinterventions are not confined to dismantling, neutralizing or ending micro- and macroaggressions alone*, but there are discernable positive outcomes that accrue to targets, allies, bystanders, institutions and society through the mere fact of taking action, as in the case of the Starbucks' example (Jones & Dovidio, 2018; Scully & Rowe, 2009; Sue, Awad, et al., 2019). This is not to deny that ending bias and discrimination is the primary aspirational goal, but when concerned citizens take visible antibias actions, the contextual influence on onlookers, targets, and the person who intervenes has a beneficial macro impact (Nelson, Dunn, & Paradies, 2011). Some scholars have suggested that even perpetrators may experience constructive benefits from having their biased beliefs and actions challenged (Goodman, 2011; Spanierman, Todd, & Anderson, 2009; Sue, 2010). Engaging in short- and long-term forms of microinterventions may, in itself, (a) produce positive outcomes for those who choose to engage in antibias actions (targets, significant others, allies and bystanders) (Byrd, 2018; Scully & Rowe, 2009), (b) establish norms intolerant of racism (Jones & Dovidio, 2018; Nelson et al., 2011), and (c) liberate perpetrator constriction (Spanierman et al., 2009; Sue, 2010). Table 3.1 not only outlines many of these benefits but also describes the negative costs of inaction.

ACTIVE ANTI-RACIST INTERVENTIONS: BENEFITS AND COSTS

On an individual psychological level, silence and inaction in the face of bias and bigotry may have internal negative consequences to those who choose not to act. On the other hand, those who engage in anti-racist actions often benefit personally in many ways. These costs and benefits may differ between groups (targets or ordinary citizens), but scholars believe they are significant (Franklin et al., 1998; Goodman, 2011).

Table 3.1   Active Anti-racist Benefits and Costs of Inaction

	BENEFITS OF MICROINTERVENTIONS	COSTS OF INACTION
Targets	• Defend worth, integrity, and self-esteem • Challenge or terminate biased behaviors or situations • Strengthen feelings of empowerment and self-efficacy • Minimize sense of helplessness and hopelessness • Validate, affirm, and acknowledge the reality of racism experiences and race-related stress • Increased sense of personal and group pride	• Loss of personal integrity • Sense of self-betrayal • Confusion and paralysis • Helplessness and hopelessness • Sense of powerlessness and futility • Negative self-evaluations • Guilt and shame
White people, Allies, and Bystanders	• Increase positive feelings for acting in a virtuous manner • Increase sense of empowerment • Challenge or terminate biased behaviors or situations • Improve self-efficacy and self-esteem • Enhance personal satisfaction and self-pride • Model to onlookers the value of respect and inclusion • Keep integrity intact • Align and reinforce values of social justice	• Self-betrayal of not acting in accordance with one's beliefs and values • Betrayal to people of color • Guilt, shame, or humiliation over one's silence and complicity • Perpetuate and contribute to the problem • Feel helpless and disempowered • Capitulate to political correctness • Lack courage and label self as a coward • Perceived by targets as being untrustworthy • Damaged relationship with people of color • Regret and self-condemnation

(Continued)

Table 3.1 *(Continued)*

	BENEFITS OF MICROINTERVENTIONS	COSTS OF INACTION
Social Norms and Contexts	• Create an inclusive environment for marginalized groups in our society • Create prosocial norms by reinforcing positive behaviors and discouraging insensitive and biases behaviors • Challenge false consensus • Targets feel welcome, seen, heard, respected, valued, supported, and affirmed • Plant seeds of acceptable or unacceptable behaviors in a social context, and positively affect social norms • Stops the perpetrators of racism and reduces its escalation • Makes the "invisible" visible and models positive behaviors for others	• Creates a norm of allowing incivilities and inequities to continue unbated • Discourages prosocial behaviors • Create an undesirable norm, and encourage even greater expression of bias • Create a "social contagion" where prejudice and discrimination can thrice and spread quickly to others • Create a hostile, invalidating, and alienating climate in numerous settings (education, employment, etc.) • Ignoring race reinforces majority group dominance and increases marginalizing for people of color
Perpetrators	• Less intimidation and fear of differences • Ability to communicate more openly with family, friends, and coworkers • Greater spiritual connectedness with all groups • Increase compassion for others • Have better interracial relations and interactions • Increase appreciation of all people of color and cultures	• Distorted perception of racial reality • Low empathy and sensitivity toward people of color • Loss of humanity • Fearful avoidance • Loss of spiritual connectedness with others • Self-deception and denial • Guilt

For Targets

Targets of micro- and macroaggressions often experience an internal struggle in which they are "Damned if you do and damned if you don't" (Sue et al., 2007). Many people of color suffer from forced compliance (Boyd-Franklin, 2010) and choose not to confront the perpetrator or to point out the unfairness of a biased policy for fear of interpersonal, social and institutional reprisals (Byrd, 2018). Protesters may be accused of being troublemakers or whiners, isolated by peers, and/or suffer economic penalties (not promoted, fired, getting a poor grade, etc.). In not acting, many people of color describe a loss of personal integrity and a sense of self-betrayal. This may be especially applicable when a strong power differential exists between perpetrator and target. In addition, targets often describe being paralyzed, confused, and at a loss of how to respond (Ashburn-Nardo, Morris, & Goodwin, 2008). Whatever the reasons for inaction, targets often suffer from negative self-evaluations (Shelton, Richeson, Salvatore, & Hill, 2006), self-disappointment, anxiety, guilt (Scully & Rowe, 2009), feelings of helplessness and hopelessness (Sue et al., 2011b), and a fatalistic belief in their inability to effect change (Williams & Williams-Morris, 2000).

For Significant Others

Likewise, it is often said that nothing is more painful for parents of color than to anticipate, recognize and witness bias and discrimination directed toward their children and young adults (Anderson & Stevenson, 2019). More devastating, however, is the feeling of confusion, impotence and the inability to ward off experiences of discrimination that sons and daughters are likely to experience in a racialized world. Unable to "protect" their children, many parents of color and significant others (family members and neighbors) suffer from constant apprehension about the fate and well-being of their children, guilt and self-blame, conflict and uncertainty about how to immunize and prepare them for the life they are to face (Anderson, 2017). How does an African American parent, for example, explain to their children why a 12-year-old Black child playing with a toy gun was shot by a police officer within seconds of arriving on the scene; the meaning of the chant, "you will not replace us" by White nationalists marching through the streets of Charlottsville; or why schoolmates never invite them to birthday parties or special occasions when all other White children in class are welcomed? Racial socialization, how to talk to children of color about race, and the use of micro-protections are parental strategies that counter the negative messages of society, empower parents and significant others, and increase self-efficacy of targets that results in functional coping and well-being (Anderson & Stevenson, 2019; Marcelo & Yates, 2018).

For White Allies

White allies may also play a significant role in combatting micro- and macro-aggressions. In general, allies are defined as dominant social group members (e.g. Whites, males, heterosexuals) who support the unjustly oppressed, and who actively work for the eradication of prejudicial practices (Broido, 2000; Brown & Ostrove, 2013). As such, part of being a White ally means a well-developed sense of social justice, a strong belief in equal access and opportunity, and a commitment to the eradication of racism at all levels (Spanierman & Smith, 2017b). Melton (2018) states, however, that allyship is not fulfilled unless the person actively intervenes when racism raises its ugly head, and the person is willing publicly to engage in advocacy. Silence and inaction not only make one complicit but also condone bias and prejudice (Aguilar, 2006). The key elements of allyship is "taking action" and being "public" when racism is expressed. Among people of color, nonactive allies are often perceived as lacking courage, untrustworthy, capitulating to political correctness, selling out their principles, and being part of the problem instead of the solution (Mio & Roades, 2003; Sue, 2017). Not acting in accordance with one's beliefs and values is a form of self-betrayal that may result in guilt, shame, humiliation, and a realization of one's complicity in the oppression of others (Jones, 1997; Sue, 2017).

For Bystanders

Some scholars suggest that bystanders represent an untapped resource to combat the "isms" of our nation (Byrd, 2018; Nelson et al., 2011; Rowe, 2008; Scully & Rowe, 2009). Bystanders are persons who become aware of and/or witness a moral transgression that is worthy of comment or action (Scully, 2005). Although anyone can be a bystander (targets and allies included), we confine our description to mainly "ordinary citizens in the majority" who may possess only a superficial understanding of prejudice, discrimination and biased institutional policies and practices. Further, there is some evidence that microinterventions from a majority group member may be more effective and persuasive than that coming from a person of color, although the findings are mixed (Czopp & Monteith, 2003; Levine, Cassidy, Brazier, & Reicher, 2002). When target group members intervene, they are often seen as overreacting, complaining, having a stake in the game, less likely to be objective, and perhaps less credible (Ashburn-Nardo et al., 2008).

One of the major barriers to action among bystanders, however, is the often-invisible nature of micro- and macroaggressions (Sue et al., 2019). Although there are many obstacles to active involvement, the invisibility of bias and the lack of anti-bias skills are two of the major factors preventing bystander intervention. However, many believe that bystander intervention is powerful, especially when it comes from a nontarget or non-ally individual for several reasons: (a) it shifts the unfair burden of anti-racism from targets to others; (b) it represents an unexpected, immediate and positive support to persons of color; (c) it communicates displeasure to perpetrators (often perceived as one of their own) in a public manner; (d) it can free other onlookers to also express their objections; and (e) it reminds onlookers of the values of respect and inclusion (Jones & Dovidio, 2018; Nelson et al., 2011; Scully & Rowe, 2009). In addition, there may be benefits to bystander prosocial actions as well. Those who fail to act often experience regret and self-condemnation, while those who choose to intervene often accumulate positive feelings of having acted in a virtuous manner consistent with egalitarian values (Hyers, 2007).

In conclusion, there is overwhelming consensus that in the face of interpersonal and systemic racism, microinterventions not only ward off the negative consequences of silence and inaction but also promote positive outcomes associated with self-respect, self-efficacy, and self-worth (Nelson et al., 2011; Scully & Rowe, 2009; Sue et al., 2019). This finding seems applicable to targets, significant others, allies, and bystanders. (a) For targets, they defend one's integrity, self-esteem, and self-worth, increase the repertoire of effective tools to take action, and contribute to a sense of control and empowerment (Byrd, 2018; Mellor, 2004). (b) For significant others (parents, relatives, neighbors), microinterventions offer opportunities to immunize targeted loved ones against the forces of racism, to communicate empathy and support, and to teach them functional survival skills (Anderson & Stevenson, 2019; Dotterer & James, 2018). (c) For allies, taking action transmits to targets and onlookers support and validation, but, more importantly, aligns with and reinforces their values of social justice and equity (Brown & Ostrove, 2013). (d) For bystanders, studies suggest that anti-racism action is associated with personal satisfaction, self-pride rather than guilt, and the knowledge of behaving in harmony with equalitarian values (Nelson et al., 2011).

Thus, while silence and inaction lead to negative psychological consequences for concerned individuals, taking action to challenge micro- and macroaggressions wards off negative thoughts about the self while enhancing a sense of self-worth and integrity.

PROSOCIAL NORMS AND CONTEXTS

At an evening social event, we clustered in a small group, laughing, sipping beverages, and making casual conversation. One of the guests had told a series of very funny jokes when he turned to us and asked, "Do you know why (Group X) always look so dirty and greasy?" I became uncomfortable knowing it was going to be a racist joke, and pictured the face of a good friend who belonged to the group being demeaned. Conflicting voices entered my head: "This is no joke coward, say something." Another voice said: "Don't be a killjoy, it's only a joke!" I was standing there frozen and paralyzed, when one person turned to his spouse and said, "Whoa, I'm not going there, I think I'd rather get another glass of wine!" He left for the bar, and I eagerly followed. Almost instantaneously, several others did likewise, leaving only a few to hear the punchline.

(Adapted from Aguilar, 2006; Ouch! That Stereotype Hurts)

When microinterventions occur in the presence of witnesses, whether it be a social event, family gathering, public occasion, or in the workplace, they encourage the positive and discourage the negative (Scully & Rowe, 2009). In the aforementioned example, it took just one voice, one person casually speaking up to communicate to bystanders that the joke was not okay, that it was disrespectful, but more powerfully, it encouraged others to mirror anti-bias behaviors and let the jokester know they disapproved.

In speaking about the intervention of bystanders, for example, Nelson et al. (2011) state: "Bystander anti-racism can aim to stop the perpetration of racism, reduce its escalation, prevent the physical, psychological, and social harms that may result, and/or *strengthen broader social norms that should reduce racism in the future*" (p. 265). Many well-intentioned people seldom consider the powerful influence of a single antibias action on other witnesses, the context of its occurrence, and the broader social norms. Hearing anti-racist comments and witnessing anti-racist actions, whether it comes from a target, ally or bystander, plant seeds of acceptable or unacceptable behaviors in a social context and may positively affect social norms (Aguilar, 2006).

Public displays of antibias behaviors may upset the apple cart of false consensus; the belief among those who deliver microaggressions that there is group support for biased words and deeds. Telling a racist joke, for example, is considered harmless fun that all can enjoy. What are unseen and unspoken, however, are the negative consequences of leaving even small offenses or an unfair policy unchallenged because it creates a norm of allowing incivilities and inequities to continue unabated (Scully & Rowe, 2009). Even more disturbing is the fact that not objecting to a public transgression may even create an undesirable norm and encourage even greater expressions of bias.

In one particular study, for example, researchers found that observing or hearing ethnic hostility among adolescents was socially contagious especially when it involves a "disliked minority" group (Bauer, Cahlíková, Chytilová, & Zelinsky, 2018). The researchers discovered that behavior that harms members of a different ethnic group is twice as contagious as behaviors that harm members of one's own group. They issue an ominous warning that even in social situations or societies with minimal interethnic hatred, witnessing biased behaviors at an interpersonal and institutional level can create a "social contagion" where prejudice and discrimination can spread rapidly and widely!

Diversity trainers and advocates have long argued that organizational climates are impacted and created by the everyday racial and gender attitudes and behaviors of employees (Rowe, 2008: Scully & Rowe, 2009). If disrespect, bias and discrimination can create a hostile, invalidating, and alienating work climate for employees of color, then why not the presence of prosocial behavior in creating anti-racist norms that are intolerant of racism (Nelson et al., 2011). We know, for example, that hearing public condemnations of racism and making egalitarian values salient increase the likelihood of others to challenge racist comments and discriminatory actions (Czopp & Monteith, 2003; Hyers, 2007; Mio & Roades, 2003). Not only are individual behaviors likely to affect the presence or absence of prosocial norms, but policies adopted by institutions can also encourage or discourage respectful or disrespectful behaviors toward employees of color. There is a common belief, for example, that colorblindness should be an aspirational goal in our society. Living in a race-neutral nation mean "forgetting about race" and judging people solely based on merit.

Unfortunately, colorblindness as a means to attain social justice and equity is highly unsuccessful (Jones, 1997; Neville, Awad, Brooks, Flores, & Bluemel, 2013). Sue et al. (2007) have argued that colorblindness is a form of micro- and macroaggressions and harms targets while fostering biased behaviors from dominant group members. In one major study, investigators tested the effects of work environments that profess the importance of either color-blindness or multiculturalism upon employees (Plaut, Thomas, & Goren, 2009). A multicultural ideology stresses the importance of group differences and celebrates their positive contributions, while a color-blind ideology stresses ignoring or minimizing group differences. Both approaches appear to argue for equality, equal access and opportunity, and the importance of fairness and justice. The findings were extremely revealing. Minimizing group differences seemed to reinforce majority group dominance and increased marginalizing employees of color. The multicultural group orientation, however, promoted inclusive behaviors among Whites, encouraged greater interactions between the groups, and reduced marginalization. Others have concluded that colorblindness is harmful to the well-being of people of color and actually results in higher incidents of racially insensitive behaviors on the part of Whites (Neville et al., 2013). The evidence is quite clear that microinterventions at both the individual and institutional levels have a profound contextual impact in creating prosocial norms and discouraging racially insensitive and biased behaviors.

PSYCHOSOCIAL COSTS OF RACISM TO WHITES: PERPETRATOR CONSTRICTION VS. LIBERATION

Some scholars and researchers have begun to note that racism has psychological and social costs to those who engage in biased actions toward marginalized group members (Spanierman et al., 2009). Although it would be an injustice to equate the victimization and harm of racism inflicted on people of color with that suffered by those with power and privilege, there are discernable costs to Whites (Kivel, 1996). Exploring the psychosocial costs of racism to White Americans appears to be a non sequitur, especially when Whites benefit from the current social arrangements associated with dominant group membership (DiAngelo, 2011; Goodman, 2011). Moreover, most studies and discussions on the topic of racism focus on the harm that perpetrators inflict on targets and rarely do they address the toll that bias has on oppressors (Jones, 1997; Sue et al., 2007). The following two passages provide clues into the discomforting reactions of Whites when microinterventions pierce their consciousness as either a perpetrator or onlooker. Sarah Winter (1977 p. 24), a White psychologist, in one of the most powerful essays on her racial awakening writes:

> We avoid Black people because their presence brings painful questions to mind. Is it OK to talk about watermelons or mention "black coffee"? Should we use Black slang and tell racial jokes? How about talking about our experiences in Harlem, or mentioning our Black lovers? Should we conceal the fact that our mother still employs a Black cleaning lady?... We're embarrassedly aware of trying to do our best but to "act natural" at the same time. No wonder we're more comfortable in all-White situations where these dilemmas don't arise.
>
> When someone pushes racism into my awareness, I feel guilty (that I could be doing so much more); angry (I don't like to feel like I'm wrong); defensive (I already have two Black friends... I worry more about racism than most whites do – isn't that enough?); turned off (I have other priorities in my life than guilt about that thought): helpless (the problems is so big – what can I do?); I HATE TO FEEL THIS WAY. That is why I minimize race issues and let them fade from my awareness whenever possible.
>
> (Winter, 1977, p. 24)

The internal struggle that many well-intentioned Whites experience when confronted by situations that bring race, racism, whiteness and White privilege to the forefront of consciousness is well illustrated in the aforementioned passages. Microinterventions make the "invisible" visible for perpetrators, threaten to puncture the protective cocoon of innocence and naiveté, and expose "White Fragility" or the inability to tolerate racial discomfort (DiAngelo, 2011). Sarah Winter's honest exposé about her racial awakening provides insights into the unpleasant truths that lie just below the surface of White consciousness: (a) realization of the pervasiveness of racism and the harm inflicted upon people of color, (b) burgeoning awareness of their roles in the oppression of others, (c) psychological exhaustion that comes from pretending they are free of biases and prejudices, (d) avoiding marginalized group members to minimize being reminded of racial inequities, and (e) feeling impotent in changing social injustices of our society. In other words, White Americans who unknowingly engage in micro- and macroaggressions are also, in a strange way, victims of racism that negatively affects their cognitive, affective, behavioral, and spiritual well-being.

Cognitive Costs to Perpetrators

Elsewhere, Sue (2010b) has argued that being perpetrators require a dimming of perceptual awareness and accuracy associated with self-deception. He notes that few oppressors are completely unaware of their roles in the oppression and degradation of others. To continue in their oppressive ways means they must engage in denial and live a false reality that allows them to function in good conscience. Second, the oppressors' empowered status over marginalized groups may have a corrupting influence in their ability to attune to the plight of those with less power (Hanna, Talley, & Guindon, 2000). The saying that "power corrupts, but absolute power corrupts absolutely" speaks to how an imbalance of power acutely affects perceptual accuracy and diminishes reality testing. In the corporate world, for example, employees of color must be constantly vigilant to understand their White counterparts lest they are evaluated negatively. Whites, however, do not need to understand the thoughts, beliefs or feelings of various marginalized groups in the organization to thrive. Their actions are not accountable to those without power and they need not understand them to function effectively.

Affective Costs to Perpetrators

In a series of insightful studies, Spanierman and colleagues (Spanierman, Poteat, Beer, & Armstrong, 2006; Spanierman et al., 2009) measured the emotional costs of racism to Whites. When racism is pushed into the consciousness of perpetrators, they are likely to experience a mix of strong and powerful disruptive emotions as those described by Winter (1977). These intense feelings represent emotional roadblocks to self-awareness and liberation from their biased cultural conditioning.

Fear, anxiety and apprehension are common and powerful feelings that arise when race and racism present themselves in public and private interactions. The fear may be internally related to revealing their own biases and prejudices and/or directed at members of marginalized groups; they are dangerous, will do harm, are prone to violence, or will take away their jobs. Thus, avoidance of certain group members and restricting interactions with them become the preferred mode of operation.

Guilt is also another strong and powerful emotion that many Whites experience when racism is brought to their awareness. An attempt to escape guilt and remorse means dulling and diminishing one's own perception. Knowledge about race-based advantages, the continued mistreatment of large groups of people, and the realization that people have personally been responsible for the pain and suffering of others elicits strong feelings of guilt. Guilt creates defensiveness and outbursts of anger in an attempt to deny, diminish and avoid such a disturbing self-revelation.

Low empathy and sensitivity toward the oppressed is another outcome of oppression for the perpetrator. The harm, damage, and acts of cruelty visited upon marginalized groups can only continue if the person's humanity is diminished; they lose sensitivity to those that are hurt; they become hard, cold and unfeeling to the plight of the oppressed; and they turn off their compassion and empathy for others. To continue being oblivious to one's own complicity in such acts means objectifying and dehumanizing people of color or other socially devalued groups. In many respects, it means distancing oneself from others, seeing them as lesser beings, and in many cases treating them like subhuman aliens.

Behavioral Costs to Perpetrators

Behaviorally, the psychosocial costs of racism include fearful avoidance of diverse groups and/or diversity activities/experiences in our society, impaired interpersonal relationships, pretense and inauthenticity in dealing with racial topics, and acting in a callous and cold manner toward fellow human beings (Spanierman & Heppner, 2004; Sue, 2015). Fearful avoidance deprives oppressors the richness of possible friendships and an expansion of educational experiences that open up life horizons and possibilities. There is great loss in depriving oneself of interracial friendships, forming new alliances, and learning about differences related to diversity. Self-segregation because of fear of certain groups in our society and depriving oneself of multicultural/diversity experiences constrict one's life possibilities and results in a narrow view of the world.

Spiritual and Moral Cost to Perpetrators

In essence, oppression inevitably means losing one's humanity for the power, wealth and status attained from the subjugation of others (Hanna et al., 2000) in exchange for the unearned benefits and privilege of dominant group membership, authenticity and the ability to form meaning relationships suffer (Edwards, 2006). It means losing the spiritual connectedness with fellow human beings. It implies a refusal to recognize the polarities of the democratic principles of equality and the inhuman and unequal treatment of the oppressed. It also means turning a blind eye to treating marginalized groups like second-class citizens, imprisoning groups on reservations, concentration camps, inferior schools, segregated neighborhoods, prisons and life-long poverty. To allow the continued degradation, harm and cruelty to the oppressed means diminishing one's humanity and lessening compassion toward others. People who oppress must, at some level, become callous, cold, hard and unfeeling toward the plight of the oppressed.

PERPETRATOR LIBERATION AND BENEFITS

Racial micro- and macroaggressions are manifestations of oppression. They remain invisible because of a cultural conditioning process that allows perpetrators to discriminate with minimal awareness of their complicity in the inequities visited upon people of color. When a perpetrator experiences a microintervention, it creates an internal struggle of defensiveness, denial and obscuration that attempt to distort truth and reality related to one's biases. The psychosocial costs of racism for perpetrators are in the cognitive, emotional, behavioral and spiritual constriction they experience and in the loss of a potentially rich and liberated life.

For many White Americans, the journey toward liberation may be unpleasant and filled with personal challenges, but those who have traveled the path often remark that they have benefited immensely (Goodman, 2011; Spanierman & Smith, 2017). Some of these benefits include increased racial literacy, less intimidation and fear of differences, a broadening of horizons, ability to communicate more openly with family, friends and coworkers, a greater spiritual connectedness with all groups, increased compassion for others, better interracial relations and interactions, and appreciation of people of all colors and cultures (President's Initiative on Race, 1999; Sue, 2010).

The process of becoming both non-racist and anti-racist is a long, arduous, and complicated journey that cannot possibly be adequately addressed in this chapter. Further, it would be a preposterous to claim that microinterventions alone could overcome the embeddedness of racist attitudes and beliefs. Yet, we are reminded of the ancient Chinese saying, "A journey of a thousand miles begins with a single step." Microinterventions in the form of personal antibias actions, and in the presence of prosocial norms and contexts, plant seeds of potential antibias change that may blossom, in the future, for perpetrators.

CHAPTER FOUR

Barriers to Combatting Micro- and Macroaggressions

Washing one's hands of the conflict between the powerful and the powerless
means to side with the powerful, not to be neutral.

– Paulo Freire

What makes it so difficult for targets, well-intentioned allies, and bystanders
to act and confront prejudice, bias and discrimination? What internal and
external fears act as barriers for them to challenge oppression and injustice?
Are the reasons for maintaining silence and inaction the same for all three
groups? What makes it so difficult for people of color and Whites, for
example, to even discuss racial matters? This last question holds the key to
unlocking and finding solutions to disarming and neutralizing micro- and
macroaggressions. Before people can even confront racism, they must be able
acknowledge that "race matters" and to talk about it. Yet, as we have seen in
the last few chapters, there is great anxiety and reluctance to engage in topics
dealing with race (Bell, 2003; Sue, 2010a).

Microintervention Strategies, First Edition. Derald Wing Sue, Cassandra Z. Calle, Narolyn Mendez,
Sarah Alsaidi, and Elizabeth Glaeser.
© 2021 John Wiley & Sons, Inc. Published 2021 by John Wiley & Sons, Inc.

Let us use the following personal narrative from a White male professor about his classroom experience in dealing with a difficult dialogue on race (adapted from Sue, 2010b).

Teaching a class in urban education, I was analyzing brief biographical sketches of Black Americans who described how race impacted their lives and the special hardships they encountered in education. Contrary to the usual class involvement, the responses were brief, tepid, and guarded. It was like "pulling teeth" to get any type of response.

Finally, a White female student observed that it was not a "race" issue and that being a woman she had also experienced low expectations from teachers. Immediately, a White male student chimed in and asked "Isn't it a social class issue?" Another White female student agreed, and went into a long monologue concerning how class issues are always neglected in discussions of social justice. She asked "Why is everything always about race?"

I could sense the energy in the classroom rise when one of the few Black female students angrily confronted the White female with these words: "You have no idea what it's like to be Black! I don't care if you are poor or not, but you have White skin. Do you know what that means? Don't tell me that being Black isn't different from being White." A Latina student also added to the rejoinder by stating "You will never understand. Whites don't have to understand. Why are White people so scared to talk about race? Why do you always have to push it aside?"

The two White female students seemed baffled and became defensive. After an attempt to clarify their points, both White female students seemed to only inflame the debate. One of the female students began to cry, and the second student indignantly got up, stated she was not going to be insulted, and left the classroom. At that point, many of the students tried to comfort the crying student while the few students of color appeared unmoved.

As a White male professor, I felt overwhelmed with anxiety and paralyzed. I was fearful about losing control of the classroom dynamics and didn't know what to do. Finally, I told everyone to calm down, not to let their emotions interfere with their learning, and to respect one another. After classmates began consoling the crying student, I suggested that we table the discussion and go on to another topic.

What is happening in this situation? What accounts for the professor's statement that talking about race was "like pulling teeth." What did the White students say or do that was so upsetting to the students of color? What could the professor have done that would facilitate a better conversation on race? What was the final outcome?

Scenes such as this or similar ones are constantly occurring not only in classrooms but also among friends and neighbors, in boardrooms, in the workplace, between political pundits on television, and even within family members. When race and racism become topics of discussion, they often push powerful emotional "hot" buttons in people, arouse defensiveness, constrict and distort perceptions, lead to avoidance of the topic, or an attempt to minimize its importance (Bell, 2003; Sue, Torino et al., 2009). These interactions and their unsuccessful resolutions lead to anger, frustration and usually a hardening of opposing racial views. In most cases, participants in racial dialogues seldom understand precisely what transpired that created the antagonisms and hard feelings.

In Chapter 3, we spoke about the importance of racial literacy, critical consciousness, or the ability to unmask the many manifestation of implicit and explicit bias, the ability to see beyond the obvious, to read between the lines, and to make sense of racial interactions (Anderson & Stevenson, 2019). Understanding the different perspectives and achieving critical consciousness to what is occurring in this situation is crucial to taking effective action. Tabling the discussion, stifling strong feelings, and allowing the conversation on race to be sidetracked (shifting the topic to gender and social class, for example) are not taking effective action. To engage in an effective microintervention requires an appreciation of the multiple internal dynamics and struggles occurring within the two groups and that of the professor.

1. From the perspective of White students, they are (a) experiencing powerful emotions such as anxiety, fear, anger, betrayal or defensiveness; (b) ambivalent about engaging the topic; (c) remaining silent or avoiding discussing race; (d) actively diluting, dismissing or negating its importance in the discussion; and (e) feeling misunderstood unjustly accused of being biased. One student even left the room and another started to cry. In essence, they were engaging in defensive maneuvers to avoid talking about race for fear of being perceived as being racist (Sue, 2015a).

2. From the perspective of students of color, however, they are (a) experiencing a denial and invalidation of their racial realities, (b) feeling that their racial integrities are being assailed, (c) frustrated that their White counterparts are so unaware of their biases and privileges, and (d)

angry and fed up with what they see as White denial and a "conspiracy of silence."

3. The professor, however, is (a) fearful of losing control of the classroom dynamics and concerned that it will become known as "the classroom from hell," (b) believes that the strong emotions expressed are antagonistic to reason and not a legitimate form of academic expression, and (c) attempts to terminate the discussion before it gets out of control and becomes disrespectful. In many respects, the professor is unaware that he has colluded with White students to avoid the many emotional and important facets of race and racism.

This singular example touches upon the many sides that impose both intentional and unintentional silence and complicity on targets, White allies, and bystanders and allows racism to thrive uninterrupted. In a series of studies aimed at unmasking the fears of discussing race, racism, whiteness and White privilege, Sue and colleagues (Sue, Lin et al., 2009; Sue, Rivera et al., 2011; Sue, Torino et al., 2009) came to the following conclusions about difficult dialogues on race.

First, topics on race and racism are anxiety provoking to targets, allies and bystanders for many different reasons. Understanding your emotive reactions whether it be anxiety, anger, defensiveness, guilt, frustration and hopelessness is key to freeing oneself to understand the perspective of others. As long as self-awareness is low, feelings remain garbled and uncontrolled, and fears dictate your behaviors, it is difficult to act or intervene effectively. In the aforementioned example, the professor was locked in an internal struggle (not being able to recognize what was happening in the classroom, fearful of losing control, and chose to terminate the classroom dynamics). In essence, he had lost the ability to intervene effectively in the situation and to make it a learning opportunity.

Second, the nature of the difficult dialogue on race remained primarily invisible to both the White professor and White students. In a series of studies conducted by Sue and colleagues (Sue, Rivera et al., 2011; Sue, Torino et al., 2009), they found that the majority of White professors and White students grappled with understanding what was occurring in a difficult dialogue on race. Although they could not put their fingers on what instigated the explosive reactions, most sensed that something was wrong, that the issue dealt with race, and that they feared showing their ignorance or bias. In general, not being able to decipher or to decode such encounters means an inability to engage in any purposeful and educational intervention.

Third, these two studies produced a multitude of rich information concerning how Whites perceive, react and deal with racial interactions in the classroom. Not only did they experience a fear of loss of control and the emotionally charged nature of the classroom climate, but also nearly all acknowledged a strong desire to facilitate difficult dialogues well, but were hindered by several factors: (a) uncertainty and confusion about what had instigated racial conflict, (b) the strong disruptive emotions of anxiety, anger, and defensiveness, and (c) the lack of knowledge or skills to properly intervene. In other words, they lacked a repertoire of antibias interventions to disarm or defuse racial incidents. Interestingly, many professors were very cognizant about their inability to handle a racial incident well. Some shared with the researchers their feelings of inadequacy: they experienced a deep sense of personal failure, disappointment in self, and feelings of inadequacy as an instructor.

Like classroom situations, responding to individual acts of bigotry (microaggressions), confronting institutional policies (macroaggressions) that oppress marginalized groups in our society, and changing ethnocentric norms are filled with potentially negative consequences that discourage individual actions (Ashburn-Nardo, Morris, & Goodwin, 2008; Goodman, 2011). It begins, however, with overcoming fears that discourage open and honest racial dialogues. Fighting against bias and discrimination seems to involve a multistage process with each offering distinctive challenges to overcome. Although listed in sequential fashion, we do not imply that these obstacles are necessarily linear, apply equally in all situations, and exhaustive. Rather, we believe they are dynamic, intersecting, and often the main reasons for inaction. Table 4.1 lists five of the major barriers to microintervention actions and the facilitative conditions (discussed in Chapter 5) that help overcome these challenges.

BEING OBLIVIOUS, INNOCENT, AND NAÏVE

First, individuals must become aware of or recognize that a prejudicial comment, racial invalidation, discriminatory action, or the application of a biased institutional policy has occurred (Sue, 2010b). One of the primary reasons for inaction, especially in the case of implicit bias or microaggressions, is their

Table 4.1 Barriers to Action and Solutions to Inaction

BARRIERS TO MICROINTERVENTION ACTIONS	SOLUTIONS TO INACTION
1. Being oblivious, innocent and naïve	1. Learning to recognize and decode hidden expressions of bias
2. Minimizing harm	2. Becoming aware of the toxicity and harmful impact of micro/macroaggressions
3. Maintaining harmony and avoiding conflict	3. Creating norms that counter conflict avoidance
4. Fearing repercussions • Isolation • Loss of position and power • Attacks of character • Psychological stress and burnout • Violent threats and physical harm	4. Seeking support and allies
5. Being paralyzed and feeling impotent	5. Obtaining skills and tactic to respond to micro/macroaggressions

invisibility. Microaggressions are frequently outside the level of conscious awareness of perpetrators and their outward manifestations are often disguised in ways that make it difficult for onlookers or even targets to clearly label racial bias (Gaertner & Dovidio, 2005), gender bias (Swim, Hyers, Cohen, & Ferguson, 2001), or sexual orientation bias (Herek, 1998).

Let us return to the opening case vignette in which two White female students felt unfairly attacked by students of color and accused of being racist. Perceiving themselves as good, moral and decent human beings, they felt hurt, humiliated, misunderstood and betrayed. One of the students walked out of the class because she was offended and staying would subject her to further "abuse." Another student was so distraught by the implied "accusation" of racism that she broke down in tears. Most of the White students, including the professor, were unaware of what had really transpired; the students of color had been the target of microinvalidations that caused their emotive statements. But more important was the metacommunication sent to students of color that they were "at fault" for the outcome.

In a revealing article, "When White Women Cry: How White Women's Tears Oppress Women of Color," Accapadi (2007) describes how tears from

White women in a verbal exchange automatically stops the original dialogue and refocus actions to consoling the person. First, the actual issue involved in the dialogue (existence of implicit bias via microaggressions) is sidetracked and no longer the center of attention. In most cases, such diversions ultimately prevent a return to the topic because of the discomfort that may again ensue. Second, the remainder of the class meeting was spent on consoling the female student and, by default, suggested she was not at fault or wrong. In other words, she was the one being supported and validated. Third, the outcome of the debate is likely to place responsibility and blame on students of color. They were *so antagonistic that they made someone cry*. Because people of color are often exposed to the "White vulnerability" card, they recognize such defensive maneuvers as the methods often used by Whites to detract from the topic at hand and to "blame the victim." So, by sitting at their desks being *unmoved and unfeeling*, they were further blamed for lacking humanity and compassion for others.

Likewise, as we have seen, macroaggressions in the form of inequitable programs, policies and practices of an organization can be concealed in SOPs that render their discriminatory nature undetectable (i.e. glass ceiling) (Jones & Dovidio, 2018). Rules or regulations that appear to apply equally to everyone may have discriminatory impact upon certain groups in our society (Jones, 1997). Some scholars have observed that there may be functional psychological reasons for majority group members to remain oblivious to the existence of bias and discrimination (Spanierman & Smith, 2017). Recognition of a personal moral transgression or unfair application of a policy can mean (a) an uncomfortable call to action (Helms, 1995), (b) realization of one's silent complicity in the oppression of others (Tatum, 1997), (c) overwhelming feelings of guilt and helplessness (Sue, 2015b), and (d) more importantly, the loss of innocence and naiveté (Jones, 1997). Challenging a perpetrator or advocating for the removal of biased practices can mean leaving one's comfort zone and placing oneself at risk. Thus, making the "invisible" visible is a challenging, but first step toward disarming prejudice and discrimination at both the individual and institutional levels (Sue, 2010a).

Minimizing the Harm

Second, even when a violation is clear and the unfairness of an organizational regulation is unmasked, the person must decide whether the transgression or possible inequity is serious enough to warrant a response or whether it is relatively harmless or insignificant. Sue et al. (2007) describe one of the major psychological dilemmas of microaggressions – their "perceived minimal harm." They are often seen by the public as "innocent acts," harmless fun, trivial, unintentional, or a mischievous joke that a target or onlooker is admonished to simply "Let it go, and do not make a big deal about it." In fact, raising the issue of a wrongdoing can result in victim blaming and accusations that the person is oversensitive, catastrophizing and "making a mountain out of a molehill" (Thomas, 2008). When many marginalized groups shared a strong sense of grief after the 2016 Presidential election, they were endlessly referred to as "crybabies" and told to "get over" themselves (Gesiotto, 2016). Interestingly, in a research paper reporting three empirical studies that tested the "hypersensitive" hypothesis, it was found that ethnic minorities were no more sensitive than their White counterparts, but that they experienced many more racial slights and insults than majority group members (West, 2019).

Likewise, macroaggressions can be deemed harmless, and that the damage inflicted toward a group is simply nonsense, exaggerated or insignificant (Steinfeldt, Hyman, & Steinfeldt, 2019). Such is the case of displaying confederate symbols and statues and sports teams using Native American mascots, nicknames and logos, or other forms of environmental macroaggressions that have proven offensive to many groups of color. Advocates of these visual symbols claim that they are not racist, they accurately reflect history, and in the case of Indian symbols, actually honor Native Americans (Steinfeldt & Steinfeldt, 2012)!

Studies on the impact of micro- and macroaggressions, however, indicate that far from being insignificant and inconsequential, their cumulative nature can assail the mental health of recipients (Ong, Burrow, Fuller-Boswell, Ja, & Sue, 2013), produce a hostile and invalidating work climate (Purdie-Vaughns, Davis, Steele, & Ditlmann, 2008; Solorzano, Ceja, & Yasso, 2000), lower work productivity and problem-solving (Dovidio, 2001; Salvatore & Shelton, 2007), and result in inequities in education, employment and health care (Jones & Dovidio, 2018). When an act or a policy is considered innocuous or a "small offense," interventions by targets and well-meaning bystanders will be discouraged and unlikely to occur.

Maintaining Harmony and Avoiding Conflict

Third, Sue (2015a) has introduced the concept of the "politeness protocol," a conversation convention in our society that discourages honest and open dialogue on topics of race/gender, racism and sexism in favor of friendly and noncontroversial topics. These social taboos in the form of rules and norms dictating when and how race, gender or other hot button topics are discussed can often leave marginalized group members feeling invisible, dismissed or invalidated. This occurs at both the individual and organization levels.

In social gatherings, for example, a societal ground rule exists that controversial topics are to be avoided in order to preserve social harmony, group balance, and pleasantries. Pointing out or objecting to a biased comment risks being potentially disruptive, divisive, creating disagreements, offending others, and ultimately endangering group cohesion (Zou & Dickster, 2013). If a microaggression was to occur, people operating under this norm may choose not to respond to it because of an unspoken rule that uncomfortable topics are to be avoided, ignored, or silenced; if, however, the topic is discussed, it is done so in a very superficial manner.

This may apply equally to macroaggressions where a biased application of a policy or regulation may result in unfair treatment of a marginalized group in places of employment. In an economic downturn, for example, a manager who is aware that the company's policy of seniority (last hired, first fired) disproportionately discriminates against employees of color may remain silent as to "not rock the boat," to avoid controversy and conflict, to maintain organizational harmony, and to keep in the good graces of upper management. Thus, the biased custom is ignored, trivialized, and seen as simply a standard operating procedure.

Fearing Repercussions

Fourth, in many respects, fearing repercussions is a dominant theme that even underlies all the previous barriers to engaging in microinterventions. Taking action involves assessing the risk potential and consequences of confronting a transgression or biased practice. For example, fear of negative consequences and retaliation are identified as major barriers to taking action (Byrd, 2018; Rasinski & Czopp, 2010). When a micro- or macroaggression occurs, both the target and onlooker need to access the potential punitive costs of their antibias actions.

Such struggles are intensified when the perpetrator or representative of an organization holds power or authority over the person. In this case, an unequal status relationship between perpetrators and targets makes it very difficult to engage in microinterventions. Relationships that involve a supervisor and employees, a professor and students, or a healthcare provider and patients are such examples. Although we can point out the serious costs of taking action from a scholarly perspective, it would be irresponsible of us not to warn antibias advocates about the real-life ramifications that may affect their social, psychological, and even physical well-being. Among those identified in the literature are isolation, loss of position, power and privilege, attacks of character, psychological stress and burnout, and violent threats and physical harm (Haley, 1964; Myers, 2017; Olle, 2018; Sue, 2017a; Tatum, 2002).

Isolation

The detrimental *social consequences* such as ostracism and rejection by family, friends or coworkers can be discouraging and powerful:

> Will I damage my friendships? Will people see me as a spoil sport and unable to take a joke? Will I be isolated from my peers and considered a trouble-maker? As a member of the dominant group, will I be accused of being a bleeding heart liberal? Will I lose my privacy and become the center of attention? As a target, will I be accused of being a "cry baby" and playing the race or gender card?
>
> (Tatum, 2002)

Taking personal action against racism often leaves family and friends baffled at the unexpected anti-racist interventions of a family member or colleague who has never shown such proclivities before. Their actions may violate traditional family, social or community norms that leave others offended, embarrassed, hurt, feeling falsely accused, or betrayed. Those who speak up against injustice must weigh the possible personal and interpersonal gains from engaging in anti-racist activities and their subsequent costs. In a study of White anti-racist allies, for example, participants indicated that among the backlash they feared most was the "break in or loss of important relationships" (Malott et al., 2019). They described feeling estranged from their peer's perceptions of reality and unable to share their new understanding of racism and oppression. With newfound racial awakening, allies often describe a state of loneliness where family, friends and colleagues no longer play a supporting role in validating their anti-racist beliefs and attitudes (Sue, 2017b). Ironically, they feel pressured to return to their "old ways and selves."

Loss of Position and Power

Microinterventions may jeopardize one's positionality, dominance, influential roles, and the rewards that follow from endorsing the "company line." White allies, for example, must ultimately face potential loss of power and privilege enjoyed as a member of the dominant group. Impediments to action may encompass potential *economic consequences*: not receiving a well-deserved raise or promotion, receiving a lower grade in class, or receiving inferior healthcare treatment. In order for allies to engage in anti-racist acts, they must acknowledge and be willing to give up power in privileged situations that may have major financial repercussions (Michael & Conger, 2009). Allies also reported that beyond being ostracized at work, they often felt that their jobs were in jeopardy (Malott, Schaefle, Paone, Cates, & Haizlip, 2019).

Speaking out against possible macroaggressions embedded in foreign policy with high political stakes, for example, can result in a severe backlash, especially when such policies have attained almost untouchable "godfather" like status. Many have wondered why the Republican Party and its members have remained relatively silent about Trump's desire to build the Southern Border wall, to ban people from predominantly Muslim countries, and to implement the inhumane Family Separation Policy. Republicans who have dared to speak against these policies were crushed by pro-Trump candidates in primaries (Representative Mark Sanford), forced to quit their party (Representative Justin Amash), or retired (Senators Jeff Flake and Bob Corker). Other critics have become ominously silent in order to preserve their jobs as senators or congressional representatives (Southern Poverty Law Center, 2019).

Attacks on Character

Social justice advocates who challenge unfair laws and speak out against oppression must be prepared for the possibility of facing attacks to their character (Hoefer, 2019). Attempts to portray protesters as flawed individuals occurred during the Civil Rights Movement and ensuing protests that erupted on college campuses in the 1960s (Caplan, 1970). Social scientists have labeled this the "riffraff theory" of protesters, and it was often used by those in power and privilege (university administrators, law enforcement, and politicians) to portray protesters as having personal flaws, thereby invalidating the legitimacy of their complaints (Caplan, 1970; Fogelson, 1970). Student protesters were often described as overly sensitive, whiners, snivelers, immature, self-pitying, and even coming from "criminal elements" (Turner & Wilson, 1976).

A more recent example of attacking the character of opponents has been the July 2019 racist tweets of President Trump demanding that four Democratic women in Congress – Representatives Alexandria Ocasio Cortez, Rashida Tlaib, Ayanna Pressley, and Ilhan Omar – "go back" to the "crime infested places from which they came." All four are women of color, American citizens, and only one born overseas. The President committed a microassault by directly stating that the group was unpatriotic, foreigners, and not true Americans. Days later, Trump again decried the four women at a rally in North Carolina and aimed much of his ire at Omar. In response to Trump's attacks, the crowd chanted, "Send her back, send her back." Soon after, he told the audience, "If they don't love it, tell them to leave it." He continued the assault upon their characters by labeling them as "insecure, weak, and incapable of loving their country."

Psychological Stress and Burnout

Engaging in anti-racist or social advocacy actions can take a heavy toll on the emotional well-being of activists (Banks et al., 2019). Whether a target, ally or bystander, the pushback from objecting to or making a transgression public can result in enormous stress. Racial battle fatigue for targets (Gorski, 2019; Smith, Hung, & Franklin, 2011) and chronic stress for allies can lead to the burnout syndrome, a term popularized by Maslach, Jackson, Leiter, Schaufeli, and Schwab (1986). They identified three dimensions of burnout that appear relevant to those who strive toward social justice and challenge individual and organizational injustices (Bemak & Chung, 2008). First, a key component of burnout is a state of emotional exhaustion where people feel so drained that they find it difficult to give of themselves to others, even with loved ones. Energy to confront even minor challenges is depleted. A second feature is depersonalization where targets and allies may develop a cynical, negative and pessimistic attitude toward others and life in general. There is increased belief that individual or systemic changes are futile. The last component of burnout is feelings of dissatisfaction and hopelessness related to a reduced sense of personal efficacy and accomplishments. These characteristics of burnout not only diminish psychological health but also render advocates ineffective in their quest for social justice.

Violent Threats and Physical Harm

As we have seen, most of the negative reactions directed toward those who seek individual or institutional change vary on a continuum from disapproval (silence, mild disagreement, or ridicule) to implied or direct threats of retaliation (name-calling, ostracism or economic consequences). Although violent threats and physical harm are always possible when people's perceptions of racial realities are challenged, they are most likely to occur during large group protests that result in public demonstrations or civil disobedience. Civil disobedience poses a threat to the rule of law and can result in protestors facing jail time, altercations, and physical harm. Martin Luther King, Jr., has argued, however, that civil disobedience for a just cause is not lawlessness, but a higher form of lawfulness (Myers, 2014). Threats of violence can also come from ordinary citizens who are angered by protesters. It is common to hear about activists who must seek police protection from individuals who disagree with the beliefs, opinions, or actions of antiracist advocates.

Black Lives Matter (BLM) activists have had to cancel events and talks due to death threats. In an email, following the cancellation of a lecture at Webster University in Missouri, Alicia Garza, a cofounder of BLM, wrote, "ultimately, the result of these threats and online attacks is that students who are hungry to learn about Black Lives Matter and how to engage meaningfully in the movement are denied the opportunity to do so" (Terrell, 2016). The ultimate threat to one's safety is a potential loss of life. Dying for a cause has always been a part of various liberation movements. In the words of Malcolm X, "if you're not ready to die for it, put the word 'freedom' out of your vocabulary" (Haley, 1964). Martin Luther King, Jr. as the de facto leader of the Civil Rights Movement was subjected to constant threats to his well-being: he was refused service, heckled, stabbed, assaulted, and finally assassinated on April 4, 1968.

BEING PARALYZED AND FEELING IMPOTENT

Fifth, should a person make a decision to intervene, the paralysis of not knowing what to do has been identified as a major barrier (Ashburn-Nardo, Morris, & Goodwin, 2008; Sue et al., 2019). Studies suggest that White professors and professors of color, for example, who witness a racial microaggression in the classroom often felt impotent, confused and at a loss of what to do (Sue et al., 2009, 2011). They felt unprepared to intervene and would often remain silent, table the discussion, quickly move to a different topic, or let the situation slide. It was not that professors did not want to make the incident a learning opportunity, but they simply admitted to being "stuck." They were fearful that their attempts to confront the transgression would result in a backlash and make the situation worse. The greatest fear was losing control of the classroom dynamics and creating the "classroom from hell" (Sue, 2015a). The lack of experience in dealing with conflicting situations, being armed with a repertoire of intervention strategies, and having rehearsed these skills were constant themes for inaction in other interpersonal interactions as well (Ashburn-Nardo, Morris, & Goodwin, 2008; Scully & Rowe, 2009).

With respect to macroaggressions where the discriminatory outcomes reside in institutions or community and societal practices, antibias actions are aimed at oppressive rules, regulations and policies, and not necessarily a specific individual. The "perpetrator" in this case may be an institution, community or societal ideological belief/norm. Microintervention strategies directed at macroaggressions most clearly fall into the category of social advocacy because it requires (a) a macro focus on systemic obstacles that block equal access and opportunity (Jones, 1997), (b) unmasking and educating others as to the unfairness in procedures and practices (Goodwin et al., 2018), (c) partnering with others for social action (Kozan & Blustein, 2018), and (d) playing new and often unfamiliar roles such as political advocacy, protest, and civil disobedience (Olle, 2018).

Most well-intentioned citizens and even socially aware professionals lack the skills and strategies required for systemic interventions whether they work within or outside of organizations (Sue, 2017b). A complicating matter is that microintervention strategies and tactics often require advocating for the creation of new policies and practices that thwart or correct the historical detrimental impact of macroaggressions. Affirmative action programs and microaggression initiatives on college campuses are such examples of attempts to (a) rectify past historical injustices and/or (b) deal with the harmful impact of current microaggressions.

CHAPTER FIVE

Overcoming Silence, Inaction and Complicity

> Silence in the face of injustice is complicity with the oppressor.
> – Ginetta Sagan

The major barriers discussed in Chapter 4 to overcoming silence and inaction each present different major challenges that need to be addressed. The urgency to respond to micro/macroaggressions is important and should not be overlooked or minimized. Although there are legitimate and real obstacles to inaction, one fact is certain – silence perpetuates racism and other forms of discrimination (Akili, 2013; DiAngelo, 2011; Sanchez-Hucles & Jones, 2005). The aforementioned quote is a call to action and directly relevant to our work on microinterventions for targets, allies, and bystanders alike. Everyone shares in the responsibility to overcome silence and inaction in moments of injustice. When asked to overcome inaction, well-intentioned individuals must be able (a) to decode the often-hidden expressions of bias, (b) to appreciate the cumulative harm wrought upon targets, (c) to break social norms of conflict avoidance, (d) to prepare for, buffer and immunize oneself against repercussions, and (e) to develop a repertoire of microintervention strategies

Microintervention Strategies, First Edition. Derald Wing Sue, Cassandra Z. Calle, Narolyn Mendez, Sarah Alsaidi, and Elizabeth Glaeser.

aimed at challenging individual and institutional racism. In this section, we briefly address the first four counteracting solutions (see Table 4.1), but reserve the latter for greater elaboration in separate chapters because of its pivotal nature in overcoming silence and inaction.

LEARN TO RECOGNIZE AND DECODE HIDDEN EXPRESSIONS OF BIAS

As scholars have indicated, many beliefs, values and practices of our society may appear race neutral, but often disguise racial biases in the self (Baron & Banaji, 2006; Dovidio & Gaertner, 2000), in others (Helms, 1995; Norton, Sommers, Apfelbaum, Pura, & Ariely, 2006), and in institutions (Jones, 1997; Jones & Dovidio, 2018). Before social justice advocates can take antibias actions, they must first recognize and be able to decode the racist messages or actions that emanate from individual behaviors or institutional policies (Anderson & Stevenson, 2019). This is especially difficult for microaggressions that arise from implicit biases, and for macroaggressions embedded as standard operating procedures in organizational structures. How can we make the "invisible" visible? Although interrelated with one another, the ability to recognize bias in the self, in others, and in our institutions is an extremely difficult task.

Many scholars have proposed that a key component of cultural competence is the ability to understand one's own worldview and the race-related biases that are culturally conditioned to it (Carter, 1995; Owen et al., 2016). This attribute is part of our earlier discussion of critical consciousness and applies equally to targets, allies and bystanders (Sue, Sue, Neville, & Smith, 2019). The hallmark of reaching cultural competence is related to the attainment of insight into one's own biased attitudes, beliefs, and assumptions (APA, 2017; DiAngelo, 2011; Sue et al., 2019). Self-awareness in identifying biases is a precondition to understanding the worldview of others, and a major component to decreasing the likelihood of racism in our society (Carter, 1995). Many educators have emphasized the importance of devising curriculum and educational training activities as consciousness raising strategies to combat bias and bigotry (Carter, 2003; Goodman, 2011; Spanierman & Smith, 2017). This self-examination involves self-reckoning and includes a holistic approach to the integration of not only a person's cognitive/belief system but also the emotive and behavioral correlates associated with racial-cultural issues (Kiselica, 1999).

In testimony before President Clinton's Race Advisory Board (President's Initiative on Race, 1998), however, Sue (2003) made the strong case that overcoming racism is more than an intellectual exercise, that cognitive understanding alone is insufficient to produce self-change, and that relying on formal education and training, while helpful, represents only part of the solution. Studies reveal, for example, that as children become older there is a disassociation between explicit and implicit bias: the former declines while the latter increases, levels off, and remains relatively unchanged in adulthood (Aboud, 1988; Baron & Banaji, 2006). These researchers concluded that implicit bias outside the level of conscious awareness is highly resistant to change. Even more disturbing, however, was a preliminary finding that formal multicultural training programs may increase cultural competency (awareness, knowledge and skills) and reduce explicit bias, but appear to have minimal impact on implicit bias (Boysen & Vogel, 2008), the source of most forms of microaggressions.

Sue (2015b) has asserted that unlearning implicit biases must involve intimate experiences that directly challenge and bring to the surface hidden behaviors and emotional fears glued together by painful associations with people of color. The key to attacking implicit bias means taking personal responsibility for change by actively seeking experiences with people of color and their communities. Sue (2003, 2015a) identified five personal actions or guidelines that address this dilemma: (1) learn about people of color from sources within the group, (2) learn from healthy and strong people of the culture, (3) learn from experiential reality, (4) learn from constant vigilance of your biases and fears, and (5) learn from being committed to personal action against racism. Under each of these categories, Sue (2015a) outlines specific daily actions that can be taken by people to overcome their racial fears and beliefs. Some of these include (a) read literature (fiction, nonfiction, and poetry) by and for people of the culture; (b) attend street fairs, educational forums, and events put on by communities of color; (c) socialize with colleagues or neighbors of color; (d) join local, state, and national organizations with diversity and inclusion goals; (e) advocate for multicultural curriculum in schools; and (f) live in diverse and integrated neighborhoods.

In essence, racial and cultural understanding and sensitivity cannot occur without lived experience and immersing oneself in the environment of people who differ in terms of race, culture and ethnicity. It requires practicing new behaviors, forming personal and intimate acquaintances with people of color, and dealing with the fears and stereotypes likely to emerge from such interactions (APA, 2017). The task is often easier when undertaken with other like-minded and supportive allies and/or with a cultural guide who can introduce people to new experiences, help process thoughts and feelings, and provide encouragement to continue the journey to self-enlightenment (APA, 2017; President's Initiative on Race, 1998; Sue, 2003). With critical consciousness comes an increased ability to recognize expressions of bias in others and in the larger context of institutional and social policies.

BECOME AWARE OF THE TOXICITY AND HARMFUL IMPACT OF MICRO/MACROAGGRESSIONS

> You may write me down in history
> With your bitter, twisted lies,
> You may tread me in the very dirt
> But still, like dust, I'll rise.
>
> You may shoot me with your words,
> You may cut me with your eyes,
> You may kill me with your hatefulness,
> But still, like air, I'll rise.
>
> Maya Angelou (Passages from *And Still I Rise*)

These poetic passages by renowned African American author and civil rights advocate Maya Angelou (1978) is a meaningful Segway into understanding the toxic and harmful nature of micro- and macroaggressions to people of color. Before addressing the negative consequences of bias, however, we first note that her poem is a testament to the resilience, strength, and courage of African Americans who suffer a lifetime of abuse, bullying, humiliation and injustice. Despite personal and historical injustices and atrocities, Maya Angelou ends each passage with an acknowledgment of the fighting spirit of African Americans: "And, still I rise."

Many who read the poem mistakenly believe she is only addressing the deliberate actions of White supremacists, Klan members, and skinheads who engage in extreme acts of prejudice and discrimination (e.g. hate crimes). Although Angelou does address blatant bias and bigotry, a closer examination of her poem and other written works (Angelou, 1969) makes clear that she is also speaking about (a) everyday subtle forms of racism that originate from well-intentioned but unaware people and (b) larger systemic expressions of bias. Although she never used the terms "microaggression" or "macroaggression," Angelou shared Pierce's (1974) conviction that the everyday racial slights, put-downs, and insults to people of color were in some ways more damaging than those originating from White supremacists. She likened microaggressions to "little murders" or "death by a thousand cuts," as opposed to the "grand execution" of hate crimes. Considerable evidence exists that subtle, ambiguous, and more nuanced forms of racism are many times more harmful and toxic to people of color than blatant and direct expressions of bias, especially in cognitive and mental functioning (Crocker & Major, 1989; Murphy, Richeson, Shelton, Rheinschmidt, & Bergsieker, 2013; Salvatore & Shelton, 2007).

Second, Maya Angelou powerfully describes the mechanisms by which macroaggressions are delivered environmentally through falsehoods and distortions in the school curriculum ("You may write me down in history with your bitter twisted lies.") and in interpersonal manifestations of verbal, ("You may shoot me with your words.") and nonverbal ("You may cut me with your eyes.") microaggressions. She makes a strong case that the school curriculum (macroaggression) is the result of knowledge construction that omits, distorts, and fabricates the real-life experiences and contributions of people of color. An ethnocentric White Western education represents the biased racial reality of White Americans that is imposed upon students of color (Sue, 2003). Rather than freeing, liberating and educating, the curriculum provides a false racial reality and sense of racial superiority for White students, but it oppresses, silences, and denigrates students of color (Sue & Spanierman, 2020).

Although the election of President Donald Trump has seen an increase in overt and blatant expressions of racial bias and bigotry (SPL, 2018), for decades race scholars have noted the morphing of blatant racism into more disguised, subtle and ambiguous forms that make their appearance more difficult to recognize and thus more acceptable (Dovidio, Kawakami, & Gaertner, 2002; Nadal, Griffin, Wong, Hamit, & Rasmus, 2014). Likewise, others have noted how contemporary forms of bias hide in our cultural belief systems and have become the fabric of institutional policies and practices (Devos & Banaji, 2005; Jones & Dovidio, 2018). The transition from overt to subtle racism and discrimination has led many well-intentioned citizens to believe that they live in *a post-racial era*, that racism is *a thing of the past*, and that anyone can succeed in society if they work hard enough (Dovidio, Gaertner, Kawakami, & Hodson, 2002; Nadal, Griffin, Wong, Hamit,

& Rasmus, 2014; Sears, 1988; Sue, 2010a). This belief has also informed the color-blind racial ideology that many individuals hold today.

While a post-racial era supported by a color-blind ideology may logistically appear beneficial to race relations, it is in reality a dangerous vehicle to perpetuate racism and discrimination. The color-blind approach blinds individuals to seeing and understanding the serious impact of "modern day racism," and the belief that equal treatment in policies of institutions could not possibly be discriminatory (Jones, 1997; Neville, Awad, Brooks, Flores, & Bluemel, 2013). The denial of the serious impact of micro- and macroaggressions: (a) gaslights those (targets, allies, and bystanders) who experience and witness microaggressions and/or note macroaggressive organizational disparities, (b) negatively affects the mental health or opportunities of targets, and (c) protects those individuals or institutions that commit and support micro- and macroaggressions from having to acknowledge biases and unfairness. Without recognizing and understanding the serious harm and impact of micro- and macroaggressions, there is no sense of urgency to change, and therefore overcoming silence and inaction in instances of bias and discrimination is near impossible (Nadal et al., 2014).

While an abundance of literature exists to document the serious impact of overt racism and discrimination, much less work has been done to demonstrate the significant consequences of micro- and macroaggressions (Nadal et al., 2014). Studies that draw connections between micro- and macroaggressions and their impact on mental and physical health are an integral part of the education needed to understand their toxicity and therefore overcome silence and inaction. With respect to microaggressions, those with power and privilege often equate them with the everyday slights and incivilities that anyone can receive from a rude person regardless of their group affiliation. Thus, in the case of microaggressions, their potential harm become trivialized. Some White scholars, for example, believe that people of color are exaggerating the harm of microaggressions, making a "mountain out of a molehill" (Thomas, 2008), being overly sensitive, and portraying themselves as weak, vulnerable and victims (Schacht, 2008) in order to manipulate others for special and preferential treatments (Campbell & Manning, 2014; Lukianoff & Haidt, 2015).

There are major differences, however, between non-group-based incivilities and race-based microaggressions (APA, 2012, 2017; Ong, Burrow, Fuller-Rowell, Ja, & Sue, 2013; Sue, 2019). First, microaggressions are constant and continual without an end date, while an everyday non-race-based hassle is time limited. Second, microaggressions are constant realities in the life of people of color. They are present from the moment of birth until death and from the time one awakens in the morning until one goes to sleep. In a recent major study, for example, West (2019) debunked the *hypersensitivity* hypothesis of critics (Lilienfeld, 2017; Lukianoff & Haidt, 2015; Schacht, 2008) by showing (a) that targets were no more sensitive to racial slights than their majority counterparts, and (b) that the harmful impact was due to the inordinately high number of microaggressions that they endured. Third, microaggressions are cumulative and any one incident may represent the feather that breaks the camel's back. Microaggressions cannot be seen in isolation from one another as they represent a lifetime of humiliation and denigration. Fourth, microaggressions are energy depleting because it requires targets to decipher double messages from perpetrators. For people of color, the constant vigilance required for psychological and physical survival results in what some call "racial battle fatigue." Fifth, microaggressions are constant reminders of a person's second-class status in society. They are treated like lesser human beings. Last, microaggressions symbolize past historic injustices perpetrated through macroaggressions (governmental policies and practices that resulted in the enslavement of African Americans, incarceration of Japanese Americans, and the taking away of land from Indigenous Peoples of this country.).

In conclusion, understanding the harmful impact of micro- and macroaggressions to marginalized group members may encourage unenlightened individuals to recognize the importance of engaging in microinterventions. Being non-racist is simply not enough unless followed by constant and continual anti-racist actions (Helms, 1990; Tatum, 1997). To understand the damaging consequences of micro/macroaggressions and the lived reality of people of color, education and personal action are necessities. Since the journey to becoming anti-racist is forever ongoing, it is necessary to understand, appreciate and comprehend the toxicity of micro- and macroaggressions at all levels, in all spaces, and at all times.

CREATE NORMS THAT COUNTER CONFLICT AVOIDANCE AND ENHANCE RACIAL DIALOGUES

Creating norms that counter conflict avoidance and offset viewing race as a taboo topic are key to honest and continuing racial dialogues, and eventually overcoming silence, inaction and complicity in the face of racism (APA, 2012;

Bell, 2003; Tatum, 1992). To claim neutrality in the face of oppression and to *stay above the fray* are to offer excuses for personal inaction, to provide cover for one's own fears of retribution, to allow and condone the actions of oppressors, and to create a climate for racial bias and discrimination to thrive unabated (DiAngelo, 2011; Sue, 2015a; Zou & Dickster, 2013). Powerful implicit social norms dictate how we talk about race, racism, whiteness and White privilege (Bell, 2003; Utsey, Gernat, & Hammer, 2005). In most cases, racial dialogues are considered taboo (Tatum, 1992), disruptive to group harmony (APA, 2012), and discussed only in a fleeting and superficial manner (Bonilla-Silva, 2006; Sue, Lin et al., 2009). As evidence of the high anxiety that conversations on race produce, Bonilla-Silva (2006) has coined the term *rhetorical incoherence* to describe the convoluted manner in which *race talk* occurs when White Americans are challenged to discuss race at deeper levels: difficulty in articulation, barely audible speech, voice constriction, stuttering, tangential and ambiguous statements, non sequitur responses, and mispronunciation of common words associated with race. Racial dialogues push powerful emotional hot buttons in people and produce elevated levels of anxiety that result in attempts to dilute, diminish, change, mystify and terminate discussions (Pasque, Chesler, Charbeneau, & Carlson, 2013; Utsey et al., 2005).

In a series of studies on the psychology of racial dialogues, Sue and colleagues (Sue et al., 2009, 2011b; Sue, Rivera, Capodilupo, Lin, & Torino, 2010; Sue, Torino et al., 2009) identified four intersecting layers of personal fears that make honest race talk difficult for many White Americans: (1) fear of appearing racist, (2) fear of realizing and acknowledging their racism, (3) fear of confronting their White privilege, and (4) fear of taking actions to combat racism. Although participants of color were more willing to talk about racial issues, they also had trepidations about bringing forth the topic with White Americans. They found the disinclination of Whites to address racial topics off-putting and infuriating. They described the superficiality of racial discussions with White cohorts as an invalidation of their racial realities and an assailing of their racial integrities. This was especially true when Whites minimized the importance of race; they often stated, "Race has nothing to do with it." Further, participants of color expressed frustration about how unaware their White counterparts seemed about their biases and privileges and were "fed up" with what they saw as White denial and a *conspiracy of silence*. Sue (2005) has observed that many White people including family, friends, neighbors, coworkers, and even educators shy away from difficult dialogues on race because they may prove divisive.

The explosive nature of racial dialogues has resulted in the creation of ground rules or societal norms that hinder constructive dialogues on race and racism (Young, 2003; Young & Davis-Russell, 2002). Society explicitly and implicitly discourages, ignores and silences honest racial dialogues through normative ground rules that protect White Americans from confronting their biases and prejudices (Bell, 2003; Sue, 2015a; Young, 2003). The code of silence on race is evident in three societal norms or protocols.

First, race talk violates the politeness protocol in that such discussions are considered impolite, improper and potentially divisive. The fear of creating disagreements and offending others is viewed as antagonistic to group harmony, especially in social, educational, and employment interactions. If, however, participants engage in a racial dialogue, superficiality and pleasantries are the rule.

Second, race talk violates the color-blind protocol in which the governing justifications for avoidance is that "race should not matter" and/or a fear that to *see* race is to risk being perceived as racist. Thus, people engage in *strategic colorblindness* and pretend not to see race in an attempt to appear unbiased (Apfelbaum, Sommers, & Norton, 2008). If one feigns not seeing race, then discussions of race and racism cannot occur. As someone once said, "To be color blind is to be color mute."

Third, race talk violates the academic protocol of scholarly objectivity, dispassionate discussions, and "rational discourse." In this respect, many in the public (hooks, 1994; Sue, 2015a) also share the dictum that *emotion is antagonistic to reason.* When difficult racial dialogues occur in classrooms, boardrooms, and other public venues, they are likely to create powerful and disturbing emotions. In academia, for example, educators frequently attempt to confine racial dialogues to intellectual discourse, and to deem that detachment from emotions should prevail. In many respects, the academic protocol hinders honest racial dialogues by refusing to *bear witness* to the lived realities of people of color, by ignoring their stories of subordination, and by minimizing their pain and suffering (Bell, 2003). As repeated throughout, confronting the emotive reactions of people of color and the nested and embedded fears of White Americans are not simply intellectual exercises. Productive race talk involves acknowledging and processing powerful, painful, and intense feelings experienced by Whites and people of color.

How do we create norms that counter conflict avoidance and enhance racial dialogues? Most of the solutions fall into four major categories: (1) appeal to moral values, (2) undertaking anti-bias education and training, (3) changing societal and institutional policies and practices, and (4) raising race-conscious children. Again, it is important to note that these endeavors are not categorically separate, but rather that they interact with one another.

Appeal to Moral Values

This approach emphasizes people's moral obligation to intervene in the face of racial transgressions, to let their voices be heard, to find the courage to step forward, and to take antibias actions (Nelson, Dunn, & Paradies, 2011; Scully & Rowe, 2009). As we have seen in the section on creating prosocial norms, courageous individual actions can undermine false consensus, discourage the negative, encourage the positive, and model and embolden others to do likewise.

Undertake Antibias Training

By far the most common methods employed to create opportunities for racial dialogues are through formal education and training programs, workshops, forums on race, community affinity groups, and civic engagement activities (Michael & Conger, 2009; President's Initiative on Race, 1999; Sue et al., 2009). Although training has many goals, one of the most important is to create a climate in which racial dialogues are no longer taboo and become an everyday part of conversations. When engaging in difficult conversations, frameworks and expectations should always be set by facilitators who have engaged in self-reflective dialogue to model perspicacity. Overall, difficult conversations in training work best when blame is avoided, when individuals are free to express and process feelings, when honestly is valued, and when the rules support these expressions. Establishing these norms can create a culture of self-reflection, feedback and insightfulness. It is important to stress that creating norms that encourage and support racial/cultural awareness is a life-long journey (Brookfield & Preskill, 2012; Sue, Lin et al., 2009).

Create Fair and Just Societal and Organizational Policies and Practices

We have already seen how the operation of macroaggressions and the use of macrointerventions can powerfully influence individual, institutional and societal racial climates that either enhance or negate our ability and willingness to acknowledge race and racism as a reality in everyday existence (Jones, 1997; Neville et al., 2013; Plaut, Thomas, & Goren, 2009). Examples include ending policies and practices that negatively impact socially marginalized groups in our society (ending color-blind philosophies) and creating ones that acknowledge and value diversity (multiculturalism).

All three approaches are valuable, but they share one major downside. They are remedial in nature and the focus is unlearning the racial biases and fears that have been culturally conditioned into everyone. Although racist attitudes and beliefs may never be completely overcome, still *prevention* is better than remediation. The best approach, many believe, is to nip racism at the bud, before it has a chance to grow and thrive (APA, 2019a).

Raising Race-Conscious Children

Many scholars and organizations suggest that race talk must begin in early childhood and discussions about race, racism, power and privilege must become normative everyday occurrences in order to break the silence (APA, 2012; Loewen, 2018b; Palmer, 2007; President's Initiative on Race, 1999; Sue, 2015a; Tatum, 2002). For people of color, early discussions on race and racism with sons and daughters have always been the norm because it (a) enhances survival (physical and mental) in a hostile and invalidating environment (Anderson, 2017; Tatum, 1992), (b) counters negative messages and misinformation (Anderson & Stevenson, 2019), and (c) promotes racial and ethnic pride (Jones & Rolon-Dow, 2018b). What has been difficult, however, is the inability of people of color to talk about race with non-defensive and open-minded majority group persons (Bell, 2003).

For White people, breaking the silence on race and racism must involve parents, family members, and teachers who are the most influential, important and significant people in the formative years of children. At home, parents, siblings, and family members through many avenues (conversations, musical preferences, food eaten, and home decorations) transmit beliefs and attitudes about race. Schools also convey how teachers and administrators view race through their educational curriculum, teaching styles and strategies, and the treatment of White and students of color. Parents who raise race-conscious children and teachers who provide a truly anti-racist curriculum can do much to minimize the acquisition of bias in later years and into adulthood. Creating a generation of race conscious youths will do much to break down the norms of conflict avoidance, the taboos of race talk, and facilitate the development of social norms that value race differences.

It is not within the scope of this chapter to conduct a detailed analysis of the strategies and techniques that parents and teachers can use to encourage open dialogues on race with their children, and the type of antibias curriculum schools need to develop and implement. Those interested in a developmental age-by-age guide to racial dialogues should begin with accessing the following insightful and helpful websites that contain resources for talking about race with children and educational approaches to an antibias education: APA Psychology Benefits Society (www.apa.org/pi/res), Recasting Race (http://recastingrace.com), APA Resilience: Uplifting Families through Healthy Communication about Race (https://www.apa.org/res/), Raising Race Conscious Children (http://www.raceconscious.org/), and the Smithsonian National Museum of African American History and Culture on *Talking about Race* (https://nmaahc.si.edu/learn/talking-about-race#.XuT6iNiaxIQ.email).

SEEK SOCIAL SUPPORT AND ALLIES

As we have previously indicated, a major obstacle to engaging in microinterventions lies in potential repercussions that targets, allies and bystanders may encounter. The fears of isolation, loss of power and privilege, attacks on character, and threats of violence are all too real (Jones, 1997; Parham, 1993). Taking antibias action disrupts the status quo (macroaggressions) and challenges the biased beliefs, attitudes, and behaviors of perpetrators (microaggressions). As such, social justice advocates face constant "pushback," resistance, and negative reactions from family, friends, neighbors, coworkers, and the larger society to end their racial protestations by returning to the protective cocoon of ethnocentrism (Banks et al., 2019; Sue, 2015b). Indeed, the idioms "go along to get along" and "don't rock the boat" are admonitions to conform to prevailing expectations so as not to disrupt or endanger one's sense of security or belonging. The sense of belonging to a "family" or community provides security, identity, social comfort, and support. It has been identified as one of the most powerful and fundamental basic human needs of people (Baumeister & Leary, 1995; Lieberman, 2013). As a result, it can also be a most potent weapon to keep members in line.

Social justice advocates whether targets or allies are often ill prepared to face the overwhelming disapproval from those in authority, but even more threatening may be the potential loss of friendship, companionship, emotional support, and validation from family and friends (Feeney & Collins, 2015; Nelson et al., 2011; Tatum, 2002). Ironically, developing a non-racist identity and undertaking anti-racist actions are often at odds with the beliefs and attitudes of prior groups who originally formed one's sense of community, but who no longer play supporting roles. In fact, former acquaintances may directly or indirectly sabotage the person's newfound non-racist identity, condemn public displays of anti-racist actions, and threaten excommunication from family, friends, and colleagues (Helms, 1995; Sue, 2017b).

To be the lone voice in the wilderness and to be "the only one" leave a person vulnerable and less effective than when confronting injustice with others. A large body of literature exists on the importance and benefits of social support and social connections as purveyors of well-being, resilience and fortitude, as well as their ability to buffer or protect against life stresses (Feeney & Collins, 2015; Kim, Sherman, & Taylor, 2008). Doing anti-racist work is exhausting unless targets and allies develop support systems (a) to fortify and encourage them to continue their struggles; (b) to validate their values of equity and fairness; (c) to immunize them against the challenges they are likely to encounter; (d) to offer emotional support, caring and empathy; and (e) to communicate they are not alone (Gorski, 2019; Houshmand, Spanierman, & De Stefano, 2019; Kim et al., 2008; Sue, 2017b).

The need for self-care in doing advocacy work can be categorized into internal (isolation, burn-out, fatigue, etc.) and external (personal attacks, punitive actions, threats of violence, etc.) challenges (Banks et al., 2019). The literature on the effectiveness of social support in protecting social justice advocates from these challenges is overwhelming. Most researchers conclude that social support is one of the most successful means by which people can cope with stressful life events (Cohen, 2004; Cohen & Wills, 1985; Feeney & Collins, 2015; Houshmand, Spanierman, & De Stephano, 2019; Ozbay et al., 2007). There are many definitions of social support, but all contain a core of common themes such as care and love, value, belonging, and close intimate interactions (Pearson, 1986).

Cohen and Willis (1985) have proposed two models of how social support promotes well-being and protects against life stresses: (1) *the main-effect explanation* and (2) *the buffering explanation*. In the former, they suggest that social support has beneficial effects regardless of stressful events that result in overall well-being. Under the buffering model, the researchers suggested that social support functions as a buffer for those who are experiencing stressful events. Through comparisons of multiple statistical models, the researchers found evidence to support both explanations. The main-effect model is evident when social support measures a person's *level of integration in social networks*. The buffering model is supported when social support assesses *perceived availability of interpersonal resources* that an individual can call on in times of crisis. Cohen and Willis (1985) conclude that despite explanatory differences, it is important to note that social support is of undeniable importance in an individual's well-being.

Social justice advocates are most likely to be effective when they (a) are socially integrated into a group that provides them with meaningful close relationships (main-effect model) and (b) have at their disposal readily available interpersonal resources to cope with challenges (buffering model) (Feeney & Collins, 2015). Social integration is more likely to be a long-term developmental process, but it plays a vital role in human flourishing, hardiness and resilience (Cohen, 2004; Ozbay et al., 2007). An abundance of empirical work reveals that social integration is correlated with better mental health, higher levels of subjective well-being, lower mortality rates, and better physical health (Balaji et al., 2007; Cobb, 1976; Cohen, 2004; Cohen & Wills, 1985; Coker et al., 2002; Jacoby & Kozie-Peak, 1997; Weinstein & Ryan, 2010).

It goes without saying that social justice advocates who are better integrated into their social networks are more able to withstand the stresses of antibias work that come from internal and external challenges. The flipside of this conclusion seems also supported: people most likely to "speak up" and intervene when witnessing uncivil or immoral behaviors tend to be better adjusted, mentally healthier, more integrated into the social and political workings of their communities, possess greater ethnic pride and identity, have a stronger sense of self-efficacy, and are better educated (Forward & Williams, 1970; Moisuc, Brauer, Fonseca, Chaurand, & Greitemeyer, 2018; Turner & Wilson, 1976).

Like social integration, the buffering function of social support is important because it speaks directly to how it immunizes or protects social advocates from the perceived or real repercussions of anti-racism work. Data suggest, for example, that the availability of coping resources derived from support groups may be more effective in protecting people from the deleterious effects of stress than their social involvement in groups (Gurung, 2006; Kessler & McCleod, 1984; Uchino, 2009). This is not to deny the importance of intimate close relations in promoting strength of character, but support groups and allies provide different benefits that moderate challenging situations that go beyond "belonging" (Feeney & Collins, 2015). Scholars have posited four different types of social support: (1) belonging social support, (2) emotional social support, (3) informational social support, and (4) tangible social support. All are intersecting in one way or another, but some are more basic to social integration and others more related to availability of interpersonal resources. Belonging social support, for example, is more related to familial connections and intimate close relationships that serve to validate and promote the sense of individual, group and universal identities (Sue et al., 2019). For anti-racist advocates, belonging provides a "home" for the person, enhances a sense of security, provides a place to relax, lowers personal defenses, enhances trust, and offers cultural nutrients to reenergize the self for future challenges to come.

Informational, emotional and tangible social supports are important in providing anti-racist advocates with interpersonal coping resources to deal with the punitive consequences of challenging individual and institutional racism. Informational social support involves members and allies sharing their experiences, giving advice on how to deal or cope with problematic situations, and suggesting who and where to consult for solutions and answers. Emotional support provides members with affirmation of their worth, validation of feelings, caring and acceptance, and a "shoulder to cry on." Tangible social support involves sharing of resources (material and financial) and the time and energy to help other members in everyday life duties (cooking, childcare duties, sharing places to stay, and other chores). Although still a rarity, some companies provide social justice benefits (paid leave to vote and engage in peaceful protests, and even travel expenses) for employees (Taylor, 2017). Considerable evidence exists, however, that the perception of the availability of these resources may be more important than whether they actually exist (Feeney & Collins, 2015; Ozbay et al., 2007). Regardless, we believe that the buffering effect of these interpersonal coping resources plays a vital role warding off stress and motivating responsible and effective problem-solving actions in the face of micro- and macroaggressions.

In addition to the benefits of social support, seeking and developing allies of like-minded and committed individuals are more likely to compel individual and systemic changes (DeLeon, 2010; Olle, 2018). The old adage that there is "strength in numbers" is a recognition that groups of people have more influence and power than any one person. Similarly, the saying that "there is safety in numbers" is the belief that being part of a large physical group protects against and minimizes the chance of a mishap, attack, or a negative outcome. Zoologists have observed that mitigation of vulnerability appears true for animals, and evidence exists that it may also apply to how humans perceive danger and threat (Cesario & Navarrete, 2014). In their study of over 300 participants, the researchers found that people who are alone judge threats as much higher than when they are in a group. For social justice advocates, if potential danger is perceived as less threatening, then risk-taking and the courage to challenge biased behaviors and practices may be enhanced. In summary, it appears that social support, social connections, and the presence of a community of collaborators are most effective in warding off psychological and physical threats to those who engage in antibias actions (Feeney & Collins, 2015; Ozbay, Johnson, Dimoulas, et al., 2007). Receiving and providing social support from like-minded individuals or groups may represent a major strategy in combatting racism.

OBTAIN SKILLS AND TACTICS TO RESPOND TO MACROAGGRESSIONS

Developing a repertoire of microintervention strategies to combat bias and discrimination represents one of the major hurdles to taking responsible action. Being motivated to help is simply not enough when well-intentioned individuals lack the necessary strategies and skills required for effective antibias actions. The "Confronting Prejudiced Response Model" developed by Ashburn-Nardo, Morris, and Goodwin (2008) nicely echoes our review of the steps to overcome inaction: (a) First and foremost, there must be an increase in detection of discrimination that includes information about its frequency, the forms it can take, and the groups affected. (b) Second, assisting others to understand the serious impact of discrimination, both its short- and long-term consequences are a necessity. (c) Third, we must create awareness of the roles all (i.e. bystanders, targets, allies) can play in combatting discrimination. (d) Fourth, advocates need to find the necessary internal fortitude and strength to overcome personal inertia and make a difference. (e) Last, social justice collaborators must learn and practice new confrontation strategies and skills in order to effectively challenge racial injustice in others and in systems of oppression. It is this last step that is deemed extremely important because few people have experience and practice in confronting bias and discrimination at the individual and systemic levels.

Social justice advocates often describe the experience of not knowing what to do and feeling paralyzed when confronted by micro- and macroaggressions (Shelton, Richeson, Salvatore, & Hill, 2006; Sue et al., 2007). The "freeze effect" is largely due to a lack of resources, tools, and tactics that aid individuals in responding. In their work on microaggressions, for example, Sue et al. (2019) argue that targets, allies, and bystanders must learn about various antibias tactics in order to overcome the immobilization that often impedes responsible actions against individual perpetrators. To combat individual expressions of bias and bigotry, they identified four strategic goals in which specific tactics or best practices are enumerated: (1) make the "invisible" visible, (2) disarm the microaggression, (3) educate the offender, and (4) seek external intervention. Those interested in a greater description of these individual antibias tactics should consult the original article. With some modifications, we use this framework to also address macroaggressions as well. Like the strategies that neutralize individual perpetrator actions, micro-interventions directed toward macro-level biased customs and practices can be categorized under a similar framework. To discuss microinterventions directed toward macro-level bias, however, it is important to note how they differ from interventions directed at microaggressions.

First, confronting macroaggressions generally requires mobilizing the efforts of large groups of concerned people in order to make a significant and effective impact on an organizational or societal policy (Broido & Reason, 2005). For example, the power of formal complaints at places of employment often depends on how many other people can corroborate the biased unfairness of a practice or procedure. Similarly, protesting social policies that advantage one group while disadvantaging another is most effective when those in authority are confronted by large segments of the population. The success of protests, strikes, rallies, and peaceful demonstrations often depends on the number of people participating. The greater the numbers demanding change, the greater is the pressure on those in authority to institute change (Maton, 2017). In this way, microinterventions directed toward macroaggressions may be initiated by a single individual, but are most effective when large numbers of like-minded citizens make their demands known.

Second, while microinterventions toward individual perpetrators aim to change the attitudes, beliefs, and actions of a single perpetrator, microinterventions directed toward macroaggressions aim to change unfair laws, policies, rules, and regulations, and/or create new ones that allow for equal access and opportunity (Jason, Beasley, & Hunter, 2015). Therefore, the target typically is not just an individual or small group of people in control, but is often directed at the general public as well whose inaction has been complicit in implementing and enforcing biased programs and policies. The goals here are to educate the populace, form collaborative allies, and use group pressure to facilitate change. The next four chapters will focus on equipping social justice advocates with the strategies and tools necessary to combat both micro- and macroaggressions.

CHAPTER SIX

Microintervention Strategy and Tactics to Make the "Invisible" Visible

> Racism is so universal in this country, so widespread and deepseated, that it is invisible because it is so normal
>
> – Shirley Chisholm

What strategies and best practices are available to targets, allies and bystanders to make bias, bigotry and racism visible, to enlist the aid of onlookers in the fight against prejudice and discrimination, and to deal with the invisibility of racism? What tactics can be used to unmask the existence of racism at the individual (microaggressions) and institutional/societal (macroaggressions) levels? Are the antibias strategies different when confronting a microaggression versus a macroaggression? In this chapter, we devote nearly all our efforts to making the "invisible" visible by outlining strategies and examples of effective intervention. We believe that the first step to social justice action is grounded in our ability to recognize the many manifestations of racism. Although each of the forthcoming chapters will address microinterventions directed at both microaggressions and macroaggressions, we spend most of our time on strategies and tactics directed

Microintervention Strategies, First Edition. Derald Wing Sue, Cassandra Z. Calle, Narolyn Mendez, Sarah Alsaidi, and Elizabeth Glaeser.

toward changing biased institutional and societal policies, programs, practices, and structures of institutions and society. However, we will summarize the most effective microintervention tools to be used against interpersonal microaggressions first. Those interested in a more detailed discussion of these antibias strategies should go to the two sources cited here (Sue et al., 2019; Sue & Spanierman, 2020).

CHALLENGING MICROAGGRESSIONS

When microinterventions are used to counteract microaggressions, they have been found to affirm the racial and group identity of targets, validate their experiential reality, reinforce their value as persons, support and encourage their beliefs or actions, and reassure them that they are "not alone." As we have noted earlier, the ability to engage in microinterventions serves to enhance psychological well-being and to provide targets, allies and bystanders with a sense of control and self-efficacy. In the face of bias and discrimination, one of the most harmful experiences is a feeling of powerlessness, helplessness and paralysis that may lead to a sense of futility and hopelessness. Microinterventions directly or indirectly provide actors with direction and a sense of power to affect problematic situations. In reviewing the literature on personal changes that are likely to be experienced by targets, allies and bystanders, some of the psychological outcomes noted were disempowered to empowered, trapped to liberated, blaming self to faulting the perpetrator, helplessness to usefulness, futility to efficacy, pessimism to optimism, timidity to confidence, and insanity to sanity.

Table 6.1 lists microintervention strategies and tactics under the heading of "Making the 'Invisible' Visible" directed toward micro- and macroaggressions. It has been a monumental undertaking to classify and organize the many tactics suggested by anti-racist activists because they are often presented as simple *comebacks* without a clear explication of their rationale. We provide a conceptual framework of microinterventions divided into five categories: *strategic goals, objectives, rationale, tactics,* and *examples.* We elaborate on some of these to illustrate the principles for their inclusion, provide examples of microintervention tactics that can be taken, and discuss their potential desired outcome. Many of the microintervention strategies were taken from Aguilar (2006) and from their excellent video, *Ouch! That Stereotype Hurts*

(Sunshower Learning, 2007). It is important to note, however, that developing microinterventions is not only a science but also an art. Implementing or using the tactics can be manifested in many ways and is most influenced by creativity and life experiences (Sue, 2015a).

Strategic Goal: Make Microaggressions Visible

It is oftentimes much easier to deal with a microaggression that is explicit and deliberate because there is no guesswork involved about the intent of the perpetrator (racial epithets or hate speech). Most microaggressions, however, contain both a conscious communication and hidden or meta-communication that is outside the level of perpetrator awareness (Nadal et al., 2014). Naiveté and innocence make it very difficult for offenders to change, if they perceive their actions as devoid of bias and prejudice (Jones, 1997). Microintervention tactics aimed at making the "invisible" visible can take many forms.

Tactic # 1 – Develop Perspicacity

For targets, allies and bystanders, the first rule of effective intervention is the quality of perspicacity (the ability to see beyond the obvious, to read between the lines, and to deconstruct conscious communications from meta-communications). In other words, the actors must be able to clearly recognize a biased statement, action or discriminatory practice that would motivate them to action. For targets, perspicacity reassures them that they are "not crazy," and that their perceptual reality is accurate. Furthermore, White allies and bystanders cannot intervene when they are unable to recognize that a microaggression has occurred. Being able to decipher the double meanings of microaggressions is often a challenging task. Sternberg (2001) describes perspicacity as a quality that goes beyond intellect but encompasses wisdom that allows for a person's clarity of vision and penetrating discernment. Racial awareness training has been found to be effective in helping individuals recognize prejudicial and discriminatory actions and to increase bystander intervention in the workplace (Scully & Rowe, 2009). Thus, allies and bystanders may be better able to offer social support and/or take other needed interventions.

Table 6.1 Strategic Goal: Make the Invisible Visible

Microinterventions for Microaggressions

Scenario: African American male enters an elevator occupied by a White heterosexual couple. The woman appears anxious, moves to the other side of her partner, and clutches her purse tightly.

Meta-communication: Black men are dangerous, potentially criminals or up to no good.

OBJECTIVES	RATIONALE	TACTICS	EXAMPLE
• Bring the micro/ macroaggression to the forefront of the person's awareness.	• Allows targets, allies, and bystanders to verbally describe what is happening in a nonthreatening manner.	1. Develop perspicacity	"Can't you see what is happening." "Do you realize what you just did when I walked in?"
• Strike back, defend yourself, or come to the defense of others.	• When allies or bystanders intervene, reassures targets they are not "crazy" and that their experiences are valid.	2. Disempower the innuendo by naming it.	"Your unconscious biases are showing. You believe Black men are dangerous." "Relax, I'm not dangerous." "Don't worry, John is a good person."
• Indicate to the perpetrator that they have behaved or said something offensive to you or others.	• When those with power and privilege respond, it has greater impact on perpetrator.	3. Undermine the meta-communication.	"You assume I am dangerous because of the way I look." "I might be Black, but that does not make me dangerous."
• Force the perpetrator to consider the impact and meaning of what was said/done or, in the case of the bystander, what was not said/done.		4. Challenge the Stereotype.	"Robberies and crimes are committed by people of all races and backgrounds."
		5. Broaden the ascribed trait.	"White men walk into elevators every day."
		6. Ask for clarification of a statement or action.	"What was that all about? Are you afraid of him?"

Microinterventions for Microaggressions

OBJECTIVES	RATIONALE	TACTICS	EXAMPLE
		7. Make the meta-communication explicit by restating/rephrasing the statement or action.	"Do you feel afraid to be in this elevator with me?"
		8. Reverse and restate the compliment, action, and role as if it was meant for the perpetrator.	Target exaggerates fear of women by huddling in the corner of the elevator.

Microinterventions for Macroaggressions

OBJECTIVES	RATIONALE	TACTICS	EXAMPLE
• Increase awareness of the unfairness of a policy, program or practice.	• Provides a method of demonstrating a need to address issues of inequities and disparities exist.	1. Monitor and document.	Monitor and keep a log of inequitable practices and report them to decision-makers (document trends around recruiting, hiring, retention, and promotion).
• Convince and motivate those in leadership positions, stakeholders, and the general public that action is required.	• Removes burden from individuals and assigns the responsibility to those in supervisory roles and holds institutions accountable.	2. Encourage implementation of systems of evaluation, accountability, and rewards.	Create partnerships with institutions to analyze data related to disparities in education, health care, and employment.
• Make stakeholders aware of the harmful impact of institutional and societal macroaggression.	• Encourages individuals with small power to work together and use their power in a collective way.	3. Leverage your power and privileged identities.	Ask questions, solicit feedback, and share data at meetings and during evaluation periods.

Tactic # 2 – Disempower the Innuendo by "Naming" It

Paulo Freire in *Pedagogy of the Oppressed* (1970) said the first step to liberation and empowerment is "naming" an oppressive event, condition or process so that it no longer holds power over those that are marginalized. It demystifies, deconstructs and makes the "invisible" visible. Naming (a) is liberating and empowering because it provides a language for people of color to describe their experiences, and (b) reassures them that they are not "crazy." It forces those with power and privilege to consider the roles they play in the perpetuation of oppression. Some examples of naming include: "That's a racist remark." "That's a microaggression." "That's a stereotype." Remember, this tactic can be used by targets who are the objects of the bias, by White allies who overhear a microaggression from a neighbor, friend or colleague, or by a bystander who informally chimes into a conversation.

Tactic # 3 – Undermine the Meta-communication

Undermining or naming the meta-communication is an example of increasing awareness of perpetrator and onlookers. For example, a White male classmate says to a third-generation Asian American student *You speak excellent English!* The meta-communication here may be *"You are a perpetual alien in your own country. You are not a true American."* In using a microintervention tactic, the student responds, *Thank you. I hope so. I was born here.*

This tactic may seem simplistic, but it does several things. It acknowledges the conscious compliment of the perpetrator, lowers defensiveness for the comeback to follow, subtly undermines the unspoken assumption of being a foreigner, and plants a *seed* of possible future awareness of false assumptions. As we have emphasized, the list of possible microintervention responses are many and only limited by the creativity of social justice advocates.

Tactic # 4 – Challenge the Stereotype

Similar to "naming," this strategy goes further by addressing, unmasking and challenging the impact of the meta-communication being sent to the target. For example, an African American male enters an elevator with a White female rider and she suddenly tenses up and clutches her purse tightly. The meta-communication is "You are potentially a dangerous criminal." A target of the microaggression may simply state to the female passenger, "Don't worry, I might be black, but that doesn't make me dangerous." White allies and bystanders may also intervene with similar responses. "Relax lady no one will harm you," or "How come you are so tense? We're all just trying to get to work." Those using this tactic, however, must be aware that the response is more challenging, confrontive and likely to evoke defensiveness. Remember that microinterventions directed at microaggressions are not necessarily meant to resolve the issue immediately. Be aware that directly challenging a stereotype can bring on a negative and antagonistic response from the perpetrator, and the advocate must decide whether to engage in a longer dialogue or to let the situation rest. Most microinterventions are meant to be "comebacks" or "checks" to microaggressions and not necessarily meant for long-term interventions.

Tactic # 5 – Broaden the Ascribed Trait to a Universal Human Behavior
Rather than pointing out the inaccuracy of a stereotype, this tact makes the trait applicable to many or all groups. The following responses are especially effective for statements that often ascribe a trait beginning with "Those people are all..."

Effective counter responses are: "I think that applies to everyone." "I don't think that's a gender thing, men do it too." Other examples are the following.
Statement: "Why are all the Black kids seated together in the cafeteria? Why do they separate themselves from us?"
Counter: "I could ask the same question about Whites. Why are all the White people sitting together in the restaurant?"
In general, the nature of stereotyping can involve selective perception of common behaviors evident in all groups, but unintentionally attributing them exclusively to socially marginalized groups in society. Usually such associations deal with negative behaviors (i.e. teasing classmates) or interpreting bothersome actions such as speaking loudly (impoliteness) as exclusive to people of color.

Tactic # 6 – Ask for Clarification of a Statement or Action
Questioning or asking for the meaning of a person's behavior throws the ball back into the perpetrator's court. It requires perpetrators to elaborate on their actions or responses, and potentially making them aware of the bias they are expressing. For example, biased intent or meaning is often couched in innuendos that allow perpetrators to deceive themselves or others. Asking for clarification unmasks and makes explicit the insinuation.

General Questions

"Robert, what exactly do you mean?"
"Come again. Did I hear you correctly?"
"Do you realize what you just said?"
"I can't believe you just said that. Tell me what you mean?"

Specific Questions

"Do you really believe all Latinos have a poor worth ethic?"
"What experiences do you have with African Americans that lead you to that conclusion?"

The intent of these questions is to (a) force the perpetrator to stop and consider what they just said or did, (b) communicate your disagreement or disapproval, and (c) encourage a further exploration of the belief or attitude of the person.

Tactic # 7 – Make the Meta-communication Explicit by Restating/ Rephrasing the Statement or Action

This practice is accomplished in a questioning tone by rephrasing the statement or action in such a manner as to make the meta-communication very explicit.

"You're telling me that you're not going to consider Jamal for the manager position because White co-workers aren't ready for a Black boss."
"In other words, you believe that women workers are less dependable than men because they will take time off to have children."
"You mean that Black students here at Columbia couldn't have gotten into the University without some accommodated admissions program."
"What you just said, makes me believe you are prejudiced against Muslims."

This method of confronting a microaggression or any form of biased state-ment is much more challenging than the previous strategies. It is meant, however, to make explicit the biased attitudes/beliefs of the person and allow them to face the meaning of their words and actions. It is meant to let the person "hear" what they may have said. It is likely to evoke defensive-ness but is aimed at peeling away naiveté or innocence of perpetrators.

Tactic # 8 – Reverse, Redirect or Mimic the Statements or Actions of the Offender as If It Was Meant for the Perpetrator

The tactic here is a form of verbal or behavioral jujitsu that reverses the roles of perpetrator and target and can be viewed as a form of humor or sarcasm. Regardless, the perpetrator now becomes the target of the remark or action, and its impact can become a learning opportunity for the offender because it unmasks the innuendo. For example, in the statement where a White student compliments an Asian American for speaking good English ("You speak excellent English."), the target says to the White classmate: "Thank you, John. You do too!" The impact of this response is quite strong, but not in a hostile or angry way. It challenges the false assumption of the perpetrator, but couches it in humor, irony, or sarcasm. Another example is the following exchange: White female teenager to a Black female friend, "You're pretty for a dark girl." Black female teenager to the White friend, "Thank you. You're pretty for a White girl." In Table 6.1 where the White female riding in an elevator tenses up and moves away as the Black passenger enters, the African American can mimic the behavior of the woman and feign fear and apprehension. Reversal statements or actions are brief, succinct comebacks that have a powerful impact upon the offender. With modifications, these types of responses can also be made by White allies or bystanders who overhear or see racial transgressions.

CHALLENGING MACROAGGRESSIONS

As we can see from the last section, confronting microaggressions is focused primarily at individual perpetrators. Challenging macroaggressions, however, means identifying numerous advocacy and antibias actions used to produce institutional or societal policy changes. Because the focus of change becomes policies and practices that reside in groups, organizations and society, microintervention actions also become more complex and group generated. Some example of these tactics are petitions, door-to-door campaigns, blogs, face-to-face meetings, letter or email writing campaigns, demonstrations, boycotts, strikes, rallies, phone calls, using social media through Facebook, Twitter, and YouTube, all aimed at particular stakeholders like elected officials, organizations, media outlets, federal, state or local governments (APA, 2014). Tactics are specific actions or best practices that represent the tools used by social advocates to produce desired change. Many are short term in nature, have small incremental actions, and when seen in isolation from a larger conceptual framework have little meaning or long-term effectiveness (Maton, 2017). Using tactics to end a discriminatory policy has little impact unless guided by strategic objectives. Successful change is most likely to occur through strategies that (a) have explicit long-term goals, (b) provide a roadmap for how they are to be achieved, and (c) categorically organize "how, when and where" the tactics are to be used (Banks et al., 2019; Maton, 2017). In this section, we provide a conceptual framework of microinterventions directed toward macroaggressions by making macroaggressions visible (see Table 6.1).

Strategic Goal: Make Macroaggressions Visible

It is difficult enough to change rules, regulations and customs that are blatantly discriminatory, but even more so when institutional and societal macroaggressions remain hidden and invisible to those who carry out unfair policies and to those who experience the advantages or disadvantages from their application. Making the "invisible" visible applies to social justice advocates and stakeholders (those individuals or groups who carry out and/ or are affected by the organizations' actions, objectives or policies). We have already spent considerable time on the importance of increasing awareness and critical consciousness of targets, allies, and bystanders who engage in social advocacy activities, so the message here is intended primarily for other stakeholders. With respect to those in leadership positions (i.e. school superintendents and school board members), it is paramount that they become cognizant of how a particular policy, practice or custom discriminates and potentially harms people of color and their communities (Holder, 2019; Sue, 1995). It is equally important that consumers and the general public become aware of how macroaggressions create disparities, and how their unawareness, silence, and inaction may make them complicit in perpetrating injustice (Jones, 1997; Obear, 2017).

The major objectives of *make the invisible visible* is to increase awareness of the unfairness of a policy, program or practice and to convince and motivate those in leadership positions, stakeholders, and the general public that action is required. The rationale is that without awareness of inequities and disparities in employment, education, and health care, many will simply assume that equitable practices are being implemented. There are three main tactics often used to make the invisible visible: (1) *monitor and document*, (2) *encourage implementation of systems of evaluation and accountability*, and (3) *leverage personal power and privileged identities*. These tactics encompass many ways to make stakeholders aware of the harmful impact of institutional and societal macroaggression. Overall, these tactics require collecting data to ensure equity, advocating holding key stakeholders accountable, and highlighting one's privileged identities to leverage personal power. Unlike addressing microaggressions, social justice advocacy directed toward macroaggressions represents a much longer and complex journey. Using effective microinterventions requires partnering with others, and forming teams of concerned advocates to press for changes (Young & Anderson, 2019).

Tactic # 1 – Monitor and Document

One of the most powerful ways to make the invisible visible is by providing undisputable facts such as statistics, trends and differential outcomes that demonstrate unfair policies and/or practices within institutions and organizations (Jones & Dovidio, 2018; Sue, 1995). By monitoring and documenting trends, disparities become visible, explicit, and harder to deny. A few examples under this tactic include: (a) monitor and keep a log of inequitable practices and report them to decision-makers (document trends around recruiting, hiring, retention, and promotion); (b) create partnerships with institutions to analyze data related to disparities in education, health care, and employment; (c) ask questions and share data at meetings and during evaluation periods; and (d) solicit feedback from marginalized group members about how policies impact them.

In higher education, for example, using focus groups to actively solicit feedback from students, staff, and faculty of color may provide a rich source of information regarding campus climate issues, curriculum issues, and residential issues, which institutions may find useful in their movement toward valuing multiculturalism. Such actions also send a strong message to students and faculty of color about the importance placed on identifying their needs and concerns; it is also a powerful statement of organizational inclusion. This last example is important because it represents the *lived experience* of people of color (students, employees, citizens, etc.) that counterbalances the perception of majority group members that *everything is fine*. Although statistics and facts are important, empirical reality cannot be the sole source of data; experiential reality must be given equal consideration (Hunsberger, 2007; Schneider, 1998).

Finally, we note that these tactics are impossible for any one individual to carry out because no one person possesses all the capabilities and proficiencies to monitor and document inequities in process and outcome. However, working with a group of advocates possessing a wide range of expertise and experience can prove most effective. In many cases, the strategic goal of *seek external support* (see Table 9.1) becomes part of bringing in allies with special knowledge and competencies.

Tactic # 2 – Encourage Implementing Systems of Evaluation and Accountability

Evaluation and accountability are integral in creating systems that encourage recognition of inequities in the programs and policies of an organization. Examples of tactics include: (a) work with others to develop and implement continual evaluation of supervisors and supervisees; (b) hold peers and those in power accountable for potentially biased hiring trends, promotions, or questionable actions; and (c) engage in continual consultation and soliciting feedback for ongoing evaluations. As in all microinterventions directed at macroaggressions, the task is twofold: (a) unmask current policies and practices that are unfair and (b) create new systems of accountability that insure equitable practices (macrointervention). Institutions of higher education, for example, often strive to implement diversity initiatives through commencing an evaluation of the university culture, structure and practices (Jones & Dovidio, 2018; Huber & Solorzano, 2014).

One of the most important components for moving an institution of higher education to accomplish diversity and multicultural goals, for example, is the implementation of a system of evaluation, accountability, and reward. In his work with colleges and universities, Sue (1995) recommends that an institutional audit of programs, policies and practices be among the first steps to uncover monocultural and multicultural policies of an organization. "Multicultural organizational development" (MOD) is a term used in the business sector to refer the creation of conditions that utilize the full potential of a diverse workforce. All organizations whether business or industry, government, mental health agency, or educational institution have an organizational culture that flesh out policies (Holder, 2019; Kim, Nguyen, & Block, 2019). These cultural values and patterns are communicated to workers as the appropriate ways to perceive, think, feel, and behave in relation to organizational challenges and problems. They are often monocultural, however, and exclude the lived experience of those who differ in race, culture and ethnicity. MOD attempts to change, refine, instill or create new policies, programs, practices and structures, which are multicultural, thus moving the organization from a monocultural to a multicultural entity (Sue, 1995).

In higher education, understanding how its educational culture enhances or negates the development of multicultural goals is crucial to equal access and opportunity. In many cases, organizational customs do not value or allow the use of cultural knowledge or skills in the educational context. Educational institutions may even actively discourage, negate, or punish multicultural expressions among its faculty, staff, and students. Developing new rules, regulations, policies, practices, and structures that enhance multiculturalism is important and requires an institutional audit (Sue, 1995; 2008). The college might consider, for example, the development of a mechanism or process by which such an assessment might be accomplished (internal committee or outside evaluators). This entity would be empowered to recommend and implement new inclusive policies. Its task would not only be to conduct an audit but also to oversee the strategic action plan associated with multicultural development. Accountability could be vested in a superordinate mechanism or oversight team/group, which would be empowered to monitor the college's development with respect to the goals of multiculturalism. This would entail, for example, holding professors and administrators responsible for implementing multicultural content into their curriculum and/or recruiting, retaining and promoting professors of color within the university. With accountability must also come rewards to motivate university personnel to make real multicultural change.

Likewise, in the business sector, it has been found that one of the most effective ways to attain diversity goals is for employees to encourage companies to craft a written policy, mission or vision statement, which frames the concepts of multiculturalism and diversity into a meaningful operational definition (Jones & Dovidio, 2018; Sue, 1995). This encourages an organization to monitor its progress toward becoming more multicultural. Valuing diversity cannot be simply an "add on" but must be conceptualized in a manner that infuses the ideas throughout its operations, structures and policies. Otherwise, such declarations serve only as a cosmetic feature. If open discussions and solutions to bias, prejudice, discrimination and racism are true priorities in the workplace, then a clear message is communicated to all employees that equity, fairness and diversity are valued in the company.

Building systems of evaluation and accountability also prevents potential backsliding, a common trend of regressing back to old, traditional and familiar ways of operating. A company may recognize hiring protocols that did not favor individuals from marginalized religious backgrounds and therefore encourage the head of human resources (HR) to restructure the entire process. After a few years of the revised selection process and the subsequent employment of a new director of HR, the organization's procedure slowly begins to dissolve, and the company regresses to its old discriminatory hiring practices. Thus, implementing a system of evaluation and accountability is vital to maintaining positive change.

Tactic # 3 – Leverage Personal Power and Privileged Identities

In many respects, all of us represent many voices that can be used to enlighten, raise awareness, point out inequities, and educate those around us. Regardless of the settings, whether neighborhood events, classrooms, family gatherings, worksites, or boardrooms, opportunities exist to make observations and express opinions and concerns about observed disparities or the unfairness of a process or regulation. Wondering aloud, for example, why most managers or supervisors at a corporation are either White or male is a microintervention that makes the invisible visible to coworkers and others in positions of authority. Recognizing the unfairness of a policy toward employees of color, for example, that operates under the principle of *first fired and last hired* during an economic downturn is a necessary precondition to change.

Although targets of macroaggressions may feel disempowered because of their marginalized status, everyone possesses multiple identities that include race, gender, age, ability, sexual orientation/identity, socioeconomic status, level of education, and religious affiliation. While many individuals hold more than one marginalized identity (i.e. race, gender, sexual orientation) or a socially devalued identity that often overshadows other identities (i.e. race), almost all individuals hold at least one identity with power and privilege (Ratts et al., 2016; Young & Anderson, 2019). For example, while a highly educated gay male Asian American may be doubly disadvantaged in our society, he also holds power because of his male status, and elevated level of education. Although privileged identities do not necessarily protect a person from various forms of micro- and macroaggressions, it potentially represents power and privilege in other situations.

By elevating and leveraging these privileged identities and the power associated with them, impacting certain spaces, policies, procedures, and so on becomes a more attainable task. Highlighting one's privileged identity is essential to combatting macroaggressions. A few examples under this tactic include: (a) use your power, your ability to sit at tables that other members of the community cannot access, to voice concerns of the community and make unfair practices explicit; (b) advocate for the rights of marginalized members of your institution/organization; (c) maintain an open, supportive, and responsive environment in all spaces; (d) be deliberate about making space for voices that are not commonly heard or usually dismissed; and (e) educate dominant group members on trends or evaluation findings.

CHAPTER SEVEN

Microintervention Strategy and Tactics to Educate Perpetrators and Stakeholders

An unenlightened person cannot enlighten others. All he or she can do is
spread ignorance and misinformation.

– Derald Wing Sue

Although microinterventions often create discomfort for perpetrators, most
are not meant to be punitive, but rather educational (Sue, 2015a). In the case
of microaggressions, the ultimate hope is to reach and educate perpetrators
by engaging them in a dialogue about what they have done that has proven
offensive, what it says about their beliefs and values, and have them consider
the worldview of marginalized group members (Goodman, 2011). In the case
of macroaggressions, the major hope is to reach and educate those in power
and authority, stakeholders, potential allies, and the populace. The
expectation is that when one sees the unfairness and harm of policies and
practices, groups become motivated to support change. As in the goal of

Microintervention Strategies, First Edition. Derald Wing Sue, Cassandra Z. Calle, Narolyn Mendez,
Sarah Alsaidi, and Elizabeth Glaeser.

making the "invisible" visible, educational strategies and tactics may differ considerably between both. Table 7.1 lists the microintervention tactics directed at micro- and macroaggressions.

STRATEGIC GOAL: EDUCATE PERPETRATORS

We realize that education is a long-term process and brief encounters seldom allow an opportunity for deep discussions; nevertheless, over the long run, microinterventions plant seeds of possible change that may blossom in the future. This is especially true if they are exposed to frequent microinterventions by those around them, creating an atmosphere of inclusion and an environment that values diversity and differences (Purdie-Vaughns et al., 2008; Scully & Rowe, 2009). Many brief educational tactics can be taken by targets, allies, and bystanders to educate perpetrators.

Tactic # 1 – Help Microaggressors Differentiate between Good Intent and Harmful Impact

One of the most powerful educational tactics is to help microaggressors differentiate between good intent and harmful impact. When microaggressions are pointed out to perpetrators, a common reaction is defensiveness and shifting the focus from action to intention (Sue, 2015a). Here the person who may have engaged in behaviors or made a statement perceived as biased claims that *I did not intend it that way*. In racial dialogues, shifting the topic to intent is tactically very effective because proving biased intent is virtually impossible. To overcome the blockage, it is often helpful to refocus the discussion on impact instead of intent. Some examples are:

"I know you meant well (intent), but that really hurts (impact)."

"I know you meant it as a joke (intent), but it really offended Aisha (impact)."

" know you want the women on this team to succeed (intent), but always putting them on hospitality committees will only prevent them from developing leadership skills (impact)."

"I know you kid around a lot (intent), but think how your words affect others (impact)."

"I know you meant it to be funny (intent), but that stereotype is no joke (impact)."

Table 7.1 Strategic Goal: Educate the Offender and Stakeholder

Microinterventions for Microaggressions

Scenario: A student in a chemistry class makes the following comment about an Arab American student: "Maybe she should not be learning about making bombs and stuff."

Meta-communication: All Arab Americans are potential terrorists.

OBJECTIVES	RATIONALE	TACTICS	EXAMPLE
• Engage in a one-on-one dialogue with the perpetrator to indicate how, what, and why the comment was offensive to you or others	• Allows targets, allies, and bystanders the opportunity to express their experience while maintaining a relationship with the offender	1. Differentiate between intent and impact	"I know you didn't realize this but that comment you made was demeaning to Maryam because not all Arab Americans are a threat to national security."
		2. Contradict the group-based stereotype by personalizing the experience.	"I know Maryam personally, and she is a good, moral, and decent person like you."
• Facilitate a possibly more enlightening conversation and exploration of the perpetrator's biases	• Lowers the defense of the perpetrator and helps them recognize the harmful impact	3. Appeal to the offender's values and principles	"I know you really care about representing everyone on campus and being a good student government leader but acting in this way really undermines your intentions to be inclusive."
• Encourage the perpetrator to explore the origins of their beliefs and attitudes toward targets	• Perpetrator becomes keen to microaggressions committed by those within their social circle and educates others	4. Point out the commonality	"That is a negative stereotype of Arab Americans. Did you know Maryam also aspires to be a doctor just like you? You should talk to her; you actually have a lot in common."
		5. Promote empathy	"The majority of Arab Americans are completely against terroristic acts. How would you feel if someone assumed something about you because of your race?"
		6. Point out how they benefit	"I know you are studying clinical psychology. Learning about why those stereotypes are harmful is going to make you a better clinician."

(Continued)

Table 7.1 (Continued)

OBJECTIVES	RATIONALE	TACTICS	EXAMPLE
			Microinterventions for Macroaggressions
• Help stakeholders and decision-makers develop critical consciousness about systemic inequities • Encourage community-level educational engagement • Illuminate the gain or the advantages	• Creates opportunities for conversation and learning • Encourages institutions to look inward and address issues that typically go unnoticed • Engages stakeholders at various levels with the community	1. Raise critical thinking	• Facilitate an open discussion on how race, culture, and ethnicity affect marginalized group members. • Participate with local community centers and faith based organizations to support and facilitate open dialogues about race, racism, and legal rights • Raise consciousness by directly teaching stakeholders how to recognize discrimination • Teach people of color how to confront possible internalized beliefs
		2. Support antibias education and training	• Support formal anti-bias education and training in all organizations. • Encourage educators to include discussions of race and bias in lesson plans. • Organize reading and discussion groups around books written by authors of color. • Conduct field trips to historical places that embody the racial struggles and lessons of oppression and courage. • Encourage people to join civil rights organizations like the Southern Poverty Law Center, American Civil Liberties Union, and the Anti-Defamation League. • Publicly support policies that allow for equal access and opportunity.
		3. Highlight the benefits of diversity and equity	• Approach companies with information on how lack of diversity and multiculturalism results in lower work productivity, low morale, high employee turnover, and lost profits. • Describe the benefits of workforce diversity on education, employment, health care, and all other aspects of society.

Refocusing the dialogue from intent to impact (a) avoids an accusation of bias, thereby lowering defensiveness, (b) allows the discussion to center on the interpersonal transaction, rather than arguing over intent, (c) encourages empathic understanding of why the impact was poorly received, and (d) hopefully, results in an educational dialogue that has a lasting impact.

Tactic # 2 – Contradict the Group-Based Stereotype with Opposing Evidence by Personalizing It to Specific Individuals

Many stereotypes or negative statements are related to stereotyping an entire group; "every member shares the same trait." Taking a cognitive or data-oriented approach, at times, may or may not prove effective. Citing studies and providing information that contradict the stereotype pose the danger of moving the conversation to a purely intellectual and abstract exercise devoid of personal or experiential meaning. Opposing evidence may be better received when personalized and made concrete and specific. Asking specifically, for example, whom the person is talking about and providing personal information that contradicts the overgeneralization challenge the group stereotype. For example, "Are you talking about someone in particular?" forces the perpetrator to personalize the statement and prevent the microaggression from being abstract and ambiguous. Other examples are:

Statement: "Those Blacks just don't have a good work ethic."

Counter: "I think Eric and Juanita (both African American) work very hard and put in more time than most workers."

Statement: "Those immigrants don't even try to learn."

Counter: "Actually, I've met many immigrants who have learned to speak English well. It's not easy. Have you ever tried to learn another language?"

Tactic # 3 – Appeal to the Offender's Values and Principles

Most people are fair-minded, moral, and decent human beings who on a conscious level believe in American ideals of democracy, equity, inclusion, and equal access and opportunity. Some may disagree with this statement, but we have been raised to cherish the US Constitution, Bill of Rights, and Declaration of Independence. The belief in human rights and the abhorrence of racism are ideologies that we have been taught to uphold. Research reveals the existence of explicit and implicit biases with regard to racism. So, it is possible for people to uphold humanistic values, to denounce racism, but to be unaware of the biases they harbor. This tactic appeals to the consciously held values of equity and social justice of people, by indirectly pointing out how their implicit biases (statements or behaviors) are at odds with their values of equality, equal access and opportunity, and humane treatment of others. The following are examples.

"I know you really care about representing everyone on campus and being a good student government leader, but acting in this way really undermines your intentions to be inclusive."

"Is it fair to always assign employees of color to lower level jobs while giving White workers more desired positions? I know you are a good person and wouldn't deliberately stifle the career growth of anyone."

"John, I know you will make the right decision. You have always valued diversity and inclusion….you know what is right, and will do the right thing."

Tactic # 4 – Point Out the Commonalities

Pointing out commonalities does not mean ignoring or devaluing differences. It means helping people understand that everyone possesses three levels of identity: individual, group, and universal (Sue, Sue, Neville, & Smith, 2019). At the individual level is the fact that everyone is unique and no two individuals (even identical twins) are the same. At the group level, we are referring to the similarities and differences associated with race, gender, disability/ability, age, socioeconomic status, religious preference, and so forth. Most of these group identities are intersecting. At the universal level, we share many similarities (common life experiences, ability to use symbols, self-awareness, similar human aspirations, etc.). Racism is born from seeing differences in others as deviant, as lesser human beings, as unlike oneself, and as "the other." Stereotyping and bigotry constrict perception and only allow the person to focus upon differences that they deem undesirable. This separation and lack of connection with one another make it easy to engage in microaggressions toward socially devalued group members. The microintervention tactic here is to (a) label and correct the stereotypes, (b) point out the shared group or universal identities they possess, and (c) encourage them to act on those shared commonalities.

"That is a negative stereotype of Arab Americans. Have you actually talked to Maryam? You two have so much in common. Did you know she is also an aspiring doctor? I think she is also into cycling too. Talk to her."

"You two have so much in common (White and African American workers). Both of you are the highest producers on my team, and yes, you two have completely different backgrounds, but you approach problems similarly. Get to know Jamal. I bet if you both combined resources, our team could out produce all the others in our company."

Tactic # 5 – Promote Empathy

In Chapter 3, we spent considerable time describing the psychosocial costs of racism to perpetrators. Considerable debate surrounds the question of whether low empathy causes inhumane treatment of others, or whether racism causes insensitivity toward the oppressed. Regardless of cause or effect, racism thrives when perpetrators become insensitive to the feelings or plight of others, when they become callous, hard, and cold toward the oppressed, and when compassion and empathy are diminished. Objectifying and dehumanizing people of color allow perpetrators to become oblivious to their complicity in allowing racism to continue, and in their own harmful attitudes and discriminatory behaviors. Promoting collectivistic attitudes toward groups who differ in race, culture, and ethnicity, and helping others increase empathy and compassion are challenging tasks.

"The majority of Latinos want the same things as you. Jesus works hard and wants to advance in his job and make enough to support his family. Do you know how he must feel to be described as being lazy and be deprived of a promotion opportunity? How would you feel if that happened to you? Can you place yourself in his shoes?"

"Have you ever felt discriminated against? How did it make you feel? It wasn't pleasant, was it? Now, multiply that tenfold for what happens to Juanita. Every day she sits alone in the cafeteria at lunch time, not by choice, but by her coworkers who tease her use of English. How do you think it makes her feel to be an outcast? It must be so lonely and made to feel like a pariah."

Tactic # 6 – Point Out How They Benefit

This is a tactic that emphasizes on a personal level the benefits of differences. Too often people believe that differences are divisive, produce conflict, and interfere with personal growth or group productivity. In the next section, we will devote considerable time to pointing out the benefits of diversity, inclusion, and multiculturalism to organizations and society. On a personal level, people can be made aware of how encountering differences and integrating them into valuing diversity can result in personal growth and development. Being exposed to diverse groups and diverse ways of thinking and interacting is associated with less intimidation and fear of differences, an increased compassion for others, a broadening of their horizons, appreciation of people of all colors and cultures, and a greater sense of connectedness with all groups. Some examples of pointing out benefits are listed here.

> "I use to feel the same way. When with Black employees, I would feel uncomfortable, afraid I would say something wrong, and believed they wouldn't add much to our productivity. Imagine my surprise when I discovered that their racial perspectives enhanced the company's knowledge of Black consumers. I found myself reaching out to our Latinx employees and reached the same conclusion. But, something happened to me beyond company goals. I found myself changing. I wasn't afraid to be in the company of people of color anymore, and enjoyed our interactions. I know it sounds strange, but it was like a big weight lifted off of me. Go to lunch with me and I'll introduce you to some of my new African American and Latinx friends."

> "I know you are studying clinical psychology. Learning about why those stereotypes are harmful is going to make you a better clinician."

STRATEGIC GOAL: CHALLENGING MACROAGGRESSIONS THROUGH EDUCATION

In many respects, the strategic goals of *make the invisible visible* and *educate stakeholders* are overlapping and intimately linked to one another. For macroaggressions, however, the educational strategy goes far beyond awareness and into the larger arena of critical consciousness and perspicacity (Anderson & Stevenson, 2019; Sternberg, 2003) characteristics we explored earlier. Stakeholders are persons, organizations, social groups, or the larger society that have a *stake* in how a particular institution or business operates (Dovidio & Jones, 2018). As a group, stakeholders (elected officials, federal, state, and local governments, organizations, key decision-makers, employees, customers, and general public) can exert powerful influence on how programs, policies, and practices are perceived, created, or changed. Educating stakeholders, especially decision-makers, and having them develop critical consciousness about systemic inequities are the primary goal. Although microinterventions are commonly described as immediate, and in the moment responses, those aimed at macroaggressions emphasize the importance of longer-term development of critical consciousness, education, and diversity benefits (Ashburn-Nardo, Morris, & Goodman, 2008; Goodman, 2011; Scully & Rowe, 2009).

Diversity in institutions and society has taken on increased importance such that numerous trainings and workshops have been developed in business, industry, and education (Aguilar, 2006; Byrd, 2018). Educational curriculums have been disseminated at various institutional settings including academic libraries, higher education (Knapp, Snavely, & Klimczyk, 2012), and public/private elementary and secondary schools (Willoughby, 2012). A major component of such educational activities is to present facts on the detrimental impact of micro- and macroaggressions. For example, the Speak Up! Booklet developed by the Southern Poverty Law Center begins by providing statistics that show that instances of prejudice are not only prevalent but also have very real detrimental consequences to mental health and well-being (Willoughby, 2005).

As we have emphasized, the presence and impact of macroaggressions are difficult to discern because they are often hidden in SOPs and appear equitable and unbiased in application. Macroaggressions are also difficult to change because they reside in institutional policies and societal customs and cannot be attributed to a single perpetrator; rather their application and enforcement are carried out by decision-makers and supported by stakeholders. Because those in authority often have greater discretion in making and influencing change, microintervention objectives used to address interpersonal microaggressions are also useful in raising awareness; (a) engage in a one-on-one dialogue with leadership to explain how a policy is biased, (b) facilitate a more enlightened conversation that educates, (c) propose possible solutions, and (d) enlist the aid of those at the very top of the organization (Sue et al., 2019).

We describe three main tactics under the strategic goal of *Educate stakeholders* to an audience that goes beyond decision-makers: (1) raise critical thinking, (2) support antibias education and training, and (3) highlight benefits of diversity and inclusion. Although each tactic has their own specific objective, all may include education and training, program planning, consulting, and making explicit values, rules, and expectations.

Tactic # 1 – Raise Critical Thinking

Critical thinking, an aspect of critical consciousness, is not merely acquisition of knowledge and information, but moves beyond schooling and literacy to (a) question the source of knowledge, (b) interrogate the purpose and use of information, (c) determine who does and doesn't benefit from present arrangements, and (d) make sure it reflects reality (APA, 2019a, 2019b; El-Amin et al., 2017). Being able to recognize and analyze systems of inequality is most likely developed through building social connections with a community of activists, participating in local, state, and national organizations, and engaging others in community forums. Through engagement, communities can also increase exposure to examples of diverse cultures, which help to offset negative stereotypes and bias. Raising critical thinking for allies and bystanders not only expands racial literacy and recognition of personal biases but also emphasizes action in the face of recognizing the way power and privilege affects others.

A beginning step in this direction can be accomplished if employees at various institutions can facilitate an open discussion on how race, culture, and ethnicity affect them on the worksite. A major way that advocates of social justice can make a large impact is by organizing with local community centers and faith-based organizations to support and facilitate open dialogues. Such advocates may also work to raise awareness and reduce internalized bias within the community and provide workshops that educate members about their legal rights. For example, immediately following the Muslim ban, various community organizations across the country collaborated with legal offices to provide "know your rights" trainings and to disseminate information to the community.

Raising critical thinking is more easily advocated than fulfilled because it represents a higher-level cognitive process that involves recognizing and analyzing systems of oppression and inequality. Despite its difficulty, Freire (1970) found it to be an attainable goal in his work with oppressed Brazilian laborers with high illiteracy rates. Understanding how structural inequality subjugates people of color through privilege and oppression is a challenging task (Freire, 1970; Watts, Diemer, & Voight, 2011). Because biased social norms, organizational policies (macroaggressions), and individual behaviors (microaggressions) are the sources of inequities in society, understanding how they are maintained by external and internal dynamisms is a major first step. For example, high incarceration rates for African American men may be attributed to external structural inequities: racial profiling, increased presence of police patrols in low income neighborhoods, and harsher mandatory sentences given to African American men (Blair, Judd, & Chapleau, 2004; Plant & Peruche, 2005). Once released, however, former convicted felons continue to encounter institutionalized rules and regulations that keep them out of mainstream society; thus, homelessness, unemployment, poverty level wages, and limited access to health care lower their standard of living when compared to the mainstream populace (Jones, 1997).

As in his work with the oppressed, Freire (1970) also found internalized oppression, the acceptance of negative messages, beliefs, and values about the target population's group to be a major barrier to liberation. For targets of macroaggressions, raising consciousness may include directly teaching them how to recognize discrimination and how to confront possible internalized beliefs. Persons of color may internalize beliefs about their perceived inferiority to White individuals and may vote, support laws, and even advocate for policies that directly harm them. For example, some immigrant families may vote in favor of immigration laws and support Immigration and Customs Enforcement (ICE) because they have internalized messages about their identities or because they believe that voting in this way will deflect attention from them, will lower perception of them as "aliens," and will help them transition more easily to the mainstream. Unfortunately, many may not be aware of the harmful impact these laws and policies may ultimately have on their own lives and on communities of color. This is why critical thinking skills are required for targets, social advocates, and those with power and privilege to possess.

Tactic # 2 – Support Antibias Education and Training

Formal education and training on topics of diversity, inclusion, and implicit and explicit bias have become increasingly used in business, industry, and education to create an equitable work environment through exploration of individual and organizational biases (Jones & Dovidio, 2018; Scully & Rowe, 2009; Toporek & Worthington, 2014). Most diversity training, in the form of workshops or classroom curriculum, attempts to address one or all of the following objectives (APA, 2017; 2019c; Ratts et al., 2016; Sue, Sue, Neville, & Smith, 2019):

1. Increase the awareness of participants regarding their values, biases, and assumptions about human behavior.

    The training usually focuses on stereotypes, biased perceptions, and inaccurate beliefs about different groups of color that hinder and create the "othering" of people of color. The curriculum/content, exercises, and activities are aimed at self-exploration, self-awareness, and accepting the troubling proposition that participants are not immune from inheriting the racial biases of the society. Without insight and awareness of the self, participants may inadvertently assume that everyone shares a similar world view, and racial/cultural differences are ignored or pathologized. When this happens, those with power and privilege may become guilty of cultural oppression, imposing White Western values on people of color. Such actions may disadvantage people of color in education, employment, and health care.

2. Acquire knowledge and understanding of the worldview of culturally diverse groups and individuals.

    Training objectives move from self-exploration to understanding the worldview of people who differ from participants in terms of race, ethnicity, and culture. How do these powerful sociodemographic identities affect worldviews? Is there such a thing as an African American, Asian American, Latinx American, or American Indian worldview? Do other culturally different groups (women, the physically challenged, gays/lesbians, etc.) also have different world views? How do these differences in perspective affect people of color (employees or students)? It is important to note, however, that this objective goes beyond cultural knowledge or understanding (information on groups of color), but must focus also on topics of power and privilege, and the racialized experiences of people of color who reside in a primarily monocultural society.

3. Understand differences in communication styles, and develop culturally appropriate interaction patterns when relating to a diverse population.

    Earlier, we indicated that communication styles are often affected by group membership. Many African Americans, for example, are more direct, confrontive, and passionate in their verbal and nonverbal interactions, while many Asian Americans are more emotionally restrained, subtle, and indirect when conversing with others (Sue, Sue, Neville, & Smith, 2019). Part of training is to acknowledge these differences and prevent misunderstandings from occurring (African Americans are "angry" and "emotional," while Asian Americans are "passive" and "inhibited"). But the issue of communication patterns goes far beyond understanding these differences and not making incorrect judgments. Communication styles have implications for teaching styles, learning styles, managerial styles, and helping styles. Not understanding that teaching styles might be incompatible with culturally different learning styles, or that managerial styles might disadvantage employees of color can create unfair educational or work environments.

4. Understand how institutional policies, practices, and customs (macroaggressions) may differentially advantage or disadvantage certain groups in an organization.

   Training and education at this macro level represents getting participants to broaden their perspective from individual racism to institutional and cultural forms of racism (macroaggressions) (APA, 2019c). Focus is on how we are all impacted by the rules and regulations of an organization for better or worse. It does little good for anyone to become culturally aware and even non-racist when organizations that employ them are filled with monocultural policies and practices that oppress groups of color. The goals here are systemic in nature and represent attempts to implement macrointerventions: (a) identify SOPs that oppress and create inequities, (b) eliminate or alter them, and (c) develop new rules, regulations, policies, practices, and structures within organizations which enhance fairness and equity.

To achieve these goals, concerned scholars and students, for example, may encourage universities to make their research findings more accessible to the general public by collaborating with artists and writers. In this way, their research findings, which are typically limited to academia, can be used to develop training and workshops that aim to prevent future instances of discrimination. Individual employees could invite race scholars to conduct training or teach at their organizations. Institutions should anticipate how race, gender, sexuality, and other aspects of identity may arise in the workplace, accept responsibility to prepare employees for such scenarios, and train them with awareness and skills to deal with diversity.

An example of how an individual might use microinterventions to address macroaggressions is given in the following case:

> A female school teacher who works as part of the hiring committee realizes that many of the incoming new teachers have not had prior training and education to prepare them to work in a community that serves mainly ethnic and racial minority children. She identifies an academic institution that conducts excellent research that can be translated into trainings and workshops and she reaches out to them to conduct training at her school. The teacher also holds panel discussions where she and her fellow colleagues invite new educators to learn from current teacher experiences, highlighting values of the school and what they have learned in their tenure. The principal and other school administrators find the training incredibly beneficial to transitioning new teachers into the school culture, providing culturally relevant education teaching tips, increasing teacher morale, and improving relations with the community. The training is identified as an important aspect of employment at the school and becomes a mandated training for all future employees (macrointerventions).

Educating stakeholders oftentimes looks different depending upon the arena in which it occurs. It may also be brief and transitory because contact is time limited. If education and influence is desired at the legislative levels, for example, input can occur in face-to-face meetings (providing fact sheets), conducting seminars for legislatures, speaking at government hearings, and serving on commissions and task forces (Banks et al., 2019). Because many of these tactics may require special knowledge and expertise about the subject at hand, forming coalitions and collaborators with a range of proficiencies to address the tasks is vital to educational success.

Although we have focused primarily on formal education and training, informal community and neighborhood-based activities are also important. Antibias education and training need not just occur through formal organizationally or group-sponsored events, but can be initiated by any dedicated individual willing to address issues of bias and equity. Parents, teachers, community, and church leaders or any civic-minded persons can initiate and encourage public engagement and education through various planned microintervention activities (APA, 2017; Community Tool Box, 2019; President's Initiative on Race, 1998; Sue, 2003):

- Organize reading and discussion groups around books written by authors of color.
- Suggest relatives, friends, and neighbors attend plays or movies with multicultural themes.
- Invite colleagues, coworkers, neighbors, or students of color to social functions.
- Invite local artists, authors, entertainers, politicians, and leaders of color to address your group about race issues.
- Conduct field trips to historical places that embody the racial struggles and lessons of oppression and courage.
- Encourage educators to include discussions of race and bias in lesson plans.
- Recommend to friends and neighbors to attend ethnic museums and displays.
- Encourage people to join civil rights organizations like the Southern Poverty Law Center, American Civil Liberties Union, and the Anti-Defamation League.
- Form a community task force on valuing diversity and hold town hall meetings on the topic.
- Encourage others to vote for candidates who stand against racism and for diversity.
- Publicly support policies that allow for equal access and opportunity.

The American Psychological Association (APA, n.d.) in their publication *Psychology and Racism* outlines the many roles that citizens can play to combat racism. In many respects, the activities associated with the roles are consistent with microintervention actions in the categories of microaffirmations, microprotections, and microchallenges. A few of these are the following:

- Be an ally to people of color. Support victims of discrimination, join them in advocating for fair treatment, help their voices be heard, and stand against racial bigotry.
- Be an anti-racist parent. Raise your children to understand concepts of race and racism, introduce them to children of color, discuss race issues

openly and nondefensively, and include topics of inclusion, democracy, and anti-racism as part of their vocabulary.

- Be a role model. Have your children see you interact positively with people of color, be vocal in opposing racist views, interrupt the telling of racist jokes, and invite neighbors and friends of color to your home.
- Be a teacher. As a coworker, parent, neighbor, or friend you can teach others to value diversity and multiculturalism.
- Be a social justice activist. Speak out and object to racial injustice, challenge family, friends, and strangers about their expressed biases, serve on groups and committees that have a social justice agenda, and work to make sure that your school and worksites operate from a position of equity and fairness.

Tactic # 3 – Highlight the Benefits of Diversity and Equity

Most formal and informal attempts to educate people about racial injustice and systemic unfairness focus on the harm and detrimental consequences of bias and discrimination. Framing diversity and equity as threats to overcome is less effective in advocating for *systemic* diversity and multiculturalism than when presented as opportunities and untapped benefits (APA, 2012, *Dual Pathways to a Better America*). It is estimated that two-thirds of companies in the business sector provide diversity training (CBLO, 2006), and that there has been a progressive evolution from addressing the harm of bias and bigotry to also include the value of acquiring multicultural competence and its importance to the bottom line (Hunt, Layton, & Prince, 2015). Earlier, we discussed how individuals benefit from increased racial literacy in that they expand their perspectives, become more comfortable and less fearful of differences, improve their relations with family and friends, and feel an increased spiritual connectedness with all groups (President's Initiative on Race, 1998). Some have concluded that companies that value multiculturalism, diversity, and inclusion in their actual practices and in the workforce profit and benefit immensely over those whose operations are more traditionally monocultural (Jones & Dovidio, 2018; Martic, 2018).

As an individual employee, a social advocacy group, or even a member of the community, it may be helpful to approach companies with information on how lack of diversity and multiculturalism results in lower work productivity, low morale, high employee turnover, and lost profits (Hunt, Layton, &

Prince, 2015; Martic, 2018). Just as companies learn about the potential negative consequences of macroaggressions that manifest in their institutions, they should be made aware of the benefits that can be gained. Many institutions already recognize diversity as an important value in their mission statements, but it does not necessarily mean that diversity and inclusion are actually practiced in day-to-day operations. The many benefits of workplace diversity and an inclusive organizational culture can be seen in internal (employee morale and improved performance) and external (profits and financial advantage) outcomes.

First, having employees from all walks of life and from diverse groups create an environment of higher innovation, increased creativity, better ideas, faster problem-solving, and better decision-making (Martic, 2018). Diversity initiatives lead to better hiring results due to an increased talent pool and the perception by applicants of color that they are welcomed (Martic, 2018). High employee morale and increased engagement are aspects of feeling included and valued leading to reduced employee turnover (Hunt, Layton, & Prince, 2015). McMahon (2010) states strongly that while a diverse workforce is important, having a diverse management team is the most powerful way to signal support and commitment to diversity. Many organizational consultants believe that diversity implementation is most effective when strong leadership is exerted on behalf of multiculturalism, and when the boards at the very top levels are diverse in terms or race and gender (Roberson & Park, 2007; Jones & Dovidio, 2018; Hunt, Layton, & Prince, 2015). Faculty, staff, and students, for example, are most likely to watch the actions (not just words) of those in leadership positions for signs of real commitment. In higher education, diversity is most effective and meaningful when it is reflected in the board of trustees, provost, chancellor, president, dean, or chair of the department (Sue, 1995, 2008).

Second, diversity benefits to business and industry are not just confined to employee morale and increased internal satisfaction but also have major external implications for public relations, customer satisfaction, and company profitability. Most companies work hard to connect to the communities around them, to foster goodwill, and to ultimately build or enhance their brand and reputation. Higher diversity in companies has been found (a) to improve the company's national and international reputation; (b) to increase investor confidence; (c) to be perceived as more interesting, humane, and socially responsible; (d) to enhance ability to open new markets; and (e) to increase forming new and profitable business partners (Martic, 2018; Roberson & Park, 2007). Being connected to the community may also mean better customer orientation and improved ability to reach key purchasing decision-makers, to anticipate the implications of the changing complexion of society (Sue, Parham, & Santiago, 1998), and to respond to changing preferences for goods and services (Hunt, Layton, & Prince, 2015).

Third, profitability is probably the most important driving rationale for companies to make major changes in their organizational culture and to hire a diverse workforce. It would make sense that lower employee turnover, better decision-making, increased productivity, and positive perception by customers would all translate into better financial performance and increased profitability for companies. In companies with a diverse leadership team and workforce, for example, researchers found a significant correlation to better financial returns. Companies in the top quartile of gender diversity were 15% more likely to have higher returns than their national industry median; those in the top quartile of racial/ethnic diversity were 35% more likely to be above the national industry median (Hunt, Layton, & Prince, 2015). What is surprising, however, is that companies in the bottom quartile of gender and race diversity were less likely to achieve above average returns when compared with companies scoring just average on diversity!

Achieving the benefits of diversity are challenging, but the positive results on individual, institutional, and societal levels are many. The world is much more diverse than that in the past, technological changes have increased exposure to one another, and social, economic, and political interdependence have increased. Diversity, inclusion, multiculturalism, and antibias values are paramount in unleashing the full potential of individuals, institutions, and ultimately society. In summarizing the social psychological studies on the overall benefits of diversity to our society, Jones and Dovidio (2018) supply the following list: (a) improves interactions with other groups; (b) increases opportunities to learn; (c) promotes flexibility, adaptability, and creativity; and (d) promotes civic mindedness. In their review, such positive benefits accrue to education, employment, health care, and nearly every aspect of society.

CHAPTER EIGHT

Microintervention Strategy and Tactics to Disarm Microaggressions and Macroaggressions

In a racist society it is not enough to be nonracist, we must be anti-racist.
— Angela Davis

Disarming micro- and macroaggressions are tactics used to more directly confront the perpetrator or institutional practice that harms, denigrates, and maligns target groups. In many cases, the destructive quality of the bias is so pressing that more immediate and forceful action is required. On a personal level (microaggressions), the potential injurious nature of the interpersonal affront must be instantly stopped. On an institutional or societal level, programs or policies that cause harm to people of color are so substantial and life threatening that group protest and demonstrations are called for. In this chapter, we first address the tactics used toward individual expressions of bias, and then turn our attention to describing microintervention strategies aimed at changing biased polices, practices, programs, and customs in institutions and society. Table 8.1 lists the tactics used to disarm micro- and macroaggressions.

Microintervention Strategies, First Edition. Derald Wing Sue, Cassandra Z. Calle, Narolyn Mendez, Sarah Alsaidi, and Elizabeth Glaeser.
© 2021 John Wiley & Sons, Inc. Published 2021 by John Wiley & Sons, Inc.

Table 8.1 Strategic Goal: Disarm the Micro/Macroaggression

Microinterventions for Microaggressions

Scenario: A colleague makes the following statement about a new employee with a visible disability: "He only got the job because he's handicapped."

Meta-communication: People with disabilities only receive opportunities through special accommodations rather than through their own capabilities or merits.

OBJECTIVES	RATIONALE	TACTICS	EXAMPLE
• Instantly stop or deflect the microaggression	• Provides targets, allies, and bystanders with a sense of control and self-efficacy to react to perpetrators in the here and now	1. Interrupt and redirect	"Whoa, let's not go there. Maybe we should focus on the task at hand."
• Force the perpetrator to immediately consider what they have just said or done	• Preserves targets' well-being and prevents traumatization by or preoccupation with what transpired	2. State values and set limits	"You know that respect and tolerance are important values in my life and, while I understand that you have a right to say what you want, I'm asking you to show a little more respect for me by not making offensive comments."
• Communicate your disagreement or disapproval toward the perpetrator in the moment	• Allows perpetrator to think before they speak or behave in future encounters with similar individuals	3. Express disagreement	"I don't agree with what you just said." "That's not how I view it."
		4. Describe what is happening	"Every time I come over, I find myself becoming uncomfortable because you make statements that I find offensive and hurtful."
		5. Nonverbal communication	Shaking your head. Looking down or away. Covering your mouth with your hand.
		6. Use an exclamation	"Ouch!" "Ahhh, C'mon!"
		7. Remind them of the rules	"That behavior is against our code of conduct and could really get you in trouble."

Microinterventions for Macroaggressions

OBJECTIVES	RATIONALE	TACTICS	EXAMPLE
• Provide a potent and effective means to confront biases in institutional or societal policies • Applies pressure on key stakeholders to institute change through persuasion • Utilizes coercion and disruption to cause embarrassment and/or inconvenience and motivate change	• Raise public awareness through media • Persuade and demand change from stakeholders and decision-makers • Make an impact through collective organizing that cannot be dismissed or ignored	1. Protest and persuade	Deliver a public speech or create a mass petition. Utilize advertisement to challenge stereotypes and inform individuals on injustices (editorials, radio, television, print, op-ed pieces, news, billboards etc.). Protest by displaying or wearing symbolic images. For example hanging a LGBTQ flag in your office or wearing a Black Lives Matter t-shirt. Hold vigils and memorials to put pressure on officials and/or cause inconvenience to initiate change. Organize legal public assemblies, protests, teach-ins, town halls or silent protests, walkouts, strikes, and boycotts.
		2. Engage in civil disobedience	Boycotts, refusal taxes or rent, refusal to pay fees or dues, slowdown strikes, resignations, excommunication, social isolation, hunger strikes, overload facilities, nonviolent sabotage, reluctance, or slow compliance, office invasions, blockades.

(Continued)

Table 8.1 *(Continued)*

OBJECTIVES	RATIONALE	TACTICS	EXAMPLE
		3. Challenge the status quo through media	• Disseminate research on disparity trends to general public and media. • Utilize traditional media (television, radio, and print) as well as social media (YouTube, Twitter, Facebook, Instagram, etc.). • Write a letter or hold a press-release. Offer to hold an interview with a news paper. • Work with other artists to create documentaries, posters, and pamphlets.
		4. Enhance collective action	• Exercise your rights in government and politics and encourage others to do the same (vote, serve on boards, attend town halls, revise, and veto community policies, call elected officials, etc.). • Create caucuses for targets and allies. • Create local affiliates for organizations that support your beliefs. • Focus efforts on building a sense of community and collective identity to enhance collective action.

STRATEGIC GOAL: DISARM MICROAGGRESSIONS

A more direct means of dealing with microaggression is to disarm them by stopping or deflecting the comments or actions through expressing disagreement, challenging what was said or done, and/or pointing out its harmful impact. This more confrontive approach is usually taken because of the immediate injurious nature to targets and those who witness it.

Tactic # 1 – Interrupt the Communication and Redirect It

During the course of a conversation when a biased or misinformed statement is made, simply interrupt it by directly or indirectly stopping the monologue and communicating your disagreement or displeasure. This is very effective when (a) racist or sexist comments are made, or when (b) racist jokes are being told. An example of using this tactic is given to an ensuing racist rant overheard by coworkers.

> A White male colleague becomes angry at work left undone by Latinx workers. He begins to rant and rave at their "laziness" and "stupidity." As he continues his diatribe, he makes increasingly racist statements around coworkers.

Interrupting and disarming the monologue is illustrated here:

> "Stop right there! I don't appreciate those sorts of comments. They are hurtful and vile. Now, if you really want to solve this issue, let's focus on the task at hand."

In this scenario, another coworker whether bystander or White ally (a) stops the demeaning comments, (b) expresses personal disapproval, (c) briefly indicates their "hurtfulness" or impact, and (d) redirects it to the problem at hand. Note that this approach avoids a direct argument about the character of socially marginalized group members, but is clear that the intervener does not agree. A similar tactic can be very effective when racist jokes are told. It is actually most effective when the intervention occurs during the process of telling the joke, and before the punchline is delivered. During the COVID-19 pandemic, anti-Asian sentiment was strong and a number of jokes blaming the Chinese for causing the virus dealt with their "diet on bats."

> "Hey everyone (at a social gathering), have you heard this joke about why the Chinese are to blame for spreading COVID-19? There were two Chinese men who entered a Chinese restaurant and ordered a bat delicacy, but it was rare and undercooked. Well, do you know what they did?"

Because racist jokes are usually at the expense of marginalized group members, use stereotypes and misinformation and demean the group, allowing them to go uninterrupted contributes to false consensus. In these situations, microinterventions need not be long or involved, but can be short and effective. Same examples are to the joke above are:

"Whoa, let's not go there."
"Danger, quick sand ahead."
"I don't want to hear the punchline, or that type of talk."
(Removing yourself from the conversation.)
Shaking your head and physically leaving the situation.

Tactic # 2 – State Values and Set Limits
In this situation, using yourself as the instrument or tool to combat microaggressions can be very effective. The values you hold on diversity, inclusion, and fairness can be used to set limits on the actions of others. This is especially effective when you have a working relationship or more than a casual one with the person making biased statements or engaging in discriminatory actions.

"You know that respect and tolerance are important values in my life and while I understand that you have a right to say what you want, I'm asking you to show a little more respect for me by not making offensive comments."

Tactic # 3 – Express Disagreement

It is always better to do something in the face of a moral transgression than to simply let things slide. Remaining silent and allowing microaggressions to occur make you complicit to the actions and impact. Again, simple short comebacks are usually easier for the target, ally, and bystander to make than long and elaborate ones. The main thing is to communicate disagreement or disapproval. Some examples are as follows:

"That's not how I view the situation."
"I don't agree with what you just said (or did)."
"That doesn't sound right to me."
"I don't think that's true at all."
"I think you're making an erroneous assumption."

Tactic # 4 – Describe What Is Happening

This technique involves stepping back to see the larger picture, becoming an enlightened observer, describing what you see happening, and the possible impact it has on the perpetrator, ally, and target.

> "Every time I come over, I find myself becoming uncomfortable because you make statements I find offensive and hurtful."
>
> "What's going on with you? You never seem to give due consideration to any of the ideas presented by the women on you work team."
>
> "You always start off our group meetings with a joke, and the team members really enjoy them. But when you make sexist jokes, the women on the team smile, but deep inside they don't like being the butt of those type of jokes. Do you realize how they must perceive you?"

Tactic # 5 – Nonverbal Communication

Nonverbal communications are powerful means of showing interest, attentiveness, and agreement with a speaker. It can also be used to display disinterest and disagreement as well. Communication specialists suggest that only 30–40% of what is communicated is done so verbally (Ramsey & Birk, 1983; Singelis, 1994). This means that some 60–70% of meaning and intent is nonverbal. Thus, without even speaking, a person can communicate either agreement or disagreement with a perpetrator. The nonverbal disagreement to a biased statement can be a frown, a shaking of one's head in disapproval, or even removing oneself from the infraction. An effective way to disarm a racist joke, for example, can be silence to the punchline, not laughing, looking away, or physically leaving the group. The unspoken nature of nonverbal communication is that they send a counteracting meta-communication to the biased statement and often leaves the perpetrator puzzled, confused, and uncomfortable. But the important thing is that they realize they have committed a transgression that is disapproved by others.

Tactic # 6 – Use an Exclamatory Short Expression

Say "Ouch" or something like "Aaah C'mon" taken from *Ouch! That Stereotype Hurts* (SunShower Learning 2007). One technique advocated by Aguilar (2006) is to state loudly and emphatically, "Ouch!" This is a very simple tactic intended to (a) indicate to the perpetrator that they have said something offensive, (b) force the person to consider the impact and meaning of what they have said or done, and (c) facilitate a possible more enlightened conversation and exploration of his/her biases. Some examples are the following.

> "Those people all look alike." Counter: "Ouch!"
> "He only got the job because he's Black." Counter: "Aahh, C'mon!"
> "I'm putting you on the finance committee, because you people (Asian American) are good at that." Counter: "Ouch!"

Tactic # 7 – Remind Them of the Rules

Similar to Tactic # 2 where personal values are used as a tool to counteract the microaggression, organizational values and codes of conduct exist in most institutions whether education, employment, or health care. Reminding them of company policies on diversity and inclusion can be used to counter microaggressions.

> "That behavior is against our code of conduct and could really get you into trouble."
> "In our company, we don't tolerate denigrating behaviors to any employee. We expect everyone to abide by those rules."

CHALLENGING MACROAGGRESSIONS

Of the three types of microinterventions (microaffirmations, microprotections, and microchallenges), the use of microchallenges is most applicable to the strategic goal of disarming macroaggressions. It is the most direct and potent method in contesting and confronting biases in institutional or societal policies by pressuring key stakeholders to institute change. Disarming macroaggression tactics are often enhanced by the strategies of making the invisible visible and educating stakeholders. Awareness of the unfairness of policies (visibility) and understanding their dynamics (critical thinking) may act as motivating forces for direct action in encouraging change (disarm). Likewise, disarm the macroaggression tactics (rallies/demonstrations, letter writing campaigns, using social media, etc.) can increase awareness and educate stakeholders. Thus, similar tactics may be overlapping and can be used in numerous ways to fulfill different strategic goals.

Although awareness and education are important aspects of disarming macroaggressions, change in policies often requires tactics that range from education, collaborative guidance, to persuasion and forceful coercion (Banks et al., 2019; Turner & Killian, 1987; Kriesberg, 2007). Tactics vary on a continuum from the amount of pressure, force, or confrontation brought to bear upon key decision-makers. Macroaggressions often call for more confrontational approaches when (a) education or persuasion fail to result in changes, (b) a segment of powerful stakeholders refuse to relinquish or share power, (c) rules or regulations are codified in law, or (d) the opposition perceives change to attack cherished values (Jason, Beasley, & Hunter, 2015; Olle, 2018). When apathy, delay, and counter-resistance from those in power prevent change from occurring, greater force by dedicated social advocates is required.

NONVIOLENT AND VIOLENT ACTIONS

It is important for us to distinguish, however, between nonviolent actions that involve the exercise of power through using symbolic protests, noncooperation, and defiance from those of physical violence (Albert Einstein Institution, 2019; Chenoweth & Stephan, 2011). Although not always the case, nonviolent microinterventions seem to be more effective than using extreme methods, especially those that result in violence (throwing smoke bombs, knocking down barriers, destroying property, and encouraging violence against the police) (Ayres, 2018; Brownlee, 2017; Chenoweth & Stephan, 2011). Directly after the murder of George Floyd, for example, protests and demonstrations were punctuated by violence (burning police cars, smashing windows, looting, and physical assaults) during the mass demonstrations. Organizers, including the BLM, realized that such actions discredited the legitimacy of the protests and sought to quell the carnage. The family of George Floyd and many others appealed for an end to the destruction of property and looting and to turn their attention to police reform. The violence and extreme nonviolent measures have been found to (a) undermine activists' goals of attracting more people to their side, (b) discourage more moderate people from joining or supporting a cause, (c) increase support for the opposition, (d) lose the moral high ground, (e) make cause less legitimate and attractive, (f) escalate the number of casualties, and (g) increase repression (Khazan, 2017; Nepstad, 2004; Smithey & Kurtz, 2003).

Two of the major historical figures who advocated and effectively used nonviolence actions as a means to overturn unjust customs and laws were Mohandas Gandhi and Martin Luther King, Jr. Both used nonviolent protests successfully; Gandhi led the nationalist movement against British rule in India, and Dr. King led the Montgomery bus boycott and many other civil rights causes. Both denounced the use of violence as a means to an end and advocated actions that involve nonviolent means: (a) acts of omission (refusal to perform acts they are expected by custom or law to perform – strikes, work stoppage, sit-ins) and/or (b) acts of commission (engage in actions forbidden by custom or law to perform – public disrobings, rude gestures, stopping traffic, etc.) (Albert Einstein Institution, 2019).

Strategic Goal: Disarming Macroaggressions

Keeping the aforementioned points in mind, we describe four major tactics under the heading *disarm the macroaggression*: (1) protest and persuade, (2) engage in civil disobedience, (3) challenge the status quo through media, and (4) enhance collective action. The latter two tactics could actually be subsumed under one of the first two headings, but their importance and the roles they play in social advocacy justify separate categories.

Tactic # 1 – Protest and Persuade
For the majority of social advocates, demanding change through protest and persuasion is the major form of microinterventions taken when confronting macroaggressions. Most of the tactics are intended to bring attention to a cause by creating inconvenience for groups of stakeholders, causing them humiliation, shame, and embarrassment, and/or persuading them to support and implement changes. These tactics fall within the law and are usually considered expressions of free speech guaranteed by the constitution. They encourage individuals to use their civilian rights such as the right to vote or to protest, persuade, and demand change. Social justice advocates are often unaware of the many nonviolent microinterventions or antibias actions available to them. A part of feeling empowered to intervene is the ready availability of microinterventions at their disposal. In one of the most comprehensive conceptual frameworks developed on nonviolent methods,

Gene Sharp (1973) identified nearly 200 tactics. Under *Nonviolent Protest and Persuasion*, he listed 10 categories of tactics:

1. *Formal statements*: public speeches, letters of opposition or support, group or mass petitions, organizational statements, declarations of indictment and intention, and so on.
2. *Communications with a wider audience*: slogans, caricatures and symbols, banners and posters, leaflets, pamphlets and books, newspapers and journals, skywriting, records, radio and television, social media, and so on.
3. *Group representations*: deputations, mock awards, group lobbying, picketing, and so on.
4. *Symbolic public acts*: displaying and wearing symbols, prayer and worship, protest disrobings, symbolic sounds, display of portraits, destruction of own property, rude gestures, and so on.
5. *Pressures on individuals*: haunting officials, taunting officials, vigils, and so on.
6. *Drama and music*: humorous skits and pranks, singing, performance, plays and music, and so on.
7. *Processions*: marches, parades, motorcades, pilgrimages, religious processions, and so on.
8. *Honoring the dead*: political mourning, mock funerals, homage at burial places, and so on.
9. *Public assemblies*: assemblies of protest and support, protest meetings, teach-ins, town halls, and so on.
10. *Withdrawal and renunciation*: walk-outs, silence, turning one's back, renouncing honors, and so on.

Noncooperation is another category of persuasion that represents an increased level of intensity and pressure to compel stakeholders to support negotiation and change. Some powerful methods often employed are work slowdowns, strikes, and boycotts that are aimed at using economic losses, inconvenience, and public awareness of issues as a motivator. In almost all cases, protest and persuasion are used to bring those with power and influence to the table, to engage in dialogue and discussion, and to negotiate a successful outcome (Gillion, 2013). For social advocates, the successful resolution of disputes depends not only on fairness and equity but also on compromise that benefits both parties (win–win outcome). Protest and persuasion strategies are not confined to national or international issues alone, but can be used effectively to address local (homelessness), city (redlining by financial institutions), and state (gerrymandering) issues. For any given situation, some tactics may be more appropriate or effective than others (Banks et al., 2019; Smithey, 2009; Smithey & Kurtz, 2003).

Tactic # 2 – Engage in Civil Disobedience

Protest and persuasion are tactics that often merge with the actions of civil disobedience. The nonviolent tactics of civil disobedience do not necessarily mean, however, "lawful actions" because they may involve violating or sabotaging unjust laws, customs, or practices. Civil disobedience is an active refusal to obey specific laws, orders, or commands of a government or society and can be manifested by (a) *directly* breaching the law or practice they oppose or (b) *indirectly* breaching a law or practice they do not oppose, for the purpose of bringing attention to an unjust and discriminatory one (Brownlee, 2017). Trespassing and breaking into the university president's office to spray paint slogans in protest over its monocultural core curriculum is an example of the latter. Many consider civil disobedience morally defensible because of its principled outlook, concern with the interests of society, transparency rather than secrecy, its nonviolent character, and the willingness of protesters to accept punishment (Brownlee, 2017; Gillion, 2013). When arrested or charged with a transgression due to civil disobedience, all of these characteristics have been used in legal proceedings to argue the protestor's overall fidelity to just laws, and their call to conscience as opposed to outright criminal behaviors.

In the history of social movements, civil disobedience by definition is non-violent, but it represents the outer range of coercion and disruption rather than persuasion. Some have pointed out the dangers of civil disobedience because it (a) poses a threat to the rule of law, (b) may radicalize individuals into more extreme positions, (c) can create an atmosphere conducive to violence, (d) can be used to promote an unjust cause (i.e. Unite the Right rally in Charlottesville), and (e) force the will of the minority on the majority (Ayres, 2018; Smithey & Kurtz, 2003). Additionally, civil disobedience places individuals at a higher risk of personal danger that includes confrontation by police, possible arrests, and psychological stress.

Despite these downsides, civil disobedience has become part of the fabric and free principle of democratic constitutional government and is forever embedded in the American way of life as a guarantee of checks and balances against unfair policies and practices (Chenoweth & Stephan, 2011; Sharp, 1973). The ultimate benefits of civil disobedience as a form of protest have been listed as (a) protection of human rights, (b) establishment of religious freedoms, (c) protecting the rights of marginalized populations in society, (d) ensures fairness, and (e) allows one to follow their conscience (Ayres, 2018; Brownlee, 2017; Chenoweth & Stephan, 2011). Martin Luther King, Jr. has argued that civil disobedience is not lawlessness, but a higher form of divine lawfulness (Myers, 2017).

How effective, however, is civil disobedience and nonviolent methods of producing change? In a comprehensive study from 1900 to 2006 of violent and nonviolent campaigns across the world, Chenoweth and Stephan (2011) found that nonviolent civil resistance was far more effective in producing change than the use of violent means. For example, they found that strikes and boy-cotts were two of the most effective methods of changing laws, instituting more equitable policies, and even the resignation of autocratic leaders. Although their study spanned the international globe, the effectiveness of the nonviolent civil rights movement in the United States supports their findings.

Sharp (1973) outlines numerous examples of "noncooperation" and "inter-ventions" that can be used to pressure or coerce change: boycotts, refusal taxes or rent, refusal to pay fees or dues, slowdown strikes, sick-ins, resigna-tions, excommunication, social isolation, hunger strikes, overload facilities, nonviolent sabotage, reluctance or slow compliance, office invasions, block-ades, and so on. As we have cautioned earlier, the use of these tactics cannot be random, but must be carefully planned and guided by strategic goals and plans in order to be successful. Chenoweth and Stephan (2011) found that strikes and economic noncooperation were personally costly to protesters, but with careful planning, suffering could be minimized. For example, pro-testors who were successful in weathering the economic costs of a strike or boycott would spend months stockpiling food, coming up with strike funds, and forming mutual aid networks (i.e. in the Montgomery bus boycott, neighbors formed car-pooling teams to provide transportation).

Tactic # 3 – Challenge the Status Quo through Media
Traditional media (television, radio, and print), social media (YouTube, Twitter, Facebook, Instagram, etc.), and other forms of public communication (skywriting and earth writing, display of symbols, use of slogans, etc.) are important methods

for social protest through mass and/or instant communication. Using media has been shown to raise public awareness, educate stakeholders, influence decision-makers, and advocate for change (Banks et al., 2019; Stephen, 2015). Civil rights advocates have long known the power of television to reach and shape the racial realities of viewers, to bring to light racist actions and practices, to prick the conscience of White America, and to pressure decision-makers toward actions (Jost et al., 2018; Stephen, 2015). Documented contemporary and historical examples attest to the potential power and effectiveness of using television and the press to expose the injustices of racism.

Traditional Media

The media coverage of the Ferguson protests and counter reactions by law enforcement, were summed up in the chant, *the whole world is watching*, often used in the civil rights movement and in the Vietnam War protests (Gitlan, 1980). In the case of the killing of Michael Brown, George Floyd, and Rayshard Brooks, the statement was literally true. On video and in full view of witnesses, Michael Brown was shot and killed with his hands up in surrender, George Floyd was suffocated for 8 minutes and 46 seconds as a police officer knelt on his neck, and Rayshard Brooks was shot in the back two times while running away, not posing danger to anyone. These recorded and televised events demonstrated the power of media in transmitting images of police brutality, highlighting the cause of activists, garnering national and international attention, and creating sympathy and support from onlookers.

On August 9, 2014, Michael Brown, an unarmed black teenager, was shot and killed by a White police officer Darren Wilson, in Ferguson, Missouri. The incident touched off a storm of protests, and a community uprising known as the "Ferguson Riots" regarding racial injustice, police brutality, harassment of journalists, and the continued killing of unarmed Black men by law enforcement officers. Images of violent clashes between police and protesters on television were transmitted for all to see, and the results had large-scale international repercussions: (a) Palestinians saw the uprising on television, and tweeted advice to protesters on how to deal with tear gas; (b) Tibetan monks traveled to Missouri and assumed the "hands up, don't shoot pose" as a gesture of solidarity; (c) representatives of Amnesty International visited Ferguson and condemned the militarized use of police; and (d) hundreds of individuals and organizations in the United States expressed outrage over police actions and support for the demonstrators (Goldhammer, 2014).

The killing of Michael Brown, however, was only a prelude to the world-shattering events following the video recording of the murder of George Floyd by police officers in Minneapolis on May 25, 2020. Although the killing of Michael Brown and many other unarmed African Americans have sparked outrage in the past, never has the fury against police misconduct reverberated so strongly across all 50 states and internationally as well. Much of the wrath was generated by witnessing undeniable proof of a White police officer pressing his knee to Floyd's neck for 8 minutes and 46 seconds until he died. Despite lying face down on the street, his arms handcuffed from behind, and being motionless, Officer Derek Chauvin continued to exert pressure on the neck of Floyd with his knee while nonchalantly looking around in full view of the public. But the death of Floyd ignited something far bigger than police reform. Within weeks, major police reform occurred in several states, confederate statues toppled across the country, calls for an end to systemic racism increased, and a multiracial and multigenerational group denounced individual, institutional, and systemic racism in all forms. The final outcome of this cry for social justice is still to be determined.

Dr. Martin Luther King is often credited with being a master at using television as a medium to highlight the injustices of segregation and Jim Crow laws. Civil rights advocates during the 1950s and 1960s knew Whites would not take the word of Black Americans about the harm of racism and the horrors they had to endure in their everyday lives. But, television and press coverage of the civil rights marches, boycotts, sit-ins, and the violence enacted against nonviolent protestors by police and White Nationalists made the horrors a reality, set the country toward a moral reckoning, and resulted in passage of the Civil Rights Act of 1964 (Jones, 1997; Poell, 2019).

Using media, however, need not be confined to large-scale societal macroaggressions, but to almost any macroaggression or unjust policy, practice, or custom in our neighborhoods, cities, and organizations. Depending on one's level of expertise, the following are a few of the tools that can be employed using traditional mainstream media (Table 8.2) (Banks et al., 2019):

- Op-eds
- Letters to the editor
- Press releases
- News conferences
- Newspaper interviews

Table 8.2 Communication Tools for Social Advocacy: Traditional Media, Social Media, and Nontraditional Communications

MEDIA TYPE	TOOL	EXAMPLE
Traditional Media	Op-eds/letter to the editor	Students in a fourth-grade class from Friends Seminary came together with Lauren Sandler of the Op-Ed project to write an Op-Ed voicing their opinion on the NFL protests in January of 2018.
	Press release/news conference	The American Civil Liberties Union issued a statement opposing the "Fairness for All Act," which would allow discrimination against LGBTQ people in December of 2019.
	Newspaper/television/ radio interviews	Marc Lemont Hill discussed his new book "Nobody: Casualties of America's War on the Vulnerable, from Flint and Beyond" on the AM radio station The Breakfast Club in August of 2016.
	Televised protest or events	The weekend after inauguration day, hundreds of thousands of people protested Trump's presidency. The Women's March on Washington was televised worldwide.
	Documentaries	The Netflix docuseries directed by Ava DuVernay raised awareness on the false convictions of the "Exonerated Five," which led to student petitions and the resignation of Columbia Law Professor Elizabeth Lederer.
	Leaflets, pamphlets, and books	Pamphlets, books, and flyers were created by local organizations and artists to bring together various communities and raise awareness about the mission of "The Women's March on Washington."

Social Media	Twitter, Facebook, Vine, Instagram	The Audacious Young Women of Action from the Arab-American Family Support Center and Take on Hate used Facebook, Twitter, and Instagram to organize the Stop the Ban art protest on the steps of Brooklyn Borough Hall to protest Executive Order 13769 (Muslim Ban) on October 16, 2017.
	WhatsApp, SMS, GroupMe	Apps such as WhatsApp as well as other forms of communication were used to mobilize community members, and specifically lawyers willing to work pro-bono after Trumps order to support individuals stuck at the airport as well as separated families following Ice Raids.
	Podcasts	The podcast "1619" raises awareness on the economics of slavery, democratic representation, and healthcare history.
	Webinars/publish news on websites	Various Webinars as well as short and simple articles were published online that provide information on how to prepare for immigration raids and how to get help.

(Continued)

Table 8.2 (Continued)

MEDIA TYPE	TOOL	EXAMPLE
Other Communication Tools	Skits, plays, and theater	Key & Peele is an award-winning sketch series on Comedy Central that is best known for using humor to tackle issues on race.
	Movies and documentaries	Movies such as "12 year a Slave" or biographical films such as "Malcolm X" raise knowledge and awareness on critical issues. More recently, the film "Black Panther" sparked excitement across the country for Marvel's first Black superhero.
	Skywriting and Earth writing	In protest, on January 1, 2016, planes flying over the New Year's Day Rose Parade in California used sky writing with the message, "America is great. Trump is delusional."
	Protest songs and DVDs	Legendary folk singers like "Peter, Paul, and Mary," Pete Seeger, and Joan Baez protested through songs against war and conflict were used to heighten awareness and symbolized movements. Modern-day artists like J Cole, Kendrick Lamar, and Meek Mill did likewise during the rise of Black Lives Matter protests.
	Banners, protests, and other displayed communication	Many banners, flyers, and signs at the Women's March included words of support, opinions, and artwork from various local artist who wanted to express their support for marginalized communities.
	Slogans, caricatures, and symbols to mock public events	Various newspapers and online media sources used caricatures and symbols to mock the inauguration of Donald Trump.

- Radio interviews
- Television interviews
- Televised protests or events

Documentaries

- Leaflets, pamphlets, and books

Social justice advocates have long known and used the power of media to document real life images of pain, suffering, humiliation, and unjust violence directed toward peaceful protesters in order to engender compassion from viewers and to motivate them to action. Television, the press, and other means of communication can provide an opportunity for marginalized group members to make known their grievances and to allow the voices of those most silenced to be heard. On the other hand, traditional media can also serve to maintain the status quo, to prevent the voices of the oppressed from being heard, and to censor or distort coverage (Goldhammer, 2014). Gaining legitimacy in the mainstream news cycle has been problematic for many protests and movements that are portrayed in unflattering and unsympathetic ways, subject to the temporary periodic news cycle, and its focus on the negative internal attributes of protesters (criminal elements, anarchists, spoiled brats, etc.) rather than the larger cause (Forward & Williams, 1970; Poell, 2019).

Social Media
The rise of social media platforms, however, is said to have unshackled the control of traditional media by allowing the sharing of censored or distorted news stories to reach a much larger audience and by livestreaming or communicating instantaneous events or information (Jost et al., 2018). Some have speculated that social media has become the most important tool for social protests and has fundamentally changed how movements originate, communicate, motivate, and plan (Poell, 2019; Jost et al., 2018; Stephen, 2015). The #BlackLivesMatter hashtag is considered an archetypal example of the intersection of social media and protest in the modern day (Anderson, Toor, Rainie & Smith, 2018). Since its origination following the acquittal of George Zimmerman for the shooting of an unarmed Black teenager, Trayvon Martin, the hashtag has been used 30 million times (average of 17,002 tweets/day) as of May 1, 2018 (Anderson, Toor, Rainie, & Smith, 2018). Although there is no

study of the hashtag use since the murder of George Floyd in 2020, we expect that the count would be a gigantic increase over the 2018 figure. The tweets tend to increase during racial incidents and are credited with sparking serious discussions of racism, violence, and law enforcement.

It is clear that social media can be the source of uncensored, live, and raw information. Posting a video or livestreaming an event (a sit-in at the University President's Office, students confronting administrators, a violent arrest, or a protest demonstration) can be accomplished on Instagram, Twitter, Vine, or Periscope. Social media platforms can also allow social justice advocates to plan and coordinate movements publicly or in secrecy, in real time. If social justice advocates or protesters desire to plan an activity in secrecy, members can chat privately with others using GroupMe. If protesters desire to publicly mobilize many individuals to attend an event, SMS or WhatsApp can be used. Thus, social media facilitates the rapid exchange of information through many avenues such as Twitter and Facebook, and their use can influence emotional and motivational appeals, heighten collective identity, and mobilize collective action.

The importance of social media for political engagement, obtaining news and information, networking (personal and professional), and civic-related activities was recently the subject of a survey by the Pew Research Center (Anderson, Toor, Rainie, & Smith, 2018). During the year of the survey, half of Americans indicated they had been civically active on social media sites (participated in causes or issues, encouraged others to take action, etc.), but when asked about its importance, only a minority described it as very personally important. Contrarily, African Americans and Latinx Americans were more likely to value using social media because it helped vocalize their opinions, get involved with issues, express their political views, and get elected officials to pay attention. Eight in ten African Americans say it sheds light on rarely discussed issues and holds people accountable for their actions. White respondents, however, were equally likely to say the sites detracted from more important issues and perpetuated a false belief of "making a difference." Differences in racial group perceptions about the use and effectiveness of social media as a tool for protest and change indicate an understandable clash of racial realities. Groups that are most disempowered with limited resources and means to combat structural inequities are more likely to value what few tools they have available. Some of the social media platforms and internet uses are listed here.

- Twitter
- Facebook
- Instagram
- YouTube
- Vine, Periscope
- GroupMe, SMS, WhatsApp
- Publishing news on websites
- Creating videos
- Podcasts
- Webinars

Other Communication Tools

There are many other forms of communicating protests that are not readily classified under the banner of media. They are, nevertheless, communication tactics that can be used to raise social issues, invoke empathy/sympathy for a cause, arouse intense emotions, educate the populace, mock an individual or a group, engage in satire, show support and camaraderie, and motivate action. All of the tactics listed here have been the arsenal of protesters who are only limited by their own creativity in what and how to use them:

- Skits, plays, and theater
- Movies and documentaries
- Skywriting and Earth writing
- Protest songs and DVDs
- Banners, protests, and displayed communications
- Slogans, caricatures, and symbols
- Mock public events

Tactic # 3 – Enhance Collective Action

Disarming macroaggressions is rarely, if ever, achieved by the actions of a single individual, but rather through the collective efforts of many. Belonging to a group of like-minded individuals, sharing similar values and goals, and providing one another aid, comfort, and sustenance immunize and buffer members from the repercussions of anti-racism work (Gurung, 2006; Uchino, 2009). Likewise, a community of collaborators who act as a collective against macroaggressions can be more forceful in bringing pressure to bear on decision-makers (DeLeon, 2010; van Zomeren, Kutlaca, Turner-Zwinkels, 2018).

Thus, effective microintervention work must begin with identifying a spectrum of allies: Who will provide active support? How do you win over passive stakeholders? And, how do you win over the opposition? Coalition and network building become essential features of enhancing collective action (Banks et al., 2019; van Zomeren, Kutlaca & Turner-Zwinkels, 2018). With respect to targets of racism, however, potential community coalitions already exist among marginalized group members who experience daily oppression and discrimination from institutional and societal inequities.

A large body of research and scholarly work on collective action and collective identity exists in the social psychological and political literature (Milan, 2015; Smithey, 2009; van Zomeren, Kutlaca, & Turner-Zwinkels, 2018). All point to two primary conclusion: (1) successful protest and social movements are almost always achieved through collective action and (2) collective action is facilitated through a strong sense of collective identity. For people of color, collective action is the use of strategies and tactics by a group of people who share a sense of "peoplehood" and common objectives. Studies on collective identity suggest that peoplehood is a form of social identity involving cognitive, emotional, moral, and spiritual connections with others (Dovidio, Gaertner, Validzic, Matoka, Johnson, & Frazier, 1997; Smithey, 2009). Collective action and collective identity is a two-way process: collective identity is found to facilitate social action, but successful collective action increases a sense of empowerment and efficacy among group members, thereby reinforcing collective identity. Enhancing collective identity strengthens solidarity, intensifies commitment to a cause, increases incentive among members to take action, and strengthens group goals over personal ones (Smithey, 2009; van Zomeren, Kutlaca, & Turner-Zwinkels, 2018).

What does research, however, tell us about the components of collective identity? From a meta-analysis of 180 studies of collective action, van Zomeren, Postmes, and Spears (2008) identified three antecedent conditions of social group identification that were correlated with collective action: injustice, efficacy, and social identity. First, the investigators found that perceived injustice in the form of oppression and discrimination was a dominant factor in motivating action against unfair rules and regulations. The feelings of deprivation, being treated unfairly, possessing limited personal power to address systemic inequality, and having one's identity assailed generated anger and resentment that motivated collective action. Second, group efficacy beliefs (the individual's belief that group goals can be achieved through unified effort) are a positive predictor of willingness to engage in collective action. Across various contexts and populations, a group's feeling of empowerment builds confidence and a belief that group objectives are achievable (van Zomeren et al., 2018). Third, social group identity such as possessing shared historical and contemporary experiences, a sense of belonging to a collective, and having strong psychological ties with the relevant group are generally already present among people of color. Especially important to social group identity for people of color is their racialized experiences, being born and raised in a predominantly monocultural society, being excluded from the mainstream, and encountering discriminatory racial events (Anderson & Stevenson, 2019; Dovidio et al., 1997).

Thus, for marginalized group members, two of three conditions already exist to spark collective action: (1) injustice – the experience of being an unfairly socially devalued group member, and (2) social identity – a connected sense of peoplehood with a shared worldview. The third condition, group efficacy and action, can be triggered by a visionary leader, a highly visible successful protest, or a single or multiple acts of defiance by group members that convince others that dissent can result in change. Protest leaders like Cesar Chavez, Mohandas Gandhi, and Martin Luther King through their visionary leadership not only provided hope to followers but also demonstrated that group action could result in major change.

Cesar Chavez, for example, who led the United Farm Workers Movement in 1965 over inhumane working conditions, unsanitary farm labor camps, low migrant wages ($1,000/year), and harassment of women led to one of the most successful strikes and boycotts of grape growers in US history (Garcia, 2016). Although his ultimate goal was to seek justice and equity for migrant farm workers across a broad range of demands, Chavez knew that small incremental victories were important to demonstrate to followers that actions could lead to change. For example, initial picketing of grape growers led to public sympathy, personal persuasion helped forge Filipino farmworkers with their Mexican counterparts (this in turn created a multiracial coalition in which other groups of color joined the movement), he was successful in attracting support from future politicians to the movement (ala, Jerry Brown who twice became Governor of California), and lastly the support of international labor unions in Europe finally broke the power and control of farm growers.

Likewise, Mohandas Gandhi used a similar approach to protest and overcome British colonial rule in India. Rather than launch a large-scale direct frontal attack on the injustices of British rule, he knew that a "small" battle and victory would ultimately demonstrate to the people that they had the power as a collective to overcome the formidable forces of colonialism. Gandhi called for a "salt march" that bewildered not only the British but even some of his own comrades who were skeptical and compared the action to "striking a fly with a sledge hammer" (Andrews, 2019). The unfair salt tax on Indians, however, was symbolic of the unfair imposition of laws on the people. The march was successful in getting the British to relax its salt laws, but, more importantly, empowered the people to ultimately seek successful redress and independence. Successful micro- and macrointervention actions rely heavily on empathy, sympathy, support, and influence from allies, bystanders, and the general public as well. Much of the success in the United Farm Workers Movement and the overthrow of British colonial rule in India was the ability to garner support from the general public and the international audience. Martin Luther King, Jr. started by mobilizing Southern Black individuals, and then shifted to bringing in Northern Whites to their cause.

Social psychological research on intergroup conflict, intergroup harmony, and social identity provides many hypothesis, theories, and clues about creating conditions that facilitate collective identity and collective action (Dovidio et al., 1997; Gaertner, Dovidio, Anastasio, Bachman, & Rust, 1993; van Zomeren et al., 2018; Jones, 1997). The literature is so vast in this area that space does not allow us to discuss the findings in even a cursory fashion. All seem to indicate, however, that attracting followers (allies, bystanders, and stakeholders) to a cause (a) requires integrating a collective/social identity that defines "who we are" and "what we stand for" and (b) requires choosing and using appropriate tactics consistent with personal and group identity (Dovidio, et al., 1997; Smithey, 2009; van Zomeren et al., 2018).

In the former, a central feature of collective action is moral conviction – the shared stance taken on an issue that reflects the individual's core values of right and wrong. An example of the power of moral conviction was the announcement of the Muslim travel ban that motivated many people to engage in collective action because the prohibition violated the moral belief of social equity (van Zomeren et al., 2018). Likewise, the selection of tactics to protest can either bring together or deter followers from joining a cause or movement. Tactical choices (violence vs. nonviolence, using traditional vs. social media, or holding a press conference vs. blocking traffic) are filled with symbolic meanings (Kriesberg, 2007; Smithey, 2009). They are said to convey the shared ideology and values of a group through the type of actions it takes. Tactics may be chosen not only for their possible success in producing change, but may be particularly suited to building solidarity and collective action (i.e. LGBTQ – parades, marches, and drag shows). Social justice advocates must balance their choice of tactics with producing not only possible successes but also their receptivity to the wide spectrum of allies and the perception of the general public. Blocking streets, throwing rocks at police, or calling for a boycott may be acceptable to one segment of allies but may turn off others.

In summary, Satell and Popovik (2017) outline some very important characteristics of tactics used in successful protests that involve creating a community of activists.

- A clear, concrete, and explicit vision of change must be articulated and easily communicated to potential allies or followers. As evidenced by the failure of the Occupy Wall Street (OWS) movement that began in 2011 against economic inequality, the complaint against the oppressive power of corporations, while legitimate, never went beyond grievances and emotionally arousing slogans. Pointing out what is wrong in broad and abstract terms without specific solutions led to the demise of OWS.
- Enhancing collective action means creating coalitions that share your values and visions. Fairness and justice, equal access and opportunity, respect and dignity, and the interconnectedness of the human condition must be translated into meaningful and concrete terms to the objectives of the protest. The task here is not to impose one's vision on others, but sharing it with them, convincing them about the rightness or morality of the cause, and having them buy-in to the overall objective.
- Attracting potential followers rather than overpowering them and avoiding the demonization of the opposition better position advocates to make an affirmative case to all stakeholders. In addition, using "affirmative tactics" does much to pave receptivity and even positive perceptions of both the cause and protesters. As reviled as he was by the opposition, Gandhi's nonviolent tactics and willingness to endure punishment engendered great respect from many, including Winston Churchill.
- Building a pillar of power through a large active following is very much based upon the notion that "success breeds success." We have already described how successful collective action increases collective identity and attracts followers. Successful social movements have demonstrated that incremental victories over "smaller challenges" increase a sense of efficacy among protesters and insure continuing and future actions.

CHAPTER NINE

Microintervention Strategy and Tactics for Using External Support and Alliances

Remember: Oppression thrives off isolation. Connection is the only thing that can save us.

– Yolo Akili

Alone, we can do so little; together we can do so much.

– Helen Keller

There are times in which individual efforts to respond to micro- and macro-aggressions may be contraindicated, and the most effective approach is to seek external support from others, from institutional authorities, and from various human rights organizations (Brondolo et al., 2009; Mellor, 2004). Targets, allies, and bystanders oftentimes put themselves at risk by confronting others about their microaggressions, for example, are often draining (Sue,

Microintervention Strategies, First Edition. Derald Wing Sue, Cassandra Z. Calle, Narolyn Mendez, Sarah Alsaidi, and Elizabeth Glaeser.

151

2017a; 2017b). Likewise, trying to deal with macroaggressions is an enormous undertaking in which the single efforts of an individual may prove fruitless and taxing. Although the concept of racial battle fatigue is very applicable to targets, social justice advocates must also be prepared for the huge pushback likely to occur from others around them. Perpetrators may deny a target's experiential reality by claiming the person of color is *oversensitive, paranoid,* or *misreading the actions of others.* For allies and bystanders who choose to intervene, they may be accused as *White liberals,* or *troublemakers,* and consequently isolated or avoided by fellow White colleagues. A family member who objects to a racist joke told by an uncle, for example, may be admonished not to rock the boat for the sake of family harmony or threatened to be disowned by the family. Table 9.1 lists some microintervention tactics to utilize external sources to support, validate, or use group or organizational pressure to press for change.

STRATEGIC GOAL: SEEKING EXTERNAL SUPPORT/ VALIDATION IN FIGHTING MICROAGGRESSIONS

Anti-racism work is exhausting and seeking support and help from others is an aspect of self-care. Some important actions that can be taken are to find a support group, utilize community services, engage in a buddy system, or seek advice and counseling from understanding professionals. These external sources are meant to allow targets, allies, and bystanders to express their emotions in ways that are safe, to connect with others who validate and affirm their being, and to offer advice and suggestions. In many ways, these actions are meant to better prepare advocates for the challenges likely to be encountered and to immunize them to the stresses of social justice work.

On another front, microinterventions often dictate seeking help from institutional authorities, especially when (a) a strong power differential exists between perpetrator and target, (b) the microaggression is blatant and immediately harmful (microassault), (c) it would be risky to respond personally, or (d) institutional changes must be implemented. A discriminatory act by a manager may best be handled by reporting to a higher authority or seeking an advocate with the same social/employment standing as the perpetrator within the company. Reporting racist graffiti and/or hate speech to university administrators, law enforcement agencies, and other community organizations are all possible microinterventions.

Table 9.1 Strategic Goal: Seek External Support and Alliances

Microinterventions for Microaggressions

Scenario: Flight attendant asks if there is a medical doctor on board who can come to the aid of fellow passenger who has gone into cardiac arrest. A Native American female physician proceeds to the front of the plane to assist when she is abruptly stopped and asked to take her seat in order to "Make way in case there is a doctor on board."

Metacommunication: People of your race or gender are not well educated or do not hold advanced degrees.

OBJECTIVES	RATIONALE	TACTICS	EXAMPLE
• Partake in regular self-care to maintain psychological and physical wellness	• Mitigates impact of psychological and physiological harm associated with continuous exposure to microaggressions	1. Alert leadership	Ask to speak to a manager or someone who is in authority
• Check in with self and others to ensure optimal levels of functioning		2. Report	Report the incident in person or use anonymous online portals such as the Southern Poverty Law Center or use a hashtag on social media to make your experience go viral
• Send a message to perpetrators at large that bigoted behavior will not be tolerated or accepted	• Reminds targets, allies, and bystanders that they are not alone in the battle	3. Therapy/ counseling	Seek out individual counseling with culturally competent providers for self-care and well-being
	• Ensures situations of discrimination or bias do not go unnoticed	4. Spirituality/ religion/ community	Turn to your community leaders or members for support
		5. Buddy system	Choose a friend with whom you can always check in and process discriminatory experiences
		6. Support group	Join a support group such as "current events group" that meets weekly to process issues concerning minorities

(Continued)

Table 9.1 (Continued)

Microinterventions for Macroaggressions

OBJECTIVES	RATIONALE	TACTICS	EXAMPLE
• Call on human rights organizations to get involved • Take legal action when necessary to hold systems, laws, and practice accountable • Foster a sense of community support through mentoring, engagement, and alliance	• Connect with institutions to call on their support and access to resources • Provide a solution for when all else fails • Instill confidence and hope by utilizing the legal justice system to hold laws, practices, and policies or other forms of inequities accountable	1. Call on the support of human rights organizations	• Report incidents to human rights organizations and communicate with leaders in the organization directly to learn more about how they can help • Utilize resources, guides, and how-to documents provided on websites as tools for social justice advocates • Connect with other individuals who are in the organizing and mobilizing sphere to learn from them and share tools
		2. Initiate governmental action	• Communicate with Members of Congress • Advocate on behalf of your field and raise awareness of its contribution to the key issue • Challenge political leaders if they fail to act due to bias or assumptions • Research and perform your legal rights • Help file an Amicus Brief • Help write an expert brief or testify as an expert witness • Help file an administrative charge
		3. Seek community support	• Encourage students to apply for fellowships and scholarships in fields with underrepresentation • Create networking and mentoring opportunities for underrepresented employees and students • Join groups with mutual goals • Join planning committees and organizations that aim to foster and support marginalized communities • Participate in celebrations and events • Organize celebrations and events

Tactic # 1 – Alert Leadership

There are many times in which individual efforts to respond directly to microaggressions may be contraindicated. Seeking help from a higher authority or someone who can intervene on behalf of the target may prove more effective. It is important to acknowledge the history of police brutality in this country and to state that authority, in this case, does not necessarily mean the police. Leadership can include a supervisor, a person on your working team who holds a position of power in the organization. It can include the office of diversity and student affairs at your university or even a single point person in the department who can offer support with care. Alerting leadership could mean that you are making a formal complaint anonymously or that you are doing it directly with the support of others in the form of a collective petition. Alert leadership can look very different, and it is entirely dependent on the individual, their immediate needs, and what they deem would be the most effective. The microintervention tactic is usually reserved for situations in which you or someone else is in imminent danger and needs support from someone who holds authority or is in a position of power that would allow them to protect you or the individual involved from potential harm. Alerting leadership can also mean taking the first step to facilitate a more macro-level microintervention that aims to dismantle systems of oppression at your school, place of work, or any other organizational affiliation.

Tactic # 2 – Report Incident

In many cases, it is best to establish a record of disturbing incidents (i.e. racial or sexual harassment) that may best be documented for possible future actions. Informing someone with influence such as a manager, supervisor, or an ombudsperson establishes a record of undesirable and unacceptable actions; it further enhances credibility for future proceedings if needed. This tactic builds upon the first by outlining an important step in helping leadership understand the experience of marginalized groups. Creating a record of events is also helpful for targets who may worry themselves about the validity of their claims. If school or office spaces do not welcome these reports or it does not feel safe to report the incident due to power differences, make sure to keep records in another form that is officially dated.

Tactic # 3 – Seek Therapy/Counseling

Targets, allies, and bystanders oftentimes put themselves at risk by confronting others, and such efforts are oftentimes emotionally draining. For targets, racial battle fatigue may result in major emotional reactions that interfere with personal and professional functioning. Seeking formal mental health counseling may help alleviate stresses, immunize advocates against invalidations, and provide suggestions of how to handle problematic situations. It is important to seek out a therapist or counselor who has had extensive training in multicultural counseling theory and identifies as a clinician that is well versed in those theories. A clinician can work one on one with clients to process traumatic experiences associated with microaggressive encounters, to process and unpack the individual's internalized messages, to unlearn negative thinking and reframe those thoughts, to identify the impact of systems of oppression in their interpersonal lives and relationships, and to actively teach and practice microintervention actions.

Tactic # 4 – Seek Spirituality/Religion/Community Support

For targets of microaggressions, research reveals that spirituality, religion, and community attachments are monumental forms of support and validation. For social justice advocates turning to community leaders and other members also enhances resilience in the face of race-related stress. Support can be found in several avenues and one of those includes community centers, local coalitions, spiritual spaces, religious organizations, as well as nonprofit human rights organizations that serve to foster spaces for community members. These spaces can offer support in various ways. First, simply attending events that foster and celebrate diverse cultures and identities is a form of self-validation and emotional support. Second, attending these events allows for opportunities to meet others who share your values and principles, create long-lasting friendships and relationships, collaborate on meaningful projects, and opportunities for activism and organizing. Third, these centers can actively teach the use of healing tools and strategies such as prayer, yoga, healing circles, and other forms of spiritual healing. Fourth, these centers provide avenues for referrals such as social services and direct economic and legal support if needed. Several of these organizations have networks and are well connected to various legal and social services that can provide connections to resources if needed. Finally, these organizations also play an important role in mentoring and can help facilitate job applications, college applications, and many others.

Tactic # 5 – Establish a Buddy System

One of the greatest sources of invalidation and denigration is the impact of microaggressions. The result is often feelings of isolation and loneliness (being "the only one"). The experience of being the only one is often shared by allies and bystanders as well because of the reluctance or hesitation for others to act. In this case, silence is collusion. Choosing a close and intimate friend to share your thoughts and feelings with, to process the discriminatory events, and to validate your experiences strengthens your resolve and resilience. Rumination following a microaggressive encounter is common and its effects are detrimental as it can lead to the internalization of the negative messages. This tactic is a preventative measure as it aims to disarm the emotional and psychological impacts of experiencing a microaggression by providing immediate validation to the target and an opportunity to process the events that took place. These preventative measures can help reduce the likelihood of rumination and the negative effect of those ruminations. The buddy system functions as a nonverbal agreement between two or more individuals in which all parties acknowledge the incessant presence of microaggressions in their daily lives and vow to be available to each other for emotional support immediately following any and all future encounters. Previous tactics have focused on immediate responses and strategies to respond back to the perpetrator and disarm the hidden message communicated. Tactics in this chapter center the experience of targets, as the ones who typically bear the brunt of the psychological tolls associated with microaggressions, by focusing on emotional healing and self-care. The buddy system is a great example of the ways that allies and bystanders can intervene to support targets. It may be that two people of color make a pact together but it may also be that an ally vows to support another ally when they hear a microaggression and need to hear validation of their response or to think through how they could respond. It may even be that the buddy system is used to process not only microaggressive encounters but also microintervention responses. Oftentimes, when one engages in a microintervention they may not receive the desired response from the perpetrator and this may leave them with feelings of hopelessness, dissatisfaction, and anger. The buddy system offers individuals who practice microinterventions with ways to motivate, support, and validate each other, process the encounter, and brainstorm for future interventions.

Tactic # 6 – Establish or Join a Support Group

One of the most effective means of dealing with microaggressions and affirm one's desire to intervene is to seek a support group that meets regularly to offer encouragement, ideas, and sustenance in combatting bias and discrimination. Support groups can offer relief from isolation, offer corrective emotional experiences, and provide information to those in need. Additionally, affinity groups can bring together individuals of similar identities to talk about issues that may impact their unique experiences. Groups can also provide a sounding board and help individuals find their voices, especially in the face of coping with difficult microaggressions. Also, for allies and bystanders, restorative spaces can aid allies to learn microintervention tactics to use in the face of microaggressions. Groups also provide an important level of accountability for targets, allies, and bystanders to recognize microaggressions and to courageously engage in antibias actions.

MICROINTERVENTION CAUTIONS

As we discussed in Chapter 3, there are always costs, personal, and professional for any single individual to engage in anti-racist actions in our society. It would be erroneous and even dangerous for anyone to recommend microintervention strategies devoid of context and environmental considerations. Microaggressions do not occur in a vacuum and neither do anti-racism strategies. White allies, who intervene after witnessing racial microaggressions, may have a greater impact on the White perpetrator than if targets respond. Yet, it is also possible that a well-intentioned bystander might "make matters worse" by intruding on the privacy of the target (Scully & Rowe, 2009). It is important for all individuals engaging in microinterventions to operate with perspicacity and to understand the repercussions – both positive and negative. A few of these considerations are the following.

- First, *pick your battles.* Although applicable to all three groups, this imperative seems more appropriate to people of color. Responding to frequent and endless microaggressions can be exhausting and energy depleting. For the purposes of self-preservation and safety, it is important to determine which offense or abuse is worthy of action and effort.

- Second, *consider where and when you choose to address the offender*. Calling out someone on a hurtful comment or behavior in public may provoke defensiveness or cause an ugly backlash that does not end microaggressions but increases them. Determine the place (public or private) or time (immediate or later) to raise the issue with perpetrators.

- Third, *adjust your response as the situation warrants*. If something was done out of ignorance, *educate* rather than just *confront*. A collaborative rather than an attacking tone lowers defensiveness and allows perpetrators to hear alternative views.

- Fourth, *be aware of relationship factors and dynamics with perpetrators*. Interventions may vary depending on the relationship to the aggressor. Is the culprit a family member, friend, coworker, stranger, or superior? Each relationship may dictate a differential response. For a close family member, education may have a higher priority than for a stranger.

- Fifth, *always consider the consequences of microinterventions, especially when a strong power differential exists between perpetrator and target*. Although positive results can ensue from a microintervention, there is always the potential for negative outcomes that place the target, White ally, or bystander at risk.

- Last, and related to the previous point, is the need to *foster valuable allies, support groups, and others to provide personal safety and increase effectiveness*. We have already seen how there is both safety and strength in numbers. In dealing with macroaggressions, this adage seems especially applicable.

STRATEGIC GOAL: SEEKING EXTERNAL SUPPORT IN FIGHTING MACROAGGRESSIONS

So far, we have discussed three strategies of microinterventions that focus on what individuals can personally do to help address macroaggressions. There are, however, incidents or situations that may require the help of powerful and influential parties that counterbalance opposition and/or require legal or constitutional authority to make changes (Banks et al., 2019; Mellor, 2004; Sue et al., 2019). Seeking external support and help from organizations (i.e. social advocacy groups) or from one of three coequal branches of government through executive orders, legislation, and judicial rulings always remains highly viable options. Microinterventions and the specific tactics described in this section dictate seeking help from institutional authorities, social advocacy organizations, and special interest groups to exert pressure on stakeholders or pursue governmental actions/legal remedies when (a) institutional policies and practices are deeply embedded in legal or constitutional doctrine, (b) individuals and community groups lack influence to address the enormity of the task, and (c) groups of protesters lack expertise and resources to effectively deal with the intricacies and complexities of desired change. As we have indicated previously, seeking external support can also be for internal reasons (individual validation, warding off burnout, emotional nurturance, and sense of belonging) in that group membership and social integration help maintain psychological and physical well-being, emotional stability, and an increased sense of empowerment (Cohen & Willis, 1985; Feeney & Collins, 2015).

Seeking external support has three main tactics: (a) call on the assistance of human rights organizations, (b) initiate governmental actions, and (c) seek community collaboration. While these tactics differ in their specific objectives, they share a common rationale that is to enlist the help of organizations and groups to tackle micro- and macroaggressions. By calling upon governmental powers, collaborating with social advocacy organizations for special expertise, funds, and resources, and utilizing community networks, social advocates not only enhance effectiveness but also help prevent feelings of isolation, helplessness, and emotional distress. The following tactics identify ways to influence or call on the support of institutional powers to reduce disparities in health, education, and employment.

Tactic # 1 – Call on the Support of Human Rights Organizations

Various organizations including the Southern Poverty Law Center (SPLC) and the National Association for the Advancement of Colored People (NAACP) are dedicated to advocating for the elimination of healthcare disparities, increasing cultural competence, combatting prejudice and discrimination, and supporting people of color through scholarship and fellowship programs (SPLC, 2019). Social advocacy groups exist nationally and internationally, but their main purpose is to defend the legal and natural rights of people who are marginalized, defenseless, and exploited. Two well-known international groups are Oxfam International (famine relief, poverty reduction, economic development, etc.) and Amnesty International (advocacy for human rights) that maintain nationwide offices, including the United States. They can and do serve as resources for social advocates, but there are many domestic national and local social advocacy groups that can provide assistance as well. For example, there are human rights organizations that combat systemic injustices for the homeless (National Coalition for the Homeless), LGBTQ individuals/groups (Human Rights Campaign), anti-semitism (Antidefamation League), women (National Organization for Women), people with disabilities (TASH), people of color (SPLC and NAACP), and for the rights of everyone (American Civil Liberties Union).

Targets, allies, and bystanders can educate themselves about what these organizations offer: the qualifications, talents, and expertise of staff and members; existence of ongoing social justice programs (SPLC Teaching Tolerance Program); training and guidance available to community groups; learning effective microintervention strategies and tactics; and how to advocate on behalf of the community. Individuals can work directly with organizations to report incidents of unfair policies at their workplaces or educational institutions, and work with them to develop a campaign that can raise awareness and push for large-scale change. Many of these nonprofit organizations may also have documents, guides, and other tools that can be used to aid individuals as they navigate their options and understand what is available to them. These organizations can take an active role in advocating directly on behalf of causes and can also be a stepping stone to helping community social justice advocates mobilize and connect with others who have similar interests. Forming coalitions, networking with others, and using resources and the expertise of the organization can lead to a more sustained and influential mobilization effort. The mobilization of groups to fight for change is essential to creating a large-scale impact, especially when it concerns the well-being of an entire class of people.

Human rights organizations are generally more capable of channeling concerns into a single powerful voice and have the experience to strategically execute the steps needed to combat macroaggressions. These organizations are typically nongovernmental organizations that have a long history in advocating for the rights of the oppressed by identifying violations, collecting data on incidents as they occur, being involved in the publicizing of these issues, and promoting public awareness. They are skilled in the use of media and social media to disseminate information in understandable ways for public consumption. Most social advocacy groups already have a large following, established credibility and respect, and ready access to public and political spheres. Whether target, ally, or bystander, being aware of what such organizations have to offer, supporting their causes, becoming a member, collaborating with them on specific issues, learning effective tactics, and relying on their expertise (i.e. legal advice or action) might make individuals a more potent advocate.

Tactic # 2 – Initiate Governmental Action

The executive, legislative, and judicial branches of our government theoretically represent our communities and make decisions with broad implications that impact the everyday lives of its citizens. When such decisions negatively impact marginalized groups in our society that lack the power and influence "to sit at the table" and to make their wishes and concerns known, social advocacy becomes important. Attempts to influence the political and legal system can occur as individuals exercising their constitutional and legal rights, and/or through an organizational umbrella. The three coequal branches of the government all have specific powers to drastically affect the standard of living of its citizens by either creating a new policy/law and/or ending one.

First, through an executive order, the president of the United States can issue a directive that is intended to manage the operations of the federal government but which may have devastating or positive impact on a specific population. In 1942, for example, President Franklin D. Roosevelt issued Executive Order 9066 that interned 120,000 Japanese Americans, two-thirds were citizens by virtue of birth because they "posed a threat to national security" during World War II. The action by the Executive Branch of the government was not only demoralizing to Japanese Americans (considered disloyal and spies) but also destructive to their families (Sue, Sue, Neville, & Smith, 2019). Executive orders can also be used to counteract bias and protect the vulnerable. In 2014, President Obama issued an executive order on immigration intended to shield many undocumented immigrants from deportation (DACA implications). Likewise, under extreme pressure from the public (individuals, groups, and organizations), President Trump was forced in 2018 to sign an executive order ending the "Family Separation Policy" he had previously endorsed. Thus, it is clear that executive orders not only reflect the philosophical, political, and ideological views of the president but also are amenable to change when social advocates are able to make their voices heard and to pressure the executive branch of the government.

Second, Congress (House of Representatives and Senate) also has the power to pass legislation consistent with its constitutional mandate. Like executive orders, laws passed by Congress can either promote the civil rights of its citizens or impact their lives in devastating ways. The Chinese Exclusion Act was signed into law in 1882 and forbid the immigration of the Chinese to the United States under the pretense that their presence led to "a race problem," and the need to maintain "racial purity" (Sue, Sue, Neville, & Smith, 2019). Historically, many Southern states supported the "separate but equal" doctrine which in 1896, the US Supreme Court in *Plessy vs. Ferguson* declared Jim Crow Laws did not violate the 14th Amendment of the Constitution. The ruling engendered passage of many municipal and state discriminatory laws to the detriment of African Americans. Perhaps, the most significant legislation ever passed that had a liberating influence on people of color was the Civil Rights Act of 1964 signed into law by President Lyndon B. Johnson. It prohibited discrimination based on race, color, religion, sex, or national origin. But it went further by outlawing unequal voter registration. Interestingly, under the current political climate, such voter registration laws have been slowly eroded (SPLC, 2018).

Third, judicial rulings, especially at the Supreme Court level, can impact laws and policies for decades or generations to come. For example, the separate but equal doctrine was declared constitutional in 1896, but was not declared unconstitutional until 1954 during *Brown vs. Board of Education* when the court voted to overturn 60 years of discriminatory laws. The continuing battle over the constitutionality of laws or practices is a back and forth battle. In 2018, the Supreme Court declared President Trump's "Muslim Ban" from select countries constitutional and within his authority. Yet, the Supreme Court in 2020 ruled in favor of LGBTQ groups who argued that it is unconstitutional to fire anyone because of sexual orientation or sexual identity, a ruling bound to have major implications for LGBTQ rights in the United States. Almost immediately following that ruling, the Supreme Court also ruled that ending DACA could not be implemented with the reason given by the Trump Administration. The US Supreme Court has heard many arguments that touch on the topic of race, racism, affirmative action, immigration, and discrimination. Being able to be heard by the highest court in the land, to present one's case, and to influence decisions are crucial to producing laws that allow for equal access and opportunity.

Thus, it is clear that the executive, legislative, and judicial branches of the government have major impact, for better or worse, on the lives of its citizens. When one views the enormity and might of the US Government and its operations, it is easy to feel overwhelmed and powerless to affect change. But, there are many microinterventions or actions that can be taken. First, individuals can be directly involved on the municipal, state, and federal levels by attending meetings (i.e. city councils) and voicing their concerns, forming personal connections with legislators, and being active in contacting elected officials (making phone calls, sending letters, etc.) on urgent matters (opposition to biased legislation, or support of those that create equity).

At the federal level, for example, individuals can inform themselves and become aware of the legislative process and the various roles within the Senate and the House of Representatives. When and if a new bill is proposed, advocates can be involved by communicating directly with key legislators. In fact, members of Congress often seek the perspectives and voices of scholars, constituents, and interested organizations/groups. Examples include raising awareness of your field's (ala, psychology) contribution to policy issues; bringing important community concerns to the forefront of your legislator's office; providing proof, data, or specific anecdotal examples to illustrate your points; and making known your group's position on policy issues.

Depending on one's qualifications and expertise, the Community Advocacy Report (Banks et al., 2019) lists a number of roles and activities that can be undertaken by concerned and civic-minded psychologists and allies. Again, doing so with a group of collaborators who share motivation, knowledge, and expertise is most effective.

- Face-to-face meetings with lawmakers, other decision-makers, or staff as a private citizen or a professional can prove effective.
- Hold seminars for legislatures or congressional briefings by sharing research findings through your university, a social advocacy group, or your professional organization.
- Attend governmental hearings to make known concerns and issues. Either through your work, research, or organization, you might be invited by legislators to present on-record information related to a policy matter.

- Provide governmental briefings through a third party or intermediary as a panel expert. Most briefings are sponsored by a professional or advocacy organization, and being personally involved is important.
- Attend policy conferences and meetings through invitation. Although limited by invitation, psychologists, for example, who have expertise on a topic can actively work with groups to be invited.
- Participate in commissions and task forces at local, state, and federal levels. Being on a task force or commission is a very influential way to affect a policy issue because it usually produces concrete findings with specific recommendations that are officially recorded.
- Help file amicus briefs. Intended to influence the judicial branch of the government, amicus briefs (friend of the court) are written documents that involve court cases or pending legislation. An amicus brief is a legal document filed by non-litigants used to advise the court of relevant and important information (data and research findings) that should be considered when making judicial decisions. The American Psychological Association, for example, has filed numerous research-based briefs advocating for affirmative action, gay rights, and racial equity matters.
- Engage in court testimony as an expert witness. Being called as an expert witness is a rare event unless you possess a high degree of knowledge and expertise on a certain topic that is recognized by the court. Expert testimony has been sought and provided by psychologists on issues of gender discrimination and workplace discrimination.
- Provide expert reports. Similar to expert testimony, information is provided as a written document rather than a personal appearance.

Despite not having the skills and expertise to individually engage in these microinterventions, collaborating with groups and organizations will allow advocates, however, to be part of the social justice actions listed here, whether as a supporter or one who provides relevant information to social justice issues.

Tactic # 4 – Seek Community Support

We have already devoted considerable space to the importance of seeking social support and allies as a means to overcome barriers to inaction, so will only touch upon this topic briefly here. Likewise, under *support antibias education and training*, we provided information on community- and neighborhood-based activities that advocates could become involved at both formal and informal levels. We indicated how targets, allies, and dedicated individuals could collaborate with parents, teachers, community leaders, church leaders, and local community organizations to initiate and encourage public engagement and education through various planned microintervention activities. Community support is essential not only in organizing and mobilizing efforts for change but also in maintaining psychological well-being and in strengthening the internal resources of advocates for social justice work. In creating community support, targets, allies, and civic-minded individuals may feel empowered as a collective to take action. The strength of social bonds and a sense of community benefit both individuals and community groups through a series of interlocking role relationships.

Mentoring relationships, for example, have been found to be extremely valuable and important in providing psychosocial support (modeling, encouragement, friendship, and emotional support) and in the transmission of new knowledge and skills (providing advice/suggestions, teaching, and discussing goals and tactics) (Bruce & Bridgeland, 2014). They are especially helpful in transmitting knowledge from more experienced to less experienced individuals. The opportunity to mentor others or to be mentored is the basis of reciprocal benefits. Mentorship relationship help foster growth for individuals and can offer insights into the challenges of social justice advocacy and how best to navigate conflictual settings and to feel connected to a group.

Although mentorship is beneficial to everyone, its value for people of color or other marginalized group members cannot be overstated. Examples under this specific tactic are encouraging students of color to apply for fellowships and scholarships in fields with underrepresentation, creating networking and mentoring opportunities, creating Big Brother, Big Sister programs, providing information on professional development, and partnering with vocational programs. Networking and mentoring opportunities via programs that advance educational and professional development opportunities are also a valuable way to create community support. It is important because the outcome of successful mentorship increases representation in a manner that fosters support and an environment for growth. This growth, therefore, expands opportunities of the collective group and facilitates change. Although both of these examples (applying for fellowships and networking) highlight students, these tactics can easily be applied to other organizational settings as well.

Through mentoring and mutual relationships, targets and allies can encourage students to apply for scholarships and other forms of aid that aims to support underrepresented students and communities. Communities are not only made of interpersonal connections but also bonded by socially constructed groups (e.g. gender, ethnicity, race, etc.). Encouraging underrepresented students to apply for fellowships and scholarships, as well as schools with underrepresentation, allows for greater representation and, therefore, increased presence of underrepresented groups when decisions that impact people of color are presented. Their presence fosters kinship, empathy, and understanding for the needs of others and ultimately benefits all. Such examples include students applying to schools with underrepresentation and scholarships through the Minority Fellowship Program, or Posse that targets underrepresented students and implements social support throughout their college career.

Finding community empowerment spaces is also essential. Joining support groups with mutual goals, planning committees and organizations, or taking time to participate and organize celebrations and events that honor your identities allow for restoration of self and goals. Spaces that allow for the collective empowerment of a community and the opportunity for individuals in that community to become vulnerable in their journey to grow and advance are of utmost importance. These spaces allow not only for support but also for nourishment, celebration, and renewal of energy and inspiration. In a similar vein, this allows the planning and brainstorming of ideas and creates not only individual self-awareness but also strategic planning for change.

CHAPTER TEN

Microinterventions
A Call to Action for Caretakers and Teachers

Children have never been very good at listening to their elders, but they have never failed to imitate them.

— James Baldwin

Racism is a grownup disease, and we should stop using our children to spread it.

— Ruby Bridges

It's time for parents to teach young children early on that in diversity there is beauty and there is strength.

— Maya Angelou

Microinterventions offer an action-oriented perspective and contribute to the "call for action" against bias, bigotry, and discrimination. It proposes a conceptual framework that organizes antibias tactics under four different strategies aimed at neutralizing and disarming individual and systemic racism. Although the existing literature is replete with studies documenting the harm of micro- and macroaggressions to the well-being, self-esteem, group identity, and standard of living of socially devalued groups, fewer studies

Microintervention Strategies, First Edition. Derald Wing Sue, Cassandra Z. Calle, Narolyn Mendez, Sarah Alsaidi, and Elizabeth Glaeser.
© 2021 John Wiley & Sons, Inc. Published 2021 by John Wiley & Sons, Inc.

have been devoted to addressing antibias actions that can alleviate the damage associated with daily experiences of micro- and macroaggressions. Specifically, what can targets, allies, and bystanders do to ameliorate experiences of everyday and systemic racism? We believe that throughout this book we have provided readers, and especially social justice advocates, with a repertoire of intervention skills that they can use to combat bias and discrimination. But, as noted in Chapter 6, prevention is better than remediation. The quote from Ruby Bridges indicates that racism (and all forms of bias) is a "grownup disease" that is instilled in our very young from the moment of birth. Thus, how we choose to raise our children is paramount to ending bigotry. The roles of parents, caretakers, and educators (especially pre-K through 12) become instrumental in raising a generation of non-racist and anti-racist adults. Much of the focus of change, however, resides in well-intentioned parents and teachers whom themselves harbor implicit biases, stereotypes, and racial anxieties that are communicated to the young.

PRIME TIME FOR DEVELOPING MINDS

I (White female) was taking my 3-years old son to a friend's birthday party in the Upper Westside near Columbia University. Because we are new to the area, I mistakenly took the #2 train instead of the #1. Instead of getting off at the 116th street exit near Columbia University, I found myself on the other side of the park in Harlem. When I realized I was in Harlem and saw the number of Black people around me, I was overcome by a sense of dread and apprehension. I felt overcome with a hazy sense of danger! I clutched my son so tightly that he began to cry. I quickly summoned a taxi and got in. When the driver asked me where to go, I couldn't remember the address. I stammered "just get me out of here. Oh, I mean go to the Columbia campus!" The driver who was Black, looked at me with a frown. "Relax lady," he said. "Nothing to be afraid of around here." Afterward, I felt a sense of relief, but was ashamed of my reactions. I had always thought of myself as a good person who was free of bias, but this incident shattered my self-image.

Although we have covered extensively the topic of implicit bias, it is important to note the role parents and other adults play in transmitting racial beliefs, attitudes, and fears. What are the lessons and messages being sent by the mother to her son? When she told the story in our workshop, she admitted to extreme fear for her safety, and that of her child, even though she had always considered herself to be free of biases. She was glad, however, that her son was too young to understand the situation, as she wanted to raise him to be accepting of others.

But, had her young child been too young to really understand the reactions of the mother? Or, was her negative nonverbal reactions communicated to her child, and those around her (taxi driver)? Her desire to raise a non-racist child is certainly admirable, but can that be done when the mother is so trapped in her own racial anxieties? What steps must the mother take to overcome her biases and fears? This is one of the most important questions that caretakers and teachers must ask of themselves, because, whether desired or not, they serve as role models for young children (APA, 2012).

Talking Race to Children

Neuropsychologists, developmental psychologists, and social psychologists have written extensively on early development and internalization of norms and social cues as children and young adults are at their learning prime (Bandura, Ross, & Ross, 1961; Browder et al., 1986; Kolb & Whishaw, 2009; Lancy et al., 2010.) Talking to young people about race should begin early for a number of reasons. First, the presumption that "children are too young to talk about race" itself is a statement of privilege that is most often communicated by White caretakers and educators to children. The privileged nature of this statement lies in the faulted idea that all children, regardless of race, are color-blind and they seldom experience or understand racism. This belief further disregards and discredits the racialized experiences for children of color, that to be Black, for example, means something far different than being White. African American families are often very cognizant of the power of racism and actively train their children at very young ages on how to engage with police, and how to stay safe in an encounter with law enforcement officers (Anderson & Stevenson, 2019). Black parents continually have conversations at home with their children about what they should do if another child at the school touches their hair without their consent, calls them "dirty" because of their dark skin, or refuses to play with them on the playground. African American and Latinx children are not immune from internalized racism, anti-Blackness, and bias that permeate our social norms and culture. Black and other children of color should not be the only ones who engage in learning about racism from a young age, but White children and others from privileged identities should also be having conversations at home that prevent such discriminatory racial encounters from happening. Interestingly, White parents who talk to their children about race early in life seem to produce less biased individuals (Anderson & Stevenson, 2019; President's Initiative on Race, 1998).

Second, while White parents or teachers may see these conversations as "unnecessary" or unimportant for very young children, literature shows that racial awareness can be seen in infants as young as three months old. A study by Kelly and colleagues (2005) found that three-month-old babies demonstrate preferences toward adults who share their own race (i.e. White babies prefer White adults) over adults who are from a different race (The Children's Community School, 2018; Hirshfeld, 2008; Katz & Kofkin, 1997; Aboud, 2008). Denial or silence around race in the form of racial colorblindness or the idea that "people don't see color" allows bias to go unchallenged among White children and their caregivers (Dunham, 2008; The Children's Community School, 2018) perpetuating misinformation and prejudice. Conversations about race for children and adults can have dramatic impact on how people view systemic racism and may lessen future micro- and macroaggressions (Bronson & Merryman, 2009). Additionally, exposure to multicultural environments is not sufficient alone to foster cross racial relationships for young people or reduce bias in youth (Eastern Educational Research Collective). Children should have conversations early and often about race, as silence impacts subtle ways children think about themselves and others when they can observe differences between individuals (Sue, 2015a). Caretakers and educators must make conversations about race and differences an intimate part of childrearing as they grow and mature over the years.

Third, as children grow and begin to solidify their beliefs as young adults, the role of educators and caretakers is essential in continuing to teach and model ways of thinking and acting that aim to dismantle systems of oppression. Children learn best through examples, especially from those who play major roles in their upbringing, like caretakers and educators. Researchers have demonstrated the many ways in which children learn, specifically highlighting how children learn through mimicking adults' actions (Bandura, Ross, & Ross, 1961; Browder et al., 1986; Lancy et al., 2010). The classic experiment that exemplifies the power of social learning and modeling is demonstrated in the "Bobo Doll" experiments undertaken by Bandura and

Associates (Bandura et al., 1961). Their findings suggest, however, that social learning and modeling is most effective when specificity and concreteness are provided, rather than broad generalities. Multicultural curriculums in most schools, for example, have minimal impact on bias because they are simply too vague and ambiguous for children to understand and apply. "Everyone is equal" and "We are all the same under the skin" are too general. Explicit age-appropriate discussions of race are better and more effective (Eastern Educational Resource Collaborative; Community Tool Box, 2019). Children learn from *things that are said* by parents ("Don't talk about her "brown skin.""), *nonverbal behavior* (mother anxiously clutches her purse around a person of color), *emotional reactions* (discomfort or fear around people of color), and *from context and surroundings* (social gatherings where parents cluster around only White guests and avoid guests of color). For this reason, caretakers and educators must be well versed in the use of microinterventions. They should demonstrate their importance through their comfort in racial dialogues and through their own individual and observable actions (Sue, 2015a).

MICROINTERVENTION IMPLICATIONS FOR CARETAKERS AND EDUCATORS

Caretakers and educators teach the future generations of society and their influence is undeniable. Additionally, they are part of individual's lives over long periods of time in which they provide life guidance and sometimes even become lifelong mentors. Children, for example, spend 50–60% of the day in classrooms with teachers. They are often seen as role models, and as a result, the influence they hold over children, teenagers, and young adults is long lasting and crucial (Izadinia, 2012; Kohl, n.d.).

Having an arsenal of microintervention strategies at their disposal has the potential of helping caretakers, and teachers navigate, execute, and understand their roles during racial dialogues or incidents. Parents are highly influential to their children and the family system as a whole, and therefore they are those best suited to use microinterventions to raise race-conscious and non-racist children. Although we use the terms parents and caretakers interchangeably, the latter is broader and includes biological parents, adoptive parents, or other individuals who play integral roles in child rearing and caretaking of children. Under the term educator lies many individuals including (a) day care teachers; (b) elementary, middle, and high school teachers; (c) college professors; and (d) coaches. While all educators and caretakers play an important role, the approach may vary depending on the developmental stages of their audience. The following sections briefly provide guidelines on how educators and caretakers can enact microinterventions through their four major strategic goals.

Make the Invisible Visible

The goal of this strategy is to bring hidden biases, oppressive messages, and/or practices and systems to the surface of one's consciousness and awareness. Educators and caretakers must begin with their own learning to increase their critical consciousness or ability to read between the lines and identify biased hidden metacommunications (Anderson & Stevenson, 2019). Additionally, one of the most important goals under this strategy is to demystify the harmful impact of a color-blind approach. Put simply, the "invisible" messages "colorblindness" sent to Black, Indigenous, and people of color (BIPOC) are: "Your experience in the world is the same as those of all races. The obstacles you face in life as a Black person is no more challenging than that of a White person. We are all the same under the skin. Anyone who works hard enough can succeed in this society" (Sue, 2015a). While those adopting a color-blind approach often have the intention of relaying their support to BIPOC, the impact is directly the opposite. A color-blind approach denies and discredits the real and traumatic experiences of racism BIPOC experience on a daily basis. Unlearning this color-blind approach – that is encouraged by many – is a pivotal first step in *making the invisible visible.*

Educators and caretakers of children can begin to seek out formal education, training workshops, self-education through books, podcasts, and films, or on-the-job experience to uncover unconscious biases and discrimination in oneself and institutions. Additionally, they should be well-versed in effective methods in leading conversations about race and systemic injustice using language and content that is developmentally appropriate for particular age groups. One way to lead these conversations in a developmentally appropriate way is through books written about race, discrimination, and anti-racism at all age levels. A simple Google search of "books about race for all ages" provides countless articles that provide lists of age-appropriate books. For example, an article written on self.com by Ali Francis (2020) lists

"23 Books to Help Kids of All Ages Learn about Race" and includes photos, descriptions, age range, and where to purchase the books. Another article written by Ana Fader (2020) on mommypoppins.com lists "21 Kids' Books about Racism, By Age" and provides an age specific break down of books and summaries. On yet another website, acsa.org, multiple child-centered activist organizations curated a list of "26 children's books to support conversations on race, racism, & resistance." In addition to a list of books with summaries, this article also lists organizations that specifically focus on teaching children about anti-racism and activism. Finally, educators and caretakers should establish a relationship with others who represent racially diverse groups and share similar values and interests to create a network of individuals who can develop content together, review material, and provide feedback and support.

Upon developing their own foundation of racial literacy and awareness, they may become better at teaching children about subtle communications of bias and making those metacommunications explicit. Educators and caretakers can utilize microintervention tactics to make the invisible visible through classroom activities and curriculum adaptations. They could begin by reviewing their curriculum and identifying which identities are represented, which histories are validated, and which voices are missing. Educators and caretakers can advocate for the elimination of biased or incomplete textbooks from the curriculum and can provide a list of material that provides representative and accurate depictions. In their teaching of historical events, for example, they may utilize textbooks that are preassigned by their district or education system, but that do not prevent them from assigning additional readings or engaging students in conversations that encourage them to think critically about the biases embedded in the curriculum. Educators and caretakers can work to make the invisible visible by illuminating the manifestation of White supremacy in biased historical narratives and accounts. For example, a teacher can use classroom time to lead discussions on the erasure of Indigenous and Native American accounts from mainstream historical textbooks. A parent can use homework time to review the historical texts and teach the child additional narratives that were not included in the textbook and explain why such narratives are missing. He or she can help the child to begin to develop their critical consciousness and train them to consider issues of oppression, power, and privilege in all of their future learning. Several resources exist including the book *Lies My Teacher Told Me* (Loewen, 2018a; b), which educators and caretakers can use (videos, films, and podcasts) to bring the erasure of Indigenous and Black narratives to the surface. Additionally, beyond teaching the "truth" about societal racism in this country, care should be taken to include curricula that celebrate BIPOC life, and not just limited to the hardship faced by these communities in history and their current life circumstance. Likewise, educators and caretakers can think about intersectional characters (i.e. LGBTQ, ability status, religious differences) and diverse genres such as poetry and afro-futurism to include in classrooms. By using lesson-planning resources to infuse current events into lesson plans, young people and teachers alike can learn about the importance of systemic injustice and micro/macroaggressions in a developmentally appropriate way.

Educate Stakeholders

Educators and caretakers themselves must go through a process of unlearning systemic bias, racism, and inequity in order to teach developmentally appropriate lessons to future generations. As mentioned previously, they must come to their own understanding of the legacy of White supremacy, the power of implicit bias, and the operation of macroaggressions through professional development, pedagogical texts (e.g. Freire, 1970), and resources such as *How to be Anti-Racist*, by Ibram X. Kendi and *White Supremacy* by Layla Saad, which can be purchased at your local bookstore or via an online bookseller or trainings such as *Undoing Racism* (more information can be found at The People's Institute for Survival and Beyond at www.pisab.org). It may be beneficial to create an accountability circle or affinity group for White educators and caretakers to process these learnings and experiences to not burden Black and Brown colleagues with such processes while educating themselves on the voices that are missing from their experiences.

Unfortunately, not all educators and caretakers have the privilege of receiving important workshops as such, and additionally may receive pushback for suggesting training around these types of topics from departments and administration. While this is unfortunate and a disservice to students and teachers alike, it does not have to stop educators and caretakers from learning and passing down the knowledge on the topics of microaggressions, macroaggressions, and microinterventions. A quick Google search on "microaggressions," for example, will pull up over one million resources that speak about microaggressions from various fields and points of view. Various authors, such as Paulo Freire (*Pedagogy of the Oppressed*), Robin DiAngelo (*White Fragility*), Christopher Emdin (*For White Folks Who Teach in the Hood ... and the Rest of Y'all Too: Reality Pedagogy and Urban Education*), and Beverly Tatum (*Why Are All the Black Kids Sitting Together in the Cafeteria and Can We Talk about Race?*), write books speaking around social justice topics and how to navigate power and privilege in classrooms. Websites such as Teaching Tolerance (tolerance.org), Anti-Defamation League (adl.org), and Teaching for Change (teachingforchange.org) all have countless sources and lesson plans that focus specifically on topics surrounding race, discrimination, and social justice actions. Articles and books focused specifically on microaggressions, macroaggressions, and microinterventions can be accessed by searching materials written by Sue and colleagues from various years (including this very book!).

After delving into the overwhelming amount of educational resources about race, discrimination, bias, and antibias actions, how does one begin to incorporate this knowledge around these topics? There are many resources that provide educators and caretakers with specific ways to bring up these types of topics in the classroom and incorporate them into everyday lessons. A very accessible, free, easy to navigate, great starting point resource is the Teaching Tolerance website (tolerance.org). With article titles such as "Teaching First-Graders About Microaggressions: The Small Moments Add Up," "Dealing with Dilemmas: Upstanders, Bystanders, and Whistle-Blowers," and "Microaggressions Have No Place in School," it is clear that these resources provide educators and caretakers with material to learn and utilize when they receive pushback from departments and those in authority. Additionally, the Teaching Tolerance website has a specific tab titled "Classroom resources tab," which provides additional resources such as lessons, learning plans, student texts, student tasks, teaching strategies, and printable posters. If an educator is so lucky to have a supportive department and senior administrators, Teaching Tolerance also has a "Professional Development" tab with resources such as workshops, request a training, facilitator guides, self-guided learning, webinars, and podcasts. Self-education around these topics allow dedicated teachers to utilize the microintervention strategy, *disarm the micro/macroaggression*, in various spaces, not only limited to the classroom.

One of the most important microinterventions, or steps to combatting (racial) micro/macroaggressions for educators and caretakers, is educating stakeholders. The microintervention often calls for important systemic change that impacts multiple spaces. This specific call to action, regardless of how educators and caretakers carry it out, share the following objectives: (a) help stakeholders and decision-makers develop critical consciousness about systemic inequities, (b) encourage community level educational engagement, and (c) illuminate gains and advantages. With an abundance of knowledge around micro/macroaggressions and microinterventions through self-education (and possibly formal education), educators and caretakers are in a key position to pass down that knowledge to stakeholders through department/faculty meetings, PTA meetings, teacher observations by higher ups, feedback surveys, and any other opportunities to meet with/give feedback to higher ups or stakeholders. Besides having a certain level of access to stakeholders, educators and caretakers also typically have access to conversations with parents/caretakers of students in order to encourage community-level engagement around these important topics (i.e. back to school night, parent–teacher conferences, at home projects, report cards, etc.). Finally, educators and caretakers are in a unique position to be able to illuminate gains and advantages of bestowing the knowledge of micro/macroaggressions and microinterventions onto students and educators and caretakers by (a) witnessing, firsthand, changes in student and faculty behaviors, (b) being able to track student progress through various assessments, and (c) monitoring changes in instances of microaggressions (discrimination) amongst students and faculty.

Educators and caretakers, although often overlooked, hold a special, privileged place in our society. They have the opportunity to work with growing minds that absorb an abundance of information through lessons and actions of their adult role models. While the journey to disarming (racial) micro/macroaggressions through microinterventions is not a simple task, educators and caretakers have a responsibility to be one of the leaders in this journey. Through informal (personal efforts) and formal education, educators and caretakers can find like-minded peers and allies to impact systemic change.

Disarm the Micro/Macroaggression

Disarming bias in an explicit, straightforward manner is one of the most effective ways to communicate disagreement with a discriminatory action or statement. While many adults do not believe that children are sophisticated enough to understand verbal, nonverbal, and contextual expressions of bias, we have already reviewed many studies that indicate children are like sponges that absorb messages quickly. Children, for example, interpret educator's and caretakers' silence as much as they interpret their words and actions. One of the major issues with silence is that it can be understood in many ways and never fully communicates disagreement or disapproval. In fact, silence can easily be interpreted as false consensus or agreement. As a result, if a micro/macroaggression is met with silence by an educator or caretaker, children (a) cannot recognize or understand the discriminatory action or practice and/or (b) find truth in the micro/macroaggression because no disagreement is being communicated. In summary, children need explicit, direct responses to micro/macroaggressions so that they are able, from a young age, to recognize, understand, and relay disagreement when faced with/witness microaggressions or a biased practice. Educator's and caretakers' roles in disarming micro/macroaggressions are as leaders and teachers – lead by example and teach children how to disarm future micro/macroaggressions.

Educators and caretakers can disarm microaggressions by implementing microintervention into household rules or into classroom norms and rules at the beginning of the school year. By setting those norms early on, students will have clear shared expectations for classroom conduct. For example, a *disarm the micro/macroaggression* ground rule for the home or classroom for young children may be: if you hear or witness someone bullying or making fun of someone because of their race, gender, size, or what they wear (in addition to other developmentally appropriate identities), interrupt and intervene through any number of actions, say "time out," "stop," or "freeze" to halt the discriminatory or prejudicial action or statement. Follow this up with accurate messaging through dialogue, evoke empathic understanding, explore what has occurred, and finally explain to the child about the harmful impact. Moralizing or being "preachy" is to be avoided, but emphasizing "anti-racist mindset" is the goal. This ground rule allows young children to not only recognize a microaggression but also encourage other onlookers to take antibias action. Another example of a *disarm the micro/macroaggression* ground rule for the home or classroom for older, high school aged children may be: when you learn something in school, especially in history class, do not take it at face value; supplement the reading with your own reading by POC authors and bring up these discussions in the classroom. This ground rule allows older children to become aware of "invisible" macroaggressions, begin to unlearn systemic racism, and challenge White-centered narratives.

By setting ground rules and norms, children will also have very clear ideas about the shared values and principles at home and in the classroom. Educators and caretakers can also use their own learning process to model these activities with colleagues and have students reflect on their feelings around experiencing and perpetuating microaggressions to demystify the use of strategies to combat these injustices. Students and classrooms can also "choose" a larger systemic issue to focus on and thread it through the curriculum throughout the year.

Educators and caretakers can work to make research more accessible through the dissemination of graphics and media. They can work to facilitate norms and create a culture in their homes, family spaces, and classrooms that is intolerant of racist, sexist, homophobic, or any other inappropriate jokes or comments. This can be done by having open, explicit dialogue about micro/macroaggressions present in current events and everyday life experiences and how to respond to these instances in the present and future. This open dialogue is a manner to teach children how to recognize micro/macroaggressions, engage in authentic dialogue, and disarm future macro/microaggressions. Additionally, educators and caretakers can work with students to identify the ways that internalized stereotypes may impact their sense of self and the ways that societal norms perpetuate those stereotypes and harmful messages. This can be done through methods such as journaling, individual, and group therapy, and surrounding children role models who are able to authentically share their experiences with micro/macroaggressions (Community Tool Box, 2019; President's Initiative on Race, 1998).

Seek External Support

Once an educator obtains the important knowledge around microaggressions and microinterventions and has incorporated it into their everyday lessons, what are the next steps? If students are receiving lessons on microaggressions and microinterventions in one classroom, this is good; if students are receiving these lessons in multiple classrooms, this is great; but if students are receiving these lessons in almost all education spaces they encounter, this is ideal. By receiving these lessons and messages around bias and antibias, children, teenagers, and young adults will not only internalize these messages but also normalize them and therefore continue to carry the lessons onto others. Impacting larger systems may feel overwhelming for educators and caretakers, but the need to transition from individual to systemic impact is vital in the movement to disarm (racial) micro/macroaggressions through microinterventions. This process begins with small attainable goals such as finding like-minded educators and caretakers who share similar goals to create interest groups. These groups serve not only as support systems but also as a fountain of knowledge and experiences to inspire and inform new lessons for students. In addition to creating/joining interest/ support groups, a critical step in creating more systemic change is finding allies that hold positions of power in various spaces (i.e. principals, PTA members, deans, etc.). These allies are able to not only provide individual support but may also have the power to impact larger systems within education spaces. Creating support/interest groups and finding allies in the journey to disarm (racial) micro/macroaggressions are manners in which you can engage in the microintervention, *seek external support.*

For educators, caretakers, and professional development organizations, collectives such as The Conscious Kid (www.theconsciouskid.org or @ TheConsciousKid on social media) and finding community online may be available even if local, in-person resources are not. Educators and caretakers may consider speaking to unions or other elected officials if support for this work is difficult to find in their communities. This effort can also include learning from health can strong communities of color – patronizing business of color, attending community and religious meetings, engage in community to model for youth the power of community and support.

IMPLICATIONS FOR FUTURE STUDY

The concept of microinterventions and its relationship to micro- and macroaggressions not only offer practical value but also open up research opportunities for studying their practicality, efficacy, impact, education, and training. We would like to suggest possible future directions in the study of microinterventions and provide a few general observations. First, while the existing stress-coping literature has identified valuable strategies in dealing with general stress, there is little research on how targets, allies, and bystanders can cope with the constant manifestations of prejudice and discrimination. It is imperative to identify new race-related response strategies, to determine their impact on microaggressive comments or actions, and to dismantling biased institutional policies and practices. How effective, for example, are the strategies and tactics identified in previous chapters in disarming micro- and macroaggressions. It would be valuable to determine the potency of microintervention training, and whether increasing the arsenal of anti-racism strategies for targets, including allies and bystanders, have any positive effect on mental health, feelings of increased efficacy, and self-esteem. Likewise, does arming targets, allies, and bystanders with microinterventions increase the likelihood of challenging micro- and macroaggressions? A reason often given for inaction in the face of bias is "not knowing" what to do. Additionally, "Do targets always want bystanders and allies to intervene?" Are there specific instances when interventions would be harmful to targets by reducing self-efficacy and autonomy, or actually increasing microaggressions? If so, what are those situations and conditions? Further, what is the relationship of racial, cultural, and gender differences in responding to racist acts or statements? Do certain coping responses or specific microintervention strategies align better with some cultures or social identities? Lee, Soto, Swim, and Bernstein (2012) found that Asian Americans typically utilize indirect and more subtle approaches in order to maintain interpersonal harmony, while African Americans tend to confront racism more directly. To assume one is more functional than the other is to make an ethnocentric value judgment. It may be better to approach this issue by asking: "What role does race, culture, and ethnicity play in confronting discrimination, and what are the advantages and disadvantages that arise from their culture-specific use?" It is clear that the concept of microinterventions is a complex issue, and future research is needed to clarify their manifestation, dynamics, and impact.

Second, in the arena of education and training, identifying microintervention strategies and skills is not enough to produce actions on the part of well-intentioned individuals. It is clear that active interventions will only occur when other inertia and inhibitions are overcome, and when these skills are learned, practiced, and rehearsed. Some organizations in the business sector have begun "active bystander" training in confronting prejudiced responses (Aguilar, 2006; Ashburn-Nardo et al., 2008; Scully & Rowe, 2009). We believe such training would also benefit targets and White allies and suggest similar microintervention training programs for psychology, education, and other social service professions.

Third, as individuals with backgrounds in counseling psychology and as clinicians ourselves, we would be remiss to not address the role of clinicians in teaching active coping strategies and microinterventions to targets of microaggressions. The revised Multicultural and Social Justice Counseling Competencies guide (Ratts et al., 2016) describes the roles of professional clinicians as social justice advocates, but little has been done to identify ways that clinicians can integrate microinterventions into their clinical work. There are various instances that may prompt the introduction of race or experiences of discrimination into the therapy room, including noticeable identity differences between client and clinician, the type of clinical setting, or identity and discrimination as a presenting problem (Boyd-Franklin, 2010). All of which points to a great need for clinicians to be trained in effective coping interventions and response strategies to empower their clients through social advocacy and direct intervention. In fact, clinicians already engage in racial socialization messages in therapy as part of multiculturally competent work (Brown, Blackmon, Schumacher, & Urbanski, 2013). These interventions may include reminding the client of their rich heritage, modeling healthy self-acceptance, and recommending community and spiritual coping mechanisms that exist, as well as teaching tools in therapy to achieve and maintain positive mental health. A meta-analysis of the literature on interventions related to race in therapy also identified critical examination of privilege, developing positive identity, externalize, and minimize self-blame, and outreach through advocacy (Miller, Keum, Thai, Lu, Truong, Huh, Li, Yeung, Ahn, 2018).

Psychology and social justice advocacy have historical connections and roots that can inform the way we understand social justice and advocacy as it applies to counseling psychology and the practice of psychology. Nadal (2017) demonstrates the many ways that psychology research has had an impact on public opinion and societal stigma, government policies and laws, and changes in practices and policies. Nadal points to the work of Mamie Phipps Clark, the first Black woman to receive a PhD from Columbia University, who's research on black and white dolls was later cited in the 1954 Brown v. Board of Education US Supreme Court case, the work of Gregory Herek (2001, 2006, 2009) and Ilan Meyer (1995; 2003) who would influence laws regarding marriage equality, or the many feminist scholars who have greatly shaped the way psychology understands issues related to women today.

Similarly, research on microaggressions has also had a major impact on issues of discrimination and mental health. Psychologists are known for their work as educators, researchers, and clinicians, but psychologists are also social justice activists. Nadal (2017) discusses the role of a psychologist-activist and suggests that they may also actively teach racial-ethnic socialization by initiating these conversations. Racial socialization messages in therapy are considered an important aspect of multiculturally competent work with African American clients (Brown, Blackmon, Schumacher, & Urbanski, 2013). It is a psychologist's job not only to validate and empathize with the experiences of their clients but also to uplift them and empower them, through identity affirming therapy and the teaching of skills and techniques to help them cope and respond in the face of oppression and prejudice such as transgender identity affirmation and social psychological identity theory (Nutbrock, Rosenblum, & Blumenstein, 2002). Furthermore, we argue that clinicians may benefit a great deal from training and increased knowledge on microintervention strategies, response tactics aimed at disarming and disrupting microaggressions, and arming their clients with these tools for future instances.

For example, clinicians can work to help validate their clients' experiential reality by making the invisible visible if and when a client describes a microaggressive encounter. Clinicians can help arm clients with the language and tools to describe their experience and can direct them to various resources for them to learn more about microaggressions and their impact. They can engage their clients in dialogues on identity and the various manifestations of oppression on individual, cultural, and institutional levels. They can directly teach strategies to disarm microaggressions and help clients evaluate the environment, their relationship with the other person, consideration of their emotional labor, who is deserving of that emotional labor, how to make decisions around when they choose to defend and disarm, and when they choose to engage in education as an approach. Clinicians can teach effective tools for utilizing education approaches that aim to help clients be as effective as possible as well as teach strategies for seeking external support and maintaining health and well-being.

CONCLUSIONS

Our microintervention journey has consumed over a year of constant research and analysis on antibias strategies, reasons for complacency in the face of moral transgressions, conditions that facilitate individual actions, the costs of inaction, antibias benefits (for targets, allies, bystanders, and the social context), and the important distinction between micro- and macroaggressions. In this chapter, we have noted the central roles educators and caretakers play in producing non-racist and anti-racist adults. Nothing has been more profound, however, than recognizing how social advocacy and social justice are foundational to microintervention strategic goals and tactics for the entire citizenry. They are of central importance to addressing institutional and societal injustices and would be ineffective without a social justice framework from which meaning and purpose can be derived (Vasquez, 2012). In our extensive literature review, for example, we noted how antibias actions directed toward systemic bias are almost always anchored within the framework of social justice and social advocacy. Although there are many conclusions to be drawn from our work, several seem especially fundamental to the concept of microinterventions.

First, the core values of social justice involve equal access and opportunity for all citizens, elimination of systems of oppression, upholding the rights of all people, and fairness in decision-making processes (Jason, Beasley, & Hunter, 2015; Ratts, Singh, Nassar-McMillan, Butler, & McCullough, 2016). The purpose of microinterventions manifested through social advocacy is to influence decisions within political, economic, legal, and social systems and to eliminate injustice by changing policies, practices, and structures of organizations and society (Goodman et al., 2018., Kozan & Blustein, 2018). Effective use of microinterventions from a social justice perspective means confronting systems of oppression with an understanding of how social and political structures and arrangements create disparities in education, employment, health care, and other inequalities in the life of marginalized groups and communities (Banks et al., 2019; Goodman, 2011; Jason, Beasley, & Hunter, 2015). Attempts to shape public policy or institutional regulatory measures, for example, may include education, lobbying, and social/political pressure (Banks et al., 2019; Toporek, Lewis, & Crethar, 2009). In many respects, microintervention strategies and tactics fall under each of these categories and can have a powerful impact in producing change.

Second, we enter a phase in our political history where taking action through microinterventions has never been more pressing and important. A prime example of the interplay between social justice advocacy and microinterventions is evident in pressuring the Executive Branch of the Federal Government to reverse the Family Separation Policy of 2018. Earlier that year, the Department of Justice had created a policy to discourage asylum seekers from entering the United States by separating children from their parents. It was supported by the Department of Homeland Security (DHS) and implemented by the Immigration and Customs Enforcement Agency (ICE). The policy, viewed by many as racist, was created under the guise of preventing potential criminals and terrorists from entering the country through a zero-tolerance policy (SPLC, 2019).

The antibias actions undertaken by targets, allies, and bystanders to overturn the policy are an excellent illustration of the power and influence of social justice advocacy and using microinterventions to address a macroaggression (Sue & Spanierman, 2020). People who held power in leadership positions (president, attorney general, DHS secretary, ICE leadership, etc.) and the public had to be educated and lobbied about the unfairness of the policy, the detrimental impact on children, the immorality of family separations, and the racist nature of such actions. Many individuals and groups made the "invisible" visible by naming the policy as racist, biased, and discriminatory. Thus, they challenged the policy's rationale as "protecting the public from criminal elements" by presenting overwhelming statistics to the contrary.

Third, mobilizing large groups of people and organizations to engage in social advocacy, to condemn individual and systemic racism, and to pressure local, state, and federal agencies to end biased policies and practices can be extremely effective. The current renewed "Black Lives Matter" movement has attracted individual followers, business and industry, and government leaders to confront systemic racism, sparked by the murder of George Floyd and many unarmed Black men by the police, and by other vigilante actions against them. Massive nationwide protests beginning in 2020 have led to calls to "defund the police," to reform the criminal justice system, and to take down confederate statues or symbols of White supremacy and demand that institutions change biased policies and practices in all facets of employment. Many believe that the "Black Lives Matter" movement in their effort to end racism and to move toward social justice appears quantitatively and qualitatively different than some of the short-lived movements of the past. Against the backdrop of the devastating impact of the pandemic, however, the eventual outcome of these protests is still to be determined. Table 10.1 outlines many of the changes that have occurred over a one-month period since the murder of George Floyd and accompanying national and international protests. The question remains, however, will the changes outlined in Table 10.1 prove only

Table 10.1 Cosmetic Changes or Real Changes: Results of Black Lives Matter Protests – between June 1, 2020 and July 1, 2020

In just 30 days, prior to the publishing of this book, activists called for large-scale changes to address systemic racism in the United States. Specifically, activists called for police reform in terms of "defunding" police departments and reallocating funds to mental health, social services, and youth programming. In addition to movement toward structural reform, this has also been accompanied by symbolic changes.

Government and Law

• Minneapolis City Council voted to disband the police department
• New York City diverted one billion dollars from NYPD budget into youth programming and social services
• Breonna's Law is passed in Louisiana to ban no-knock warrants
• Colorado passed a law ending qualified immunity for police officers
• Removal of the confederate symbol on the Mississippi State flag
• Numerous statues of confederate, colonial, and White supremacist monuments taken down
• Arrests were made in police involved shootings
• Several states issued bans on choke holds in policing
• Several states pledged to review police practices, police body camera guidelines, and other reforms
• Several states pledged to restructure police department funding
• Congress unveiled legislation on police reform
• Several US cities banned use of tear gas by police
• Some city and town school districts ended their relationship with police departments
• Several states declared Juneteenth a state holiday

Media

• Non-Black characters in animated series who play Black characters have stepped down
• The show *Cops* cancelled after 32 seasons
• The Associated Press and *The New York Times* issued new guidelines to capitalize Black to pay homage to the impacts of systemic racism in this country and throughout the diaspora
• A group of activists aggregated data reporting for police violence
• The hacking group anonymous released documents supporting racist practices in police departments
• Popular anti-racism books have sold out across the country
• An editor of *The New York Times* resigned after publishing a conservative opinion piece on the protest movement
• An editor of *The Philadelphia Inquirer* after approving the headline: "Buildings Matter Too"
• The Grammy awards announced that they would no longer use the word "urban" to describe music of Black origin
• The group Dixie Chicks changed their name to the "Chicks"
• CEO of Bon Appetit stepped down highlighting systemic racial injustices in the food media industry

(Continued)

Table 10.1   *(Continued)*

Lifestyle

- Realtors in Texas will stop using "Master" as a bedroom and bathroom table
- PepsiCo, the brand behind Aunt Jemima, Uncle Ben's, and Eskimo Pies, discontinued the products due to its legacies of racism and pledged $400 million in investments to address systemic racism
- NFL issued a statement apologizing for actions related to Colin Kapernick and acknowledging systemic racism
- Sports franchises and university mascots depicting insensitive racial symbols are being considered for removal
- Johnson & Johnson also announced it would stop selling products that had been used by some people to lighten their skin tone
- NASCAR removed the confederate flag from its events
- Black Lives Matter murals were painted on streets in several cities
- Walmart stopped selling guns and locking up black hair care products
- Walmart, Walgreens, and CVS will stop placing African American beauty products in anti-theft cases, alongside other beauty products not given the same protections
- Sephora signed the "15% Pledge" and committed to devoting 15% of its shelf space to products from Black-owned businesses
- Popular streaming services (Netflix Hulu, HBO, etc.) removed films and TV shows with racist characters, depictions, and characters in Black face from their platforms
- Organizations, celebrities, individuals, and funding organizations have donated millions to non-profit and individual activists involved in Black Lives Matter work
- Disney will rename "Splash Mountain"
- Various companies have committed to increasing inclusivity and diversity in their staff

Academia Institutions and Public/Private Organizations

- Academics for Black Lives held a training attended by 8,000 people live and thousands more after the week it aired
- Requests for anti-racism trainings have increased dramatically
- CEO of CrossFit resigned after questioning the existence of systemic racism
- Reddit co-founder stepped down from the company's board of directors in hopes to fill his seat with Black candidate
- The CEO of The Wing resigned following months of complaints about racial inequities within the company
- Princeton University removed name of Woodrow Wilson from building
- Racism declared a public health crisis in a variety of states and cities and various professional medical groups called for an end to police brutality
- Many private organizations declared Juneteenth an official paid holiday
- Tech companies such as Apple, Amazon, and Google have updated their smart voice assistants, which now explain the Black Lives Matter movement when asked "Do Black lives matter?"

(Continued)

Table 10.1   *(Continued)*

- Colleges have pledged to support Black students and been called to combat systemic racism in educational settings
- IBM has stopped investing in facial recognition software used by police forces; Microsoft will no longer share its version with the police

Sources:
- https://www.businessinsider.com/13-concrete-changes-sparked-by-george-floyd-protests-so-far-2020-6#reddit-cofounder-alexis-ohanian-stepped-down-from-the-companys-board-of-directors-urging-the-company-to-fill-his-board-seat-with-a-black-candidate-11
- https://www.wmur.com/article/here-are-some-of-the-biggest-changes-that-have-come-since-protests-began-around-george-floyds-death/32857941#https://thehill.com/changing-america/respect/equality/502121-what-the-2020-black-lives-matter-protests-have-achieved-so
- https://justcapital.com/news/notable-corporate-responses-to-the-george-floyd-protests/

to be cosmetic and transitory, or will the changes prove to be the foretelling of our Nation living up to the promise, principles, and values of equal access and opportunities for all.

Fourth, as seen in the earlier example, microinterventions within the framework of social advocacy can be effective tools to use in addressing macroaggressions. It requires, however, overcoming personal inertial in the face of rules and regulations that seem so daunting to change. And, it requires a complex series of steps that move from policy analysis, targeting stakeholders, identifying and forming allies/collaborators, anticipating resistance, and providing self-care, to strategy development of microinterventions (Jason, Beasley, & Hunter, 2015; Melton, 2018; Ratts et al., 2016; Toporek & Ahluewalea, 2012). The integrated complexity of social justice advocacy is clearly seen in the development of an *Advocacy Toolkit* created by a joint effort between four divisions of the American Psychological Association: Division 17, the Society of Counseling Psychology; Division 27, the Society for Community Research and Action; Division 35, the Society for the Psychology of Women; and Division 45, the Society for the Psychological Study of Culture, Ethnicity, and Race (Banks et al., 2019). Our taxonomy of microintervention strategies and tactics that address macroaggressions should not be seen in isolation from the values of individual morality and responsibility, social advocacy, community advocacy, and the strategic framework provided in *Community Advocacy: A Psychologist's Toolkit for State and Local Advocacy* (Banks et al., 2019).

Last, we wish to make one final point. We have constantly asserted that it is the responsibility of all concerned civic-minded individuals to combat individual and systemic bias and discrimination through the use of microinterventions or antibias actions. As mental health practitioners and academics, our goal in producing this book was never to tease out the implications for the helping profession alone but to address the larger issue of what targets, White allies, and bystanders from all professions and walks of life could do to combat individual, institutional, and cultural racism. The helping profession and mental health practitioners are just a few of many stakeholders urged to take social justice actions. We believe that the concept of microinterventions is an important one, not only for the field of psychology but also for our society as well. It has numerous implications for research, practice, education, and training, our everyday lives, and especially the social justice arena. We are hopeful that other activists, scholars, and researchers will make microinterventions a lived reality through their research and practice in education, employment, and health care.

References

Aboud, F. E. (1988). *Children and prejudice*. Hoboken, NJ: B. Blackwell.

Aboud, F. E. (2008). A social-cognitive developmental theory of prejudice. In S. Quintana & C. McKown (Eds.), *Handbook of race, racism, and the developing child* (pp. 55–71). Hoboken, NJ: John Wiley & Sons, Inc.

Accapadi, M. M. (2007). When white women cry: How white women's tears oppress women of color. *College Student Affairs Journal, 26*(2), 208–215.

Aguilar, L. (2006). *Ouch! That stereotype hurts*. Flower Mound, TX: The Walk The Talk Company.

Akili, Y. (2013). *Dear universe: Letters of affirmation and empowerment for all of us*. Boston, MA: Michael Todd Books.

Albert Einstein Institution. (2019). Retrieved from http://www.aeinstein.org/

American Psychological Association. (2000). *Racism and psychology*. Washington, DC: Author.

American Psychological Association. (2014). A psychologist's guide to federal advocacy: Advancing psychology in the public interest. Retrieved from https://www.apa.org/advocacy/guide/federal-guide.pdf

American Psychological Association. (2017). Multicultural guidelines: An ecological approach to context, identity, and intersectionality. Retrieved from https://www.apa.org/about/policy/multicultural-guidelines

American Psychological Association. (2019a). APA psychology benefits society. Retrieved from www.apa.org/pi/res

Microintervention Strategies, First Edition. Derald Wing Sue, Cassandra Z. Calle, Narolyn Mendez, Sarah Alsaidi, and Elizabeth Glaeser.
© 2021 John Wiley & Sons, Inc. Published 2021 by John Wiley & Sons, Inc.

American Psychological Association. (2019b) APA resilience: Uplifting families through healthy communication about race. Retrieved from https://www.apa.org/res/

American Psychological Association. (2019c). Race and ethnicity guidelines in psychology: Promoting responsiveness and equity. Retrieved from www.apa.org/about/policy/summary-guidelines-race-ethnicity

American Psychological Association, Presidential Task Force on Preventing Discrimination and Promoting Diversity. (2012). Dual pathways to a better America: Preventing discrimination and promoting diversity. Washington, DC: American Psychological Association. Retrieved from http://www.apa.org/pubs/info/reports/promoting-diversity.aspx

Anderson, M., Toor, S., Rainie, L., & Smith, A. (2018). Activism in the social media age. Pew Research Center: Internet, Science & Tech. Retrieved from https://www.pewresearch.org/internet/2018/07/11/activism-in-the-social-media-age/

Anderson, N., & Svrluga, S. (2015). What a massive sexual assault survey found at 27 top US universities. The Washington Post. Retrieved from https://www.washingtonpost.com/news/grade-point/wp/2015/09/21/what-a-massive-sexual-assault-survey-showed-about-27-top-u-s-universities/

Anderson, R. (2017). "But daddy, why was he shot?" How to talk to children about race today. Psychology Benefits Society. Retrieved from www.apa.org/pi/res.

Anderson, R. E., & Stevenson, H. C. (2019). RECASTing racial stress and trauma: Theorizing the healing potential of racial socialization in families. American Psychologist, 74(1), 63. doi:10.1037/amp0000392

Andrews, E. (2019). When Gandhi's salt march rattled British colonial rule. History. Retrieved from https://www.history.com/news/gandhi-salt-march-india-british-colonial-rule

Angelou, M. (1969). I know why the caged bird sings. Random House.

Angelou, M. (1978). And still I rise: A book of poems. Random House.

Apfelbaum, E. P., Sommers, S. R., & Norton, M. I. (2008). Seeing race and seeming racist? Evaluating strategic colorblindness in social interaction. Journal of Personality and Social Psychology, 95(4), 918.

Ashburn-Nardo, L., Morris, K. A., & Goodwin, S. A. (2008). The confronting prejudiced responses (CPR) model: Applying CPR in organizations. Academy of Management Learning & Education, 7(3), 332–342. doi:10.5465/amle.2008.34251671

Ayres, C. (2018, Dec. 24). 19 Major pros and cons of civil disobedience. Connect Us. Retrieved from https://connectusfund.org/19-major-pros-and-cons-of-civil-disobedience

Balaji, A. B., Claussen, A. H., Smith, D. C., Visser, S. N., Morales, M. J., & Perou, R. (2007). Social support networks and maternal mental health and well-being. Journal of Women's Health, 16(10), 1386–1396.

Bandura, A., Ross, D., & Ross, S. A. (1961). Transmission of aggression through imitation of aggressive models. *The Journal of Abnormal and Social Psychology*, 63(3), 575.

Banks, K., Beachy, S., Ferguson, A., Gobin, R. L., Ho, I., Liang, C., ... Toporek, R. (2019). Community advocacy: A psychologist's toolkit for state and local advocacy. Retrieved from https://www.communitypsychology.com/wp-content/uploads/2019/06/2019_Community_Advocacy_A_Psychologist_Toolkit.pdf

Baron, A. S., & Banaji, M. R. (2006). The development of implicit attitudes: Evidence of race evaluations from ages 6 and 10 and adulthood. *Psychological Science*, 17(1), 53–58.

Bauer, M., Cahlíková, J., Chytilová, J., & Želinský, T. (2018). Social contagion of ethnic hostility. *Proceedings of the National Academy of Sciences*, 115(19), 4881–4886. doi:10.1073/pnas.1720317115

Baumeister, R. F., & Leary, M. R. (1995). The need to belong: Desire for interpersonal attachments as a fundamental human motivation. *Psychological Bulletin*, 117(3), 497.

Bell, L. A. (2003). Telling tales: What stories can teach us about racism. *Race, Ethnicity and Education*, 6, 3–28. doi:10.1080/1361332032000044567

Bemak, F., & Chung, R. C.-Y. (2008). New professional roles and advocacy strategies for school counselors: A multicultural/social justice perspective to move beyond the nice counselor syndrome. *Journal of Counseling & Development*, 86(3), 372–381. doi:10.1002/j.1556-6678.2008.tb00522.x

Blair, I. V., Judd, C. M., & Chapleau, K. M. (2004). The influence of Afrocentric facial features in criminal sentencing. *Psychological Science*, 15(10), 674–679. doi:10.1111/j.0956-7976.2004.00739.x

Bonilla-Silva, E. (2006). *Racism without racists: Color-blind racism and the persistence of racial inequality in the United States*. Rowman & Littlefield Publishers.

Boyd-Franklin, N. (2010). Incorporating spirituality and religion into the treatment of African American clients. *The Counseling Psychologist*, 38(7), 976–1000. doi:10.1177/0011000010374881

Boysen, G. A., & Vogel, D. L. (2008). The relationship between level of training, implicit bias, and multicultural competency among counselor trainees. *Training and Education in Professional Psychology*, 2(2), 103.

Broido, E. M. (2000). The development of social justice allies during college: A phenomenological investigation. *Journal of College Student Development*, 41(1), 3–18.

Broido, E. M., & Reason, R. D. (2005). The development of social justice attitudes and actions: An overview of current understandings. *New Directions for Student Services*, 110, 17. doi:10.1002/ss.162

Brondolo, E., Brady Ver Halen, N., Pencille, M., Beatty, D., & Contrada, R. J. (2009). Coping with racism: A selective review of the literature and a theoretical and methodological critique. *Journal of Behavioral Medicine*, 32, 64–88. doi:10.1007/s10865-008-9193-0

Bronson, P., & Merryman, A. (2009, September 4). Even babies discriminate: A nature shock excerpt. Newsweek. Retrieved from https://www.newsweek.com/even-babies-discriminate-nurtureshock-excerpt-79233

Brookfield, S. D., & Preskill, S. (2012). *Discussion as a way of teaching: Tools and techniques for democratic classrooms.* John Wiley & Sons.

Browder, D. M., Schoen, S. F., & Lentz, F. E. (1986). Learning to learn through observation. *The Journal of Special Education,* 20(4), 447–461. doi:10.1177/002246698602000406

Brown, D. L., Blackmon, S. K., Schumacher, K., & Urbanski, B. (2013). Exploring clinician's attitudes toward the incorporation of racial socialization in psychotherapy. *Journal of Black Psychology,* 39(6), 507–531.

Brown, K. T. (2015). Perceiving allies from the perspective of non- dominant group members: Comparisons to friends and activists. *Current Psychology,* 34, 713–722. doi:10.1007/s12144-014-9284-8

Brown, K. T., & Ostrove, J. M. (2013). What does it mean to be an ally?: The perception of allies from the perspective of people of color. *Journal of Applied Social Psychology,* 43(11), 2211–2222. doi:10.1111/jasp.12172

Brownlee, K. (2017, Fall Edition). Civil disobedience. The Stanford Encyclopedia of Philosophy. Retrieved from https://plato.stanford.edu/archive3s/fall2017/entries/civil-disobedience/

Bruce, M., & Bridgeland, J. (2014). *The mentoring effect: Young people's perspective on the outcome and availability of mentoring.* Washington, DC: Civic Enterprises. https://eric.ed.gov/?id=ED558065

Byrd, C. (2018). Microaggressions self-defense: A role-playing workshop for responding to microaggressions. *Social Sciences,* 7(6), 96. doi:10.3390/socsci7060096

Campbell, B., & Manning, J. (2014). Microaggression and moral cultures. *Comparative Sociology,* 13(6), 692–726.

Caplan, G. (1970). *The theory and practice of mental health consultation.* New York, NY: Basic Books.

Carter, R. T. (1995). *The influence of race and racial identity in psychotherapy: Toward a racially inclusive model* (Vol. 183). John Wiley & Sons.

Carter, R. T. (2003). Becoming racially and culturally competent: The racial-cultural counseling laboratory. *Journal of Multicultural Counseling and Development,* 31(1), 20–30. doi:10.1002/j.2161-1912.2003.tb00527.x

CDC. (2020a, February 11b). Coronavirus disease 2019 (COVID-19). Centers for Disease Control and Prevention. Retrieved from https://www.cdc.gov/coronavirus/2019-ncov/need-extra-precautions/racial-ethnic-minorities.html

CDC. (2020b). Coronavirus disease 2019 (COVID-19): Reducing stigma. Center for Disease Control and Prevention. Retrieved from https://www.cdc.gov/coronavirus/2019-ncov/daily-life-coping/reducing-stigma.html

Cesario, J., & Navarrete, C. D. (2014). Perceptual bias in threat distance: The critical roles of in group support and target evaluations in defensive threat regulation. *Social Psychological and Personality Science*, 5(1), 12–17.

Chenoweth, E., & Stephan, M. J. (2011). *Why civil resistance works: The strategic logic of nonviolent conflict*. Columbia University Press.

The Children's Community School. (2018). They're not too young to talk about race! The Children's Community School. Retrieved from http://www. childrenscommunityschool.org/wp-content/uploads/2018/02/theyre-not-too-young-1.pdf

CLBO. (2006). New data on diversity training. *Compensation & Benefits for Law Offices*, 6(2), 9.

Cobb, S. (1976). Social support as a moderator of life stress. *Psychosomatic Medicine*, 38, 300–314.

Cohen, S. (2004). Social relationships and health. *American Psychologist*, 59(8), 676.

Cohen, S., & Wills, T. A. (1985). Stress, social support, and the buffering hypothesis. *Psychological Bulletin*, 98(2), 310.

Coker, A. L., Smith, P. H., Thompson, M. P., McKeown, R. E., Bethea, L., & Davis, K. E. (2002). Social support protects against the negative effects of partner violence on mental health. *Journal of Women's Health & Gender-Based Medicine*, 11(5), 465–476.

Community Tool Box. (2019). Center for Community Health and Development at the University of Kansas. https://ctb.ku.edu/en

Cortes, C. (2013). *Multicultural America: A multimedia encyclopedia* (Vols. 1–4). Thousand Oaks, CA: Sage.

Crocker, J., & Major, B. (1989). Social stigma and self-esteem: The self-protective properties of stigma. *Psychological Review*, 96(4), 608.

Cross, W. E. (1991). *Shades of Black: Diversity in African-American identity*. Temple University Press.

Czopp, A. M., & Ashburn-Nardo, L. (2012). Interpersonal confrontations of prejudice. In A. J. Colella & E. B. King (Eds.), *The psychology of prejudice: Interdisciplinary perspectives on contemporary issues* (pp. 373–386). Hauppauge, NY: Nova Science Publishers, Inc.

Czopp, A. M., & Monteith, M. J. (2003). Confronting prejudice (literally): Reactions to confrontations of racial and gender bias. *Personality and Social Psychology Bulletin*, 29(4), 532–544. doi:10.1177/0146167202250923

DeLeon, A. P. (2010). Anarchism, sabotage, and the spirit of revolt: Injecting the social studies with anarchist potentialities. *Critical Theories, Radical Pedagogies, and Social Education*, 1–12. doi:10.1163/9789460912788_002

Devos, T., & Banaji, M. R. (2005). American= white? *Journal of Personality and Social Psychology*, 88(3), 447.

DiAngelo, R. J. (2011). White fragility. *International Journal of Critical Pedagogy*, 3(3), 54–70.

Dickter, C. L. (2012). Confronting hate: Heterosexuals' responses to anti-gay comments. *Journal of Homosexuality*, 59(8), 1113–1130. doi:10.1080/00918369.2012.712817

Dickter, C. L., & Newton, V. A. (2013). To confront or not to confront: Non-targets' evaluations of and responses to racist comments. *Journal of Applied Social Psychology*, 43(S2), E262–E275. doi:10.1111/jasp.12022

Dorn, A. V., Cooney, R. E., & Sabin, M. L. (2020). COVID-19 exacerbating inequalities in the US. *The Lancet*, 395(10232), 1243–1244. doi:10.1016/s0140-6736(20)30893-x

Dotterer, A. M., & James, A. (2018). Can parenting microprotections buffer against adolescents' experiences of racial discrimination? *Journal of Youth and Adolescence*, 47(1), 38–50. doi:10.1007/s10964-017-0773-6

Dovidio, J. F. (2001). On the nature of contemporary prejudice: The third wave. *Journal of Social Issues*, 57(4), 829–849. doi:10.1111/0022-4537.00244

Dovidio, J. F., Gaertner, S. E., Kawakami, K., & Hodson, G. (2002). Why can't we just get along? Interpersonal biases and interracial distrust. *Cultural Diversity and Ethnic Minority Psychology*, 8(2), 88. doi:10.1037/1099-9809.8.2.88

Dovidio, J. F., & Gaertner, S. L. (2000). Aversive racism and selection decisions: 1989 and 1999. *Psychological Science*, 11(4), 315–319.

Dovidio, J. F., Gaertner, S. L., Validzic, A., Matoka, K., Johnson, B., & Frazier, S. (1997). Extending the benefits of recategorization: Evaluations, self-disclosure, and helping. *Journal of Experimental Social Psychology*, 33(4), 401–420. doi:10.1006/jesp.1997.1327

Dovidio, J. F., Kawakami, K., & Gaertner, S. L. (2002). Implicit and explicit prejudice and interracial interaction. *Journal of Personality and Social Psychology*, 82(1), 62.

Dunbar, A. (2017). Black pain, black joy, and racist fear: Supporting Black children in a hostile world [American Psychologist Association web long post]. Retrieved from https://psychologybenefits.org/2017/08/30/encouraging-black-childrens-self-expression/

Dunham, Y., Baron, A. S., & Banaji, M. R. (2008). The development of implicit intergroup cognition. *Trends in Cognitive Sciences*, 12(7), 248–253.

Edwards, K. E. (2006). Aspiring social justice ally identity development: A conceptual model. *NASPA Journal*, 43(4), 39–60. doi:10.2202/0027-6014.1722

El-Amin, A., Seider, S., Graves, D., Tamerat, J., Clark, S., Soutter, M., … Malhotra, S. (2017). Critical consciousness: A key to student achievement. *Phi Delta Kappan*, 98(5), 18–23. doi:10.1177/0031721717690360

Eligon, J. (2016). After racist episodes, blunt discussions on campus. The New York Times, p. 3.

Ellis, J. M., Powell, C. S., Demetriou, C. P., Huerta-Bapat, C., & Panter, A. T. (2019). Examining first-generation college student lived experiences with microaggressions and microaffirmations at a predominately White public research university. *Cultural Diversity and Ethnic Minority Psychology*, 25(2), 266. doi:10.1037/cdp0000198

Fader, A. (2020). 21 Kids' books about racism, by age. Mommy Poppins. Retrieved from https://mommypoppins.com/Childrens-kids-books-about-racism-preschoolers-teens

Farago, F., Davidson, K. L., & Byrd, C. M. (2019). Ethnic-racial socialization in early childhood: The implications of color-consciousness and colorblindness for prejudice development. In *Handbook of children and prejudice* (pp. 131–145). Cham: Springer.

Feeney, B. C., & Collins, N. L. (2015). A new look at social support: A theoretical perspective on thriving through relationships. *Personality and Social Psychology Review*, 19(2), 113–147.

Fogelson, R. M. (1970). Violence and grievances: Reflections on the 1960s riots. *Journal of Social Issues*, 26(1), 141–163. doi:10.1111/j.1540-4560.1970.tb01284.x

Forward, J. R., & Williams, J. R. (1970). Internal-external control and black militancy1. *Journal of Social Issues*, 26(1), 75–92.

Fox, D. (2011). Reflections on occupying. *Journal for Social Action in Counseling and Psychology*, 3, 129–137.

Francis, A. (2020, June 12). 23 Books to help kids of all ages learn about race. Self.com. Retrieved from https://www.self.com/gallery/childrens-books-on-race

Franklin, A. J. (2004). *From brotherhood to manhood: How Black men rescue their relationships and dreams from the invisibility syndrome*. Hoboken, NJ: John Wiley & Sons.

Franklin, J. H., Chavez-Thompson, L., Johnson Cook, S. D., Kean, T. H., Oh, A. E., & Winter, W. E. (1998). One America in the 21st century: The President's Initiative on Race. Retrieved from https://clintonwhitehouse2.archives.gov/Initiatives/OneAmerica/PIR.pdf

Freire, P. (1970). *Pedagogy of the oppressed*. New York, NY: Continuum.

Gaertner, S. L., & Dovidio, J. F. (2005). Understanding and addressing contemporary racism: From aversive racism to the common ingroup identity model. *Journal of Social Issues*, 61(3), 615–639. doi:10.1111/j.1540-4560.2005.00424.x

Gaertner, S. L., Dovidio, J. F., Anastasio, P. A., Bachman, B. A., & Rust, M. C. (1993). The common ingroup identity model: Recategorization and the reduction of intergroup bias. *European Review of Social Psychology*, 4(1), 1–26. doi:10.1080/14792779343000004

Garcia, M. (2016). Cesar Chavez and the united farm workers movement. *Oxford Research Encyclopedia of American History*. doi:10.1093/acrefore/9780199329175.013.217

Gassam, J. (2019). *Diversity without inclusion is useless*. Forbes.

Gesiotto, M. (2016). Campus chaos: A message to campus crybabies. The Washington Times. Retrieved from https://www.washingtontimes.com/news/2016/nov/16/message-campuscrybabies

Gillion, D. Q. (2013). *The political power of protest: Minority activism and shifts in public policy*. Cambridge University Press.

Gitlin, T. (1980). *The whole world is watching: Mass media in the making and unmaking of the new left, with a new preface (first edition, with a new preface edition)*. University of California Press.

Goldhammer, Z. (2014). The whole world is watching Ferguson. The Atlantic. Retrieved from https://www.theatlantic.com/international/archive/2014/08/the-whole-word-is-watching-ferguson/378729/

Goodman, D. J. (2011). *Promoting diversity and social justice: Educating people from privileged groups*. New York, NY: Routledge. doi:10.4324/9780203829738

Goodman, L. A., Wilson, J. M., Helms, J. E., Greenstein, N., & Medzhitova, J. (2018). Becoming an advocate: Processes and outcomes of a relationship-centered advocacy training model. *The Counseling Psychologist, 46*(2), 122–153. doi:10.1177/0011000018757168

Gorski, P. C. (2019). Racial battle fatigue and activist burnout in racial justice activists of color at predominately white colleges and universities. *Race, Ethnicity and Education, 22*(1), 120.

Gurung, R. A. R. (2006). *Health psychology: A cultural approach*. Belmont, CA: Thomson Wadsworth.

Haley, A. (1964). *The autobiography of Malcolm X: As told to Alex Haley*. New York, NY.

Hanna, F. J., Talley, W. B., & Guindon, M. H. (2000). The power of perception: Toward a model of cultural oppression and liberation. *Journal of Counseling & Development, 78*(4), 430–441. doi:10.1002/j.1556-6676.2000.tb01926.x

Harris-Britt, A., Valrie, C. R., Kurtz-Costes, B., & Rowley, S. J. (2007). Perceived racial discrimination and self-esteem in African American youth: Racial socialization as a protective factor. *Journal of Research on Adolescence, 17*(4), 669–682. doi:10.1111/j.1532-7795.2007.00540.x

Hartocollis, A., & Bidgood, J. (2015). Racial discrimination protests ignite at colleges across the US. The New York Times. Retrieved from https://www.nytimes.com/2015/11/12/us/racial-discrimination-protests-ignite-at-colleges-across-the-us.html

Helms, J. E. (Ed.). (1990). *Contributions in Afro-American and African studies, no. 129. Black and White racial identity: Theory, research, and practice*. Greenwood Press.

Helms, J. E. (1995). An update of Helm's White and people of color racial identity models. In J. G. Ponterotto, J. M. Casas, L. A. Suzuki, & C. M. Alexander (Eds.), *Handbook of multicultural counseling* (pp. 181–198). Sage Publications, Inc.

Herek, G. M. (Ed.). (1998). *Stigma and sexual orientation: Understanding prejudice against lesbians, gay men and bisexuals*. Thousand Oaks, CA: SAGE Publications, Inc. doi:10.4135/9781452243818

Herek, G. M. (2001). Homosexuality. In W. E. Craighead & C. B. Nemeroff (Eds.), *The Corsini encyclopedia of psychology and behavioral science* (Vol. 2, 3rd ed., pp. 683–688). New York, NY: John Wiley and Sons.

Herek, G. M. (2006). Legal recognition of same-sex relationships in the United States: A social science perspective. *American Psychologist, 61*(6), 607–621.

Herek, G. M. (2009). Hate crimes and stigma-related experiences among sexual minority adults in the United States: Prevalence estimates from a national probability sample. *Journal of Interpersonal Violence*, 24, 54–74.

Hinton, E. L. (2004, March/April). Microinequities: When small slights lead to huge problems in the workplace. Diversity Inc. Retrieved from http://www.magazine. org/content/files/Microinequities.pdf

Hirschfeld, L. A. (2008). Children's developing conceptions of race. In S. Quintana & C. McKown (Eds.), *Handbook of race, racism, and the developing child* (pp. 37–54). John Wiley & Sons, Inc.

Hoefer, R. (2019). *Advocacy practice for social justice*. Oxford University Press.

Holder, A., Jackson, M. A., & Ponterotto, J. G. (2015). Racial microaggression experiences and coping strategies of Black women in corporate leadership. *Qualitative Psychology*, 2, 82–164. doi:10.1037/qup0000024

Holder, R. (2019b). On the intersectionality of religious and racial discrimination: A case study on the applicability of ICERD with respect to China's Uyghur Muslim Minority. *Religion & Human Rights*, 14(1), 1–30.

hooks, B. (1994). *Teaching to transgress: Education as the practice of freedom*. Routledge.

Houshmand, S., Spanierman, L. B., & De Stefano, J. (2019). "I have strong medicine, you see": Strategic responses to racial microaggressions. *Journal of Counseling Psychology*, 66, 651–664.

Huber, L. P., & Solorzano, D. G. (2014). Racial microaggressions as a tool for critical race research. *Race, Ethnicity and Education*, 18, 297–320. doi:10.1080/13613324.201 4.994173

Hunsberger, P. H. (2007). Reestablishing clinical psychology's subjective core. *The American Psychologist*, 62(6), 614–615.

Hunt, V., Layton, D., & Prince, S. (2015). Diversity matters. *McKinsey & Company*, 1(1), 15–29.

Hussain, S. (2020). Fear of coronavirus fuels racist sentiment targeting Asians. LA Times. Retrieved from https://www.latimes.com/california/story/2020-02-03/ fear-panic-around-the-coronavirus-fuels-racist-sentiment

Hyers, L. (2010). Alternatives to silence in face-to-face encounters with everyday heterosexism: Activism on the interpersonal front. *Journal of Homosexuality*, 57(4), 539–565. doi:10.1080/00918361003608749

Hyers, L. L. (2007). Resisting prejudice every day: Exploring women's assertive responses to anti-Black racism, anti-semitism, heterosexism, and sexism. *Sex Roles*, 56(1), 1–12. doi:10.1007/s11199-006-9142-8

Izadinia, M. (2012). Teacher educators as role models: A qualitative examination of student teacher's and teacher educator's views towards their roles. *Qualitative Report*, 17. Retrieved from https://eric.ed.gov/?id=EJ981479

Jacoby, J. E., & Kozie-Peak, B. (1997). The benefits of social support for mentally ill offenders: Prison-to-community transitions. *Behavioral Sciences & the Law*, 15(4), 483–501.

James, A. G. (2016). Parenting and protecting. Advocating microprotections toward loving and supporting Black parent-child relationships. National Council on Family Relations Report. Retrieved from https://www.ncpr.org/ncfr-report/focus/family-cultural-seachange–and-families/parenting-and-protecting-advocating

Jason, L. A., Beasley, C. R., & Hunter, B. A. (2015). Advocacy and social justice. In V. C. Scott & S. M. Wolfe (Eds.), Community psychology: Foundations for practice, 262–289.

Jean-Baptiste, C. O., & Green, T. (2020). Commentary on COVID-19 and African Americans. The numbers are Just a Tip of a Bigger Iceberg. SSRN Electronic Journal. doi:10.2139/ssrn.3596097

Johnson, D. J. (2004). Racial socialization strategies of parents in three Black private schools. In J. Bobo, C. Hudley, & C. Michel (Eds.), The black studies reader (pp. 391–400). Routledge.

Jones, C., & Shorter-Gooden, K. (2003). Shifting: The double lives of Black women in America. New York, NY: Harper Collins.

Jones, J. M. (1972). Prejudice and racism. Addison Wesley Publishers.

Jones, J. M. (1997). Prejudice and racism (2nd ed.). McGraw-Hill.

Jones, J. M., & Dovidio, J. F. (2018). Change, challenge, and prospects for a diversity paradigm in social psychology. Social Issues and Policy Review, 12(1), 7–56. doi: 10.1111/sipr.12039

Jones, J. M., & Rolon-Dow, R. (2018). Multidimensional models of microaggressions and microaffirmations. In G. C. Torino, D. P. Rivera, C. M. Capodilupo, K. L. Nadal, & D. W. Sue (Eds.), Microaggression theory: Influence and implications. (pp. 32–47). Hoboken, NJ: Wiley. doi:10.1002/9781119466642.

Jost, J. T., Barberá, P., Bonneau, R., Langer, M., Metzger, M., Nagler, J., ... Tucker, J. A. (2018). How social media facilitates political protest: Information, motivation, and social networks. Political Psychology, 39(S1), 85–118. doi:10.1111/pops.12478

Katz, P. A., & Kofkin, J. A. (1997). Race, gender, and young children. Developmental Psychopathology: Perspectives on Adjustment, Risk, and Disorder, 21, 51–74.

Kaur, H. (2020, May 8). The coronavirus pandemic is hitting black and brown Americans especially hard on all fronts. CNN. Retrieved from https://www.cnn.com/2020/05/08/us/coronavirus-pandemic-race-impact-trnd/index.html

Kawakami, K., Dunn, E., Karmali, F., & Dovidio, J. F. (2009). Mispredicting affective and behavioral responses to racism. Science, 323, 276–278. doi:10.1126/science.1164951

Kelly, D. J., Quinn, P. C., Slater, A. M., Lee, K., Gibson, A., Smith, M., ... Pascalis, O. (2005). Three-month-olds, but not newborns, prefer own-race faces. Developmental Science, 8(6), F31–F36.

Kessler, R. C., & McLeod, J. D. (1984). Sex differences in vulnerability to undesirable life events. American Sociological Review, 49, 620–631.

Khazan, O. (2017). Percent of women killed by husbands or boyfriends. The Atlantic. Retrieved from https://www.theatlantic.com/health/archive/2017/07/homicides-women/534306/

Kim, H. S., Sherman, D. K., & Taylor, S. E. (2008). Culture and social support. *American Psychologist, 63*(6), 518.

Kim, J. Y., Nguyen, D., & Block, C. (2019). The 360-degree experience of workplace microaggressions: Who commits them? How do individuals respond? What are the consequences? In *Microaggressions Theory: Influence and Implications*. Hoboken, NJ: Wiley. doi:10.1002/9781119466642.ch10

Kiselica, M. S. (1999). *Confronting prejudice and racism during multicultural training*. ACA.

Kivel, P. (1996). *Uprooting racism: How White people can work for racial justice*. New Society.

Knapp, J. A., Snavely, L., & Klimczyk, L. (2012). Speaking up: Empowering individuals to promote tolerance in the academic library. *Library Leadership & Management, 26*, 1. doi:10.5860/llm.v26i1.5508

Kohl, S. (n.d.). Modeling positive behavior in the classroom. NEA. Retrieved from http://www.nea.org//tools/52062.htm

Kolb, B., & Whishaw, I. Q. (2009). *Fundamentals of human neuropsychology*. Macmillan.

Kozan, S., & Blustein, D. L. (2018). Implementing social change: A qualitative analysis of counseling psychologists' engagement in advocacy. *The Counseling Psychologist, 46*(2), 154–189. doi:10.1177/0011000018756882

Kriesberg, L. (2007). *Constructive conflicts: From escalation to resolution*. Rowman & Littlefield.

Lancy, D. F., Bock, J., & Gaskins, S. (2010). *The anthropology of learning in childhood*. Rowman Altamira.

Latané, B., & Darley, J. M. (1968). Group inhibition of bystander intervention in emergencies. *Journal of Personality and Social Psychology, 10*, 215–221. doi:10.1037/h0026570

Latané, B., & Darley, J. M. (1970). *The unresponsive bystander: Why doesn't he help?* Appleton-Century-Crofts.

Laughter, J. (2014). Toward a theory of micro-kindness: Developing positive actions in multicultural education. *International Journal of Multicultural Education, 16*(2), 2–14. doi:10.18251/ijme.v16i2.842

Laurencin, C. T., & McClinton, A. (2020). The COVID-19 pandemic: A call to action to identify and address racial and ethnic disparities. *Journal of Racial and Ethnic Health Disparities, 7*(3), 398–402. doi:10.1007/s40615-020-00756-0

Lazarus, R. S. (2000). Toward better research on stress and coping. *American Psychologist, 55*, 665–673. doi:10.1037/0003-066X.55.6.665

Lazarus, R. S., & Folkman, S. (1984). *Stress, appraisal, and coping*. New York, NY: Springer.

Lee, E. A., Soto, J. A., Swim, J. K., & Bernstein, M. J. (2012). Bitter reproach or sweet revenge: Cultural differences in response to racism. *Personality & Social Psychology Bulletin*, 38(7), 920–932. doi:10.1177/0146167212440292

Lerner, M. (2016). What happened on election day. The New York Times. Retrieved from https://www.nytimes.com/interactive/projects/cp/opinion/election-night-2016/stopshaming-trump-supporters

Levine, M., Cassidy, C., Brazier, G., & Reicher, S. (2002). Self-categorization and bystander non-intervention: Two experimental studies1. *Journal of Applied Social Psychology*, 32(7), 1452–1463. doi:10.1111/j.1559-1816.2002.tb01446.x

Lieberman, M. D. (2013). *Social: Why our brains are wired to connect*. Oxford: OUP.

Liu, W. M., Liu, R. Z., Garrison, Y. L., Kim, J. Y. C., Chan, L., Ho, Y. C. S., & Yeung, C. W. (2019). Racial trauma, microaggressions, and becoming racially innocuous: The role of acculturation and White supremacist ideology. *American Psychologist*, 74(1), 143–155. doi:10.1037/amp0000368

Loewen, J. W. (2018a). *Lies my teacher told me: Everything your American history textbook got wrong*. The New Press.

Loewen, J. W. (2018b). *Sundown towns: A hidden dimension of American racism*. The New Press.

Lukianoff, G., & Haidt, J. (2015). The coddling of the American mind. *The Atlantic*, 316(2), 42–52.

Malott, K. M., Schaefle, S., Paone, T. R., Cates, J., & Haizlip, B. (2019). Challenges and coping mechanisms of whites committed to antiracism. *Journal of Counseling & Development*, 97(1), 86–97.

Marcelo, A. K., & Yates, T. M. (2018). Young children's ethnic/racial identity moderates the impact of early discrimination behaviors on child behavior problems. *Cultural Diversity and Ethnic Minority Psychology*, 9(1), C2–C2. doi:10.1037/1099-9809.9.1.c2

Martic, K. (2018). Top 10 benefits of diversity in the workplace. Retrieved from https://www.talentlyft.com/en/blog/article/244/top-10-benefits-of-diversity-in-the-workplace-infographic-included

Maslach, C., Jackson, S. E., Leiter, M. P., Schaufeli, W. B., & Schwab, R. L. (1986). *Maslach burnout inventory* (Vol. 21, pp. 3463–3464). Consulting Psychologists Press.

Maton, K. I. (2017). *Influencing social policy: Applied psychology serving the public interest*. Oxford University Press.

Mazzula, S. L., & Campón, R. R. (2018). Microaggressions: Toxic rain in health care. In *Microaggression theory: Influence and implications* (pp. 178–193). Hoboken, NJ: Wiley. doi:10.1002/9781119466642.ch11

McMahon, A. M. (2010). Does workplace diversity matter? A survey of empirical studies on diversity and firm performance, 2000–09. *Journal of Diversity Management*, 5(2), 37–48. doi:10.19030/jdm.v5i2.808

Mellor, D. (2004). Responses to racism: A taxonomy of coping styles used by Aboriginal Australians. *American Journal of Orthopsychiatry*, 74(1), 56–71. doi:10.1037/0002-9432.74.1.56

Melton, M. L. (2018). Ally, activist, advocate: Addressing role complexities for the multiculturally competent psychologist. *Professional Psychology: Research and Practice*, 49(1), 83. doi:10.1037/pro0000175

Meyer, I. H. (1995). Minority stress and mental health in gay men. *Journal of Health and Social Behavior*, 36(1), 38–56.

Meyer, I. H. (2003). Prejudice, social stress, and mental health in lesbian, gay, and bisexual populations: Conceptual issues and research evidence. *Psychological Bulletin*, 129(5), 674–697.

Michael, A., & Conger, M. C. (2009). Becoming an anti-racist White ally: How a White affinity group can help. *Perspectives on Urban Education*, 6(1), 56–60.

Milan, S. (2015). From social movements to cloud protesting: The evolution of collective identity. *Information, Communication & Society*, 18(8), 887–900. doi:10.1080/1369118X.2015.1043135

Miller, C. T., & Major, B. (2000). Coping with stigma and prejudice. In T. F. Heatherton, R. E. Kleck, M. R. Hebl, & J. G. Hull (Eds.). *The Social Psychology of Stigma*, 243–272. New York: Guilford Press.

Miller, M. J., Keum, B. T., Thai, C. J., Lu, Y., Truong, N. N., Huh, G. A., … Ahn, L. H. (2018). Practice recommendations for addressing racism: A content analysis of the counseling psychology literature. *Journal of Counseling Psychology*, 65(6), 669–680. doi:10.1037/cou0000306

Mio, J. S., & Roades, L. A. (2003). Building bridges in the 21st century: Allies and the power of human connection across demographic divides. In J. S. Mio & G. Y. Iwamasa (Eds.), *Culturally diverse mental health: The challenges of research and resistance* (pp. 105–117). Brunner-Routledge.

Moisuc, A., Brauer, M., Fonseca, A., Chaurand, N., & Greitemeyer, T. (2018). Individual differences in social control: Who 'speaks up' when witnessing uncivil, discriminatory, and immoral behaviours?. *British Journal of Social Psychology*, 57(3), 524–546.

Murphy, M. C., Richeson, J. A., Shelton, J. N., Rheinschmidt, M. L., & Bergsieker, H. B. (2013). Cognitive costs of contemporary prejudice. *Group Processes & Intergroup Relations*, 16(5), 560–571.

Myers, P. C. (2014). Martin Luther King, Jr. and the American dream. The Heritage Foundation. Retrieved from http://thf-media.s3.amazonaws.com/2014/pdf/FP50.pdf

Myers, P. C. (2017). The limits and dangers of civil disobedience: The case of Martin Luther King, Jr. The Heritage Foundation. Retrieved from https://www.heritage.org/civil-society/report/the-limits-and-dangers-civil-disobedience-the-case-martin-luther-king-jr

Nadal, K. L. (2017). "Let's get in formation": On becoming a psychologist–activist in the 21st century. *American Psychologist*, 72(9), 935.

Nadal, K. L., Griffin, K. E., Wong, Y., Hamit, S., & Rasmus, M. (2014). The impact of racial microaggressions on mental health: Counseling implications for clients of color. *Journal of Counseling & Development*, 92(1), 57–66. doi:10.1002/j.1556-6676.2014.00130.x

Nelson, J. K., Dunn, K. M., & Paradies, Y. (2011). Bystander anti-racism: A review of the literature. *Analyses of Social Issues and Public Policy*, 11(1), 263–284.

Nepstad, S. E. (2004). Religion, violence, and peacemaking. *Journal for the Scientific Study of Religion*, 43(3), 297–301.

Neville, H. A., Awad, G. H., Brooks, J. E., Flores, M. P., & Bluemel, J. (2013). Color-blind racial ideology: Theory, training, and measurement implications in psychology. *American Psychologist*, 68(6), 455.

Neville, H. A., Gallardo, M. E., & Sue, D. W. (2016). *The myth of racial color blindness.* Washington, DC: American Psychological Association.

Norton, M. I., Sommers, S. R., Apfelbaum, E. P., Pura, N., & Ariely, D. (2006). Color blindness and interracial interaction: Playing the political correctness game. *Psychological Science*, 17(11), 949–953.

Nuttbrock, L., Rosenblum, A., & Blumenstein, R. (2002). Transgender identity affirmation and mental health. *International Journal of Transgenderism*, 6(4), 117–120.

Obear, K. (2017). ... *But I'm NOT racist!: Tools for well-meaning whites.* Difference Press.

Olle, C. D. (2018). Breaking institutional habits: A critical paradigm for social change agents in psychology. *The Counseling Psychologist*, 46(2), 190–212. doi:10.1177/0011000018760597

Ong, A. D., Burrow, A. L., Fuller-Rowell, T. E., Ja, N. M., & Sue, D. W. (2013). Racial microaggressions and daily well-being among Asian Americans. *Journal of Counseling Psychology*, 60(2), 188.

Owen, J., Tao, K. W., Drinane, J. M., Hook, J., Davis, D. E., & Kune, N. F. (2016). Client perceptions of therapists' multicultural orientation: Cultural (missed) opportunities and cultural humility. *Professional Psychology: Research and Practice*, 47(1), 30.

Ozbay, F., Johnson, D. C., Dimoulas, E., Morgan, C. A., III, Charney, D., & Southwick, S. (2007). Social support and resilience to stress: From neurobiology to clinical practice. *Psychiatry (Edgmont)*, 4(5), 35.

Palmer, P. J. (2007). *The courage to teach: Exploring the inner landscape of a teacher's life* (10th Anniversary edition). Jossey-Bass.

Parham, T. A. (1993). White researchers conducting multicultural counseling research: Can their efforts be "Mo Betta"? *The Counseling Psychologist*, 21(2), 250–256. doi:10.1177/0011000093212009

Pasque, P. A., Chesler, M. A., Charbeneau, J., & Carlson, C. (2013). Pedagogical approaches to student racial conflict in the classroom. *Journal of Diversity in Higher Education*, 6(1), 1.

Pearson, J. E. (1986). The definition and measurement of social support. *Journal of Counseling & Development*, 64, 390–394.

Pérez Huber, L., & Solorzano, D. G. (2015). Racial microaggressions as a tool for critical race research. *Race Ethnicity and Education*, 18(3), 297–320. doi:10.1080/1361332 4.2014.994173

Pierce, C. M. (1974). Psychiatric problems of the Black minority. In S. Aneti & G. Caplan (Eds.), *American handbook of psychiatry*, 2nd ed. (pp. 512–523). New York: Basic Books.

Plant, E. A., & Peruche, B. M. (2005). The consequences of race for police officers' responses to criminal suspects. *Psychological Science*, 16(3), 180–183. doi:10.1111/ j.0956-7976.2005.00800.x

Plaut, V. C., Thomas, K. M., & Goren, M. J. (2009). Is multiculturalism or color blindness better for minorities? *Psychological Science*, 20(4), 444–446.

Plous, S. (2000). Responding to overt displays of prejudice: A role-playing exercise. *Teaching of Psychology*, 27(3), 198–200. doi:10.1207/S15328023TOP2703_07

Poell, T. (2019). Social media, temporality, and the legitimacy of protest. *Social Movement Studies*, doi:10.1080/14742837.2019.1605287

Potok, M. (2017). The Trump effect: The campaign language of the man who would become president sparks hate violence, bullying, before and after the election. *Southern Poverty Law Center Intelligence Report*, 162. https://www.google.com/ search?client=firefox-b-1-d&q=Potok%2C+M.+%282017%29.+The+Trump+effect% 3A+The+campaign+language+of+the+man+who+would+become+president+spa rks+hate+violence%2C+bullying%2C+before+and+after+the+election.+Southern+ Poverty+Law+Center+Intelligence+Report%2C+162.

Powell, C., Demetriou, C., & Fisher, A. (2013). Micro-affirmations in Academic Advising: Small Acts, Big Impact. *Mentor: An Academic Advising Journal*, 15. doi: 10.26209/MJ1561286

President's Initiative on Race. (1998). One America in the 21st century. Washington, DC: U. S. Government Printing Office. Retrieved from https://www.ncjrs.gov/ pdffiles/173431.pdf

President's Initiative on Race. (1999). Pathways to one America in the 21st century. Washington, DC: U. S. Government Printing Office. Retrieved from https:// clintonwhitehouse5.archives.gov/media/pdf/ppreport.pdf

Purdie-Vaughns, V., Steele, C. M., Davies, P. G., Ditlmann, R., & Crosby, J. R. (2008). Social identity contingencies: How diversity cues signal threat or safety for African Americans in mainstream institutions. *Journal of Personality and Social Psychology*, 94(4), 615. doi:10.1037/0022-3514.94.4.615

Ramsey, S., & Birk, J. (1983). Preparation of North Americans for interactions with Japanese: Considerations of language and communication style. In D. Landis & R. W. Brislin (Eds.), *Handbook of intercultural training, volume III* (pp. 227–259). Pergamon.

Rasinski, H. M., & Czopp, A. M. (2010). The effect of target status on witnesses' reactions to confrontations of bias. *Basic and Applied Social Psychology*, 32(1), 8–16. doi:10.1080/01973530903539754

Ratts, M. J., Singh, A. A., Nassar-McMillan, S., Butler, S. K., & McCullough, J. R. (2016). Multicultural and social justice counseling competencies: Guidelines for the counseling profession. *Journal of Multicultural Counseling and Development*, 44(1), 28–48. doi:10.1002/jmcd.12035

Reason, R. D., & Broido, E. M. (2005). Issues and strategies for social justice allies (and the student affairs professionals who hope to encour- age them). *New Directions for Student Services*, 110, 81–89. doi:10.1002/ss.167

Rhodan, M. (2018). Here are the facts about President Trump's family separation policy. Time Magazine, p. 20. Retrieved from https://time.com/5314769/family-separation-policy-donald-trump/

Roberson, Q. M., & Park, H. J. (2007). Examining the link between diversity and firm performance: The effects of diversity reputation and leader racial diversity. *Group & Organization Management*, 32(5), 548–568. doi:10.1177/1059601106291124

Rowe, M. (2008). Micro-affirmations and micro-inequities. *Journal of the International Ombudsman Association*, 1(1), 45–48.

Salvatore, J., & Shelton, J. N. (2007). Cognitive costs of exposure to racial prejudice. *Psychological Science*, 18(9), 810–815.

Sanchez-Hucles, J., & Jones, N. (2005). Breaking the silence around race in training, practice, and research. *The Counseling Psychologist*, 33(4), 547–558.

Satell, G., & Popovic, S. (2017). How protests become successful social movements. Harvard Business Review. Retrieved from https://hbr.org/2017/01/how-protests-become-successful-social-movements

Schacht, T. E. (2008). A broader view of racial microaggression in psychotherapy. *The American Psychologist*, 63(4), 273. doi:10.1037/0003-066x.63.4.273

Schneider, K. J. (1998). Toward a science of the heart: Romanticism and the revival of psychology. *American Psychologist*, 53(3), 277. doi:10.1037/0003-066x.53.3.277

Scully, M. (2005). Bystander awareness: Skills for effective managers. In D. Ancona, T. Kochan, M. Scully, J. Van Maanen, & D. E. Westney *Managing for the future: Organizational behavior and processes* (pp. M11: 18–27). Cincinnati, OH: Southwestern.

Scully, M., & Rowe, M. (2009). Bystander training within organizations. *Journal of the International Ombudsman Association*, 2(1), 1–9.

Sears, D. O. (1988). Symbolic racism. In P. A. Katz & D. A. Taylor (Eds.), *Eliminating racism perspectives in social psychology (A series of texts and monographs)* (pp. 53–84). Springer. doi:10.1007/978-1-4899-0818-6_4

Sharp, G. (1973). *The politics of nonviolent action: The dynamics of nonviolent action.* P. Sargent Publisher.

Shelton, J. N., Richeson, J. A., Salvatore, J., & Hill, D. M. (2006). Silence is not golden: The intrapersonal consequences of not confronting prejudice. In S. Levin & C. van Laar (Eds.), *The Claremont symposium on Applied Social Psychology. Stigma and group inequality: Social psychological perspectives* (pp. 65–81). Washington, DC: Lawrence Erlbaum Associates Publishers,

Shorter-Gooden, K. (2004). Multiple resistance strategies: How African American women cope with racism and sexism. *The Journal of Black Psychology*, 30, 406–425. doi:10.1177/0095798404266050

Singelis, T. M. (1994). Nonverbal communications in intercultural interactions. In R. W. Brislin & T. Yoshida (Eds.), *Improving intercultural interactions* (pp. 268–294). Sage.

Smith, W. A., Hung, M., & Franklin, J. D. (2011). Racial Battle Fatigue and the miseducation of black men: Racial microaggressions, societal problems, and environmental stress. *The Journal of Negro Education*, 80(1), 63–82.

Smithey, L. (2009). Social movement strategy, tactics, and collective identity. *Sociology Compass*, 3(4), 658–671. doi:10.1111/j.1751-9020.2009.00218.x

Smithey, R. A., & Kurtz, L. R. (2003). Parading persuasion: Nonviolent collective action as discourse in Northern Ireland. *Research in Social Movements, Conflict and Change*, 24, 319–359. doi:10.1016/S0163-786X(03)80029-0

Solorzano, D., Ceja, M., & Yosso, T. (2000). Critical race theory, racial microaggressions, and campus racial climate: The experiences of African American college students. *The Journal of Negro Education*, 69(1/2), 60–73.

Southern Poverty Law Center. (2018). America the trumped: 10 ways the administration attacked civil rights in year one. Retrieved from https://www.splcenter.org/20180119/america-trumped-10-ways-administration-attacked-civil-rights-year-one

Southern Poverty Law Center. (2019). Family separation. Retrieved from https://www.splcenter.org/our-issues/immigrant-justice/family-separation

Spanierman, L. B., & Heppner, M. J. (2004). Psychosocial costs of racism to Whites scale (PCRW): Construction and initial validation. *Journal of Counseling Psychology*, 51(2), 249. doi:10.1037/0022-0167.51.2.249

Spanierman, L. B., Poteat, V. P., Beer, A. M., & Armstrong, P. I. (2006). Psychosocial costs of racism to whites: Exploring patterns through cluster analysis. *Journal of Counseling Psychology*, 53(4), 434–441. doi:10.1037/0022-0167.53.4.434

Spanierman, L. B., & Smith, L. (2017). Confronting white hegemony: A moral imperative for the helping professions. *The Counseling Psychologist*, 45(5), 727–736. doi:10.1177/0011000017719550

Spanierman, L. B., Todd, N. R., & Anderson, C. J. (2009). Psychosocial costs of racism to Whites: Understanding patterns among university students. *Journal of Counseling Psychology*, 56(2), 239–252. doi:10.1037/a0015432

Speight, S. L. (2007). Internalized racism: One more piece of the puzzle. *The Counseling Psychologist*, 35, 126–134. doi:10.1177/0011000006295119

Steinfeldt, J. A., Hyman, J., & Steinfeldt, M. C. (2019). Environmental microaggressions: Context, symbols, and mascots. In *Microaggression theory: Influence and limitations* (pp. 213–225). Wiley. doi:10.1002/9781119466642.ch13

Steinfeldt, J. A., & Steinfeldt, M. C. (2012). Components of a training intervention designed to produce attitudinal change toward native-themed mascots, nicknames, and logos. *Counselor Education and Supervision*, 51, 17–32. doi:10.1002/j.1556-6978.2012.00002.x

Stephen, B. (2015). How Black Lives Matter uses social media to fight the power. *Wired*. Retrieved from https://www.wired.com/2015/10/how-black-lives-matter-uses-social-media-to-fight-the-power/

Sternberg, R. J. (2001). *Wisdom, intelligence, and creativity synthesized*. Cambridge University Press.

Sternberg, R. J. (2003). WICS as a model of giftedness. *High Ability Studies*, 14(2), 109–137. doi:10.1080/1359813032000163807

Sue, D. W. (1995). Multicultural organizational development: Implications for the counseling profession.

Sue, D. W. (2003). *Overcoming our racism: The journey to liberation*. John Wiley & Sons.

Sue, D. W. (2005). Racism and the conspiracy of silence: Presidential address. *The Counseling Psychologist*, 33(1), 100–114. doi:10.1177/0011000004270686

Sue, D. W. (2006). The invisible whiteness of being: Whiteness, white supremacy, white privilege, and racism. In M. Constantine & D. W. Sue (Eds.), *Addressing racism: Facilitating cultural competence in mental health and educational settings* (pp. 15–30). Hoboken, NJ: John Wiley & Sons Inc.

Sue, D. W. (2008). Multicultural organizational consultation: A social justice perspective. *Consulting Psychology Journal: Practice and Research*, 60(2), 157–169. doi:10.1037/0736-9735.60.2.157

Sue, D. W. (2010a). Microaggressions, marginality, and oppression. In D. W. Sue (Ed.). *Microaggressions and marginality* (pp. 3–22).

Sue, D. W. (2010b). *Microaggressions in everyday life: Race, gender, and sexual orientation*. John Wiley & Sons.

Sue, D. W. (2015a). *Race talk and the conspiracy of silence: Understanding and facilitating difficult dialogues on race*. Hoboken, NJ: John Wiley & Sons. doi:10.1080/15210960.2016.1125273

Sue, D. W. (2015b). Therapeutic harm and cultural oppression. *The Counseling Psychologist*, 43(3), 359–369.

Sue, D. W. (2017a). Microaggressions and "evidence": Empirical or experiential reality? *Perspectives on Psychological Science*, 12(1), 170–172. doi:10.1177/1745691616664437

Sue, D. W. (2017b). The challenges of becoming a White Ally. *The Counseling Psychologist*, 45(5), 706–716. doi:10.1177/0011000017719323

Sue, D. W. (2019). Microaggressions and student activism. In G. C. Torino, D. P. Rivera, C. M. Capodilupo, K. L. Nadal, & D. W. Sue (Eds.), *Microaggression theory: Influence and implications* (pp. 229–243). Hoboken, NJ: John Wiley & Sons. doi:10.1002/9781119466642.ch14

Sue, D. W., Alsaidi, S., Awad, M. N., Glaeser, E., Calle, C. Z., & Mendez, N. (2019). Disarming racial microaggressions: Microintervention strategies for targets, White allies, and bystanders. *American Psychologist*, 74(1), 128.

Sue, D. W., Capodilupo, C. M., Torino, G. C., Bucceri, J. M., Holder, A., Nadal, K. L., & Esquilin, M. (2007). Racial microaggressions in everyday life: Implications for clinical practice. *American Psychologist*, 62(4), 271.

Sue, D. W., Lin, A. I., Torino, G. C., Capodilupo, C. M., & Rivera, D. P. (2009). Racial microaggressions and difficult dialogues on race in the classroom. *Cultural Diversity and Ethnic Minority Psychology*, 15(2), 183. doi:10.1037/a0014191

Sue, D. W., Parham, T. A., & Santiago, G. B. (1998). The changing face of work in the United States: Implications for individual, institutional, and societal survival. *Cultural Diversity and Mental Health*, 4(3), 153–164. doi:10.1037/1099-9809.4.3.153

Sue, D. W., Rivera, D. P., Capodilupo, C. M., Lin, A. I., & Torino, G. C. (2010). Racial dialogues and White trainee fears: Implications for education and training. *Cultural Diversity and Ethnic Minority Psychology*, 16(2), 206.

Sue, D. W., Rivera, D. P., Watkins, N. L., Kim, R. H., Kim, S., & Williams, C. D. (2011). Racial dialogues: Challenges faculty of color face in the classroom. *Cultural Diversity and Ethnic Minority Psychology*, 17(3), 331–340. doi:10.1037/a0024190

Sue, D. W., & Spanierman, L. (2020). *Microaggressions in everyday life* (2nd ed.). Wiley.

Sue, D. W., & Sue, D. (2015). *Counseling the culturally diverse: Theory and practice* (7th ed.). John Wiley & Sons.

Sue, D. W., Sue, D., Neville, H. A., & Smith, L. (2019). *Counseling the culturally diverse: Theory and practice* (8th ed.). John Wiley & Sons.

Sue, D. W., Torino, G. C., Capodilupo, C. M., Rivera, D. P., & Lin, A. I. (2009). How White faculty perceive and react to difficult dialogues on race: Implications for education and training. *The Counseling Psychologist*, 37(8), 1090–1115. doi:10.1177/0011000009340443

Sue, S., Sue, D. W., Zane, N., & Wong, H. Z. (1985). Where are the Asian American leaders and top executives?. *P/AAMHRC Review*, 4, 13–15.

Sunshower Learning. (2007). *Ouch! That Stereotype Hurts.* International Training and Development, LLC. www.Ouch-Video.com.

Swim, J. K., Hyers, L. L., Cohen, L. L., & Ferguson, M. J. (2001). Everyday sexism: Evidence for its incidence, nature, and psychological impact from three daily diary studies. *Journal of Social Issues*, 57(1), 31–53. doi:10.1111/0022-4537.00200

Tatum, B. D. (1992). Talking about race, learning about racism: The application of racial identity development theory in the classroom. *Harvard Educational Review*, 62(1), 1–24. doi:10.17763/haer.62.1.146k5v980r703023

Tatum, B. D. (1997). *Why are all the Black kids sitting in the cafeteria? And other conversations about race.* New York, NY: Basic Books. doi:10.2202/1940-1639.1132

Tatum, B. D. (2002). Breaking the silence. In P. S. Rothenberg (Ed.) *White privilege: Essential readings on the other side of racism* (pp. 115–120). Worth Publishers. doi:10.4324/9780429494772-2

Taylor, S. J. (2017). Could "social justice benefits" be the newest employment trend? *Fast Company.* Retrieved from https://www.fastcompany.com/40407672/could-social-justice-benefits-be-the-newest-employment-trend

Terrell, K. (2016). Say what? Black lives matter event cancelled due to death threats. *Hello Beautiful.* Retrieved from https://hellobeautiful.com/2855225/say-what-black-lives-matter-event-cancelled-due-to-death-threats

Thomas, K. R. (2008). Macrononsense in multiculturalism. *American Psychologist*, 63(4), 274275. doi:10.1037/0003-066X.63.4.274

Toporek, R. L., & Ahluwalia, M. K. (2012). *Taking action, creating social change through strength, solidarity, strategy, & sustainability.* Cognella Press.

Toporek, R. L., & Worthington, R. L. (2014). Integrating service learning and difficult dialogues pedagogy to advance social justice training. *The Counseling Psychologist*, 42(7), 919–945. doi:10.1177/0011000014545090

Torino, G. C., Rivera, D. P., Capodilupo, C. M., Nadal, K. L., & Sue, D. W. (2018). *Microaggression theory: Influence and implications.* Hoboken, NJ: Wiley. doi:10.1002/9781119466642

Turner, C. B., & Wilson, W. J. (1976). Dimensions of racial ideology: A study of urban black attitudes. *Journal of Social Issues*, 32(2), 139–152.

Turner, R. H., & Killian, L. M. (1987). *Collective behavior* (Subsequent edition). Englewood Cliffs, NJ: Pearson College Div.

Uchino, B. N. (2009). Understanding the links between social support and physical health: A life-span perspective with emphasis on the separability of perceived and received support. *Perspectives on Psychological Science*, 4(3), 236–255.

Utsey, S., Gernat, C. A., & Hammer, L. (2005). Examining white counselor trainees' reactions to racial issues in counseling and supervision dyads. *The Counseling Psychologist*, 33(449), 478.

van Zomeren, M., Kutlaca, M., & Turner-Zwinkels, F. (2018). Integrating who "we" are with what "we" (will not) stand for: A further extension of the Social Identity Model of collective action. *European Review of Social Psychology*, 29(1), 122–160. doi: 10.1080/10463283.2018.1479347

van Zomeren, M., Postmes, T., & Spears, R. (2008). Toward an integrative social identity model of collective action: A quantitative research synthesis of three socio-psychological perspectives. *Psychological Bulletin*, 134, 504–535. doi:10.1037/0033-2909.134.4.504

Vasquez, M. J. (2012). Psychology and social justice: Why we do what we do. *American Psychologist*, 67(5), 337. doi:10.1037/e692142011-001

Warren, J. W. (2000). Masters in the field: White talk, White privilege, White biases. In F. W. Twine & J. W. Warren (Eds.), *Racing research, researching race: Methodological dilemmas in critical race studies* (pp. 135–164). New York University Press. doi:10.2307/3089378

Waters, A. (2010). Book review. *Injustice. Local Economy*, 25, 523–525. doi:10.1080/0269 0942.2010.525995

Watts, R. J., Diemer, M. A., & Voight, A. M. (2011). Critical consciousness: Current status and future directions. *New Directions for Child and Adolescent Development*, 2011(134), 43–57. doi:10.1002/cd.31

Weinstein, N., & Ryan, R. M. (2010). When helping helps: Autonomous motivation for prosocial behavior and its influence on well-being for the helper and recipient. *Journal of Personality and Social Psychology*, 98(2), 222.

West, K. (2019). Testing hypersensitive responses: Ethnic minorities are not more sensitive to microaggressions, they just experience them more frequently. *Personality and Social Psychology Bulletin*, 45(11), 1619–1632.

Williams, D. R., & Williams-Morris, R. (2000). Racism and mental health: The African American experience. *Ethnicity & Health*, 5(3–4), 243–268. doi:10.1080/713667453

Willoughby, B. (2005). Speak up: Responding to everyday bigotry. Southern Poverty Law Center. Retrieved from https://www.splcenter.org/20150125/speak-responding-everyday-bigotry

Willoughby, B. (2012). Speak up at school: How to respond to everyday prejudice, bias and stereotypes. A guide for teachers. Retrieved from https://eric.ed.gov/?id=ED541256

Winter, S. (1977). Rooting out racism. *Issues in Radical Therapy*, 17, 24–30.

Young, G., & Davis-Russell, E. (2002). The vicissitudes of cultural competence: Dealing with difficult classroom dialogue. In E. Davis-Russell (Ed.), *The California School of Professional. Psychology handbook of multicultural education, research, intervention, and training* (pp. 37–53). Jossey-Bass.

Young, K. S., & Anderson, M. R. (2019). Microaggressions in higher education: Embracing educative spaces. In G. Torino, D. Rivera, C. Capodilupo, K. NadaL, & D. W. Sue (Eds.), *Microaggression theory: Influence and limitations* (pp. 291–305). Hoboken, NJ: Wiley. doi:10.1002/9781119466642.ch18

Young, R. J. (2003). *Postcolonialism: A very short introduction.* Oxford: OUP.

Zou, L. X., & Dickter, C. L. (2013). Perceptions of racial confrontation: The role of color blindness and comment ambiguity. *Cultural Diversity and Ethnic Minority Psychology*, 19(1), 92. doi:10.1037/a0031115

Name Index

Aboud, F. E., 75, 172
Accapadi, M. M., 64
Aguilar, L., 50, 52, 53, 92, 115, 131, 182
Ahluwalia, M. K., 189
Ahn, L. H., 183
Akili, Y., 73
Albert Einstein Institution, 133, 134
American Psychological Association
   (APA), 2, 36, 37, 74, 76, 78, 79, 80, 83,
   99, 116, 118, 119, 121, 122, 171
Anastasio, P. A., 148
Anderson, C. J., 46
Anderson, M., 143, 144
Anderson, M. R., 25, 26, 49, 51, 101, 104
Anderson, N., 25
Anderson, R. E., 29, 34, 35, 37, 38, 49, 50,
   61, 74, 83, 114, 147, 171, 172, 174
Andrews, E., 148
Angelou, M., 76
APA. *See* American Psychological
   Association (APA)

Apfelbaum, E. P., 74, 81
Ariely, D., 74
Armstrong, P. I., 56
Ashburn-Nardo, L., 21, 39, 49, 51, 63,
   72, 88, 115, 182
Awad, G. H., 54, 78
Ayres, C., 133, 136, 137

Bachman, B. A., 148
Balaji, A. B., 86
Banaji, M. R., 74, 75, 77, 172
Bandura, A., 171, 172, 173
Banks, K., 70, 84, 85, 100, 120, 133, 136,
   138, 139, 146, 159, 164, 185, 189
Baron, A. S., 74, 75, 172
Bauer, M., 53
Baumeister, R. F., 84
Beasley, C. R., 90, 133, 185, 189
Beatty, D., 6
Beer, A. M., 56
Bell, L. A., 59, 61, 80, 81, 83

Microintervention Strategies, First Edition. Derald Wing Sue, Cassandra Z. Calle, Narolyn Mendez, Sarah Alsaidi, and Elizabeth Glaeser.

Lin, A. I., 62, 80, 82
Liu, W. M., 36
Loche, L., 32
Loche, R. W., 32
Loewen, J. W., 83, 175
Lu, Y., 183
Lukianoff, G., 29, 78, 79

Major, B., 39, 77
Malott, K. M., 68, 69
Manning, J., 29, 78
Marcelo, A. K., 36, 50
Martic, K., 122, 123, 124
Maslach, C., 70
Matoka, K., 146
Maton, K. I., 89, 99, 100
Mazzula, S. L., 17
McClinton, A., 13
McCullough, J. R., 2, 185
McLeod, J. D., 87
McMahon, A. M., 123
Medzhitova, J., 3
Mellor, D., 6, 17, 18, 51, 151, 159
Melton, M. L., 50, 189
Merryman, A., 172
Meyer, I. H., 183
Michael, A., 69, 82
Milan, S., 146
Miller, C. T., 39
Miller, M. J., 29, 32, 183
Mio, J. S., 50, 53
Moisuc, A., 86
Monteith, M. J., 51, 53
Morris, K. A., 21, 49, 63, 72, 88, 115
Murphy, M. C., 77
Myers, P. C., 68, 71, 137

Nadal, K. L., 3, 77, 78, 93, 183, 184
Nassar-McMillan, S., 2, 185

Navarrete, C. D., 88
Nelson, J. K., 46, 50, 51, 52, 53, 82, 85
Nepstad, S. E., 134
Neville, H. A., 3, 23, 25, 46, 54, 74, 78, 83,
    112, 118, 119, 162, 163
Newton, V. A., 39
Nguyen, D., 16, 102
Norton, M. I., 74, 81
Nuttbrock, L., 184

Obear, K., 2, 18, 20, 39, 100
Olle, C. D., 2, 40, 68, 72, 88, 133
Ong, A. D., 66, 78
Ostrove, J. M., 2, 19, 50, 52
Owen, J., 74
Ozbay, F., 85, 86, 87, 88

Palmer, P. J., 83
Panter, A. T., 32
Paone, T. R., 69
Paradies, Y., 46, 82
Parham, T. A., 84, 124
Park, H. J., 123, 124
Pasque, P. A., 80
Pearson, J. E., 85
Pencille, M., 6
Pérez Huber, L., 7, 9, 29, 32
Peruche, B. M., 117
Pierce, C. M., 9, 77
Plant, E. A., 117
Plaut, V. C., 54, 83
Plous, S., 40
Poell, T., 139, 143
Ponterotto, J. G., 17
Popovic, S., 149
Postmes, T., 146
Poteat, V. P., 56
Potok, M., 3, 5, 12
Powell, C. S., 32, 33

Subject Index

Note: Page numbers in "t" refer to tables.

Microintervention Strategies, First Edition. Derald Wing Sue, Cassandra Z. Calle, Narolyn Mendez, Sarah Alsaidi, and Elizabeth Glaeser.
© 2021 John Wiley & Sons, Inc. Published 2021 by John Wiley & Sons, Inc.